Contemporary Body Psychotherapy

Contemporary Body Psychotherapy: The Chiron Approach looks at the ground-breaking work of the London-based Chiron Centre for Body Psychotherapy, a training centre recognised worldwide by professionals in the field. The book brings together Chiron trainers and therapists, describing how their integrative approach has enabled cutting-edge thinking.

Divided into two parts, the book deals with topics including:

- The roots and the development of the Chiron approach.
- Self-regulation – an evolving concept at the heart of body psychotherapy.
- The evolution of an embodied, integral and relational approach to psychotherapy.
- Moving towards an integrative model of trauma therapy.

At a time when the psychotherapeutic profession has turned its interest towards the body and its intrinsic psychological dimension, *Contemporary Body Psychotherapy: The Chiron Approach* offers a timely and valuable contribution to the literature. It will provide essential reading for those practising or involved with body psychotherapy, offering a new synthesis with the psychoanalytic tradition, as well as appealing to a wider audience of mental health professionals and academics with an interest in the area.

Linda Hartley is a UKCP registered Psychotherapist, an ADMP-UK senior registered Dance Movement Psychotherapist, and an ISMETA registered Somatic Movement Therapist. She runs a transpersonal and body psychotherapy practice in Cambridge and Norfolk, and is the author of three books.

Contemporary Body Psychotherapy

The Chiron Approach

Edited by Linda Hartley

Routledge
Taylor & Francis Group

LONDON AND NEW YORK

First published 2009
by Routledge
27 Church Road, Hove, East Sussex BN3 2FA

Simultaneously published in the USA and Canada
by Routledge
270 Madison Ave, New York NY 10016

Routledge is an imprint of the Taylor & Francis Group, an Informa business

Typeset in Times by
RefineCatch Limited, Bungay, Suffolk
Printed and bound in Great Britain by
TJ International Ltd, Padstow, Cornwall
Paperback cover design by Aubergine Creative Design

British Library Cataloguing in Publication Data
A catalogue record for this book is available from the British Library

Library of Congress Cataloging-in-Publication Data
Contemporary body psychotherapy : the Chiron approach / edited by Linda Hartley.
    p. ; cm.
    Includes bibliographical references.
    ISBN 978-0-415-43938-1 (hbk.) – ISBN: 978-0-415-43939-8 (pbk.)
    1. Chiron centre for Body Psychotherapy. 2. Mind and body therapies.
    3. Eclectic psychotherapy. I. Hartley, Linda, 1953–
    [DNLM: 1. Chiron Centre for Body Psychotherapy. 2. Psychotherapy—methods—London. 3. Mental Health Services—London.
    4. Mind–Body Relations (Metaphysics)—London. WM 420 C7605 2008]
    RC489.M53C68 2008
    616.89′14—dc22
                                                        2008005767

ISBN: 978–0–415–43938–1 (hbk)
ISBN: 978–0–415–43939–8 (pbk)

This book is dedicated to Bernd and Jochen,
holders of the Crucible, with love and gratitude.

The editor's personal dedication is in memory
of Sally Byford, dear friend and colleague

Contents

Contributors

Carmen Joanne Ablack is a UKCP Integrative Body Psychotherapist, Director of the Centre for Integral-Relational Learning and for the last twelve years has been a trainer and supervisor at the Chiron Centre. She teaches on masters' programmes nationally and internationally, was Chair of the Chiron Association for Body Psychotherapists, and currently Chairs the Standards Board and Training Standards Committee of the UKCP. www.cirl.org.uk

Shoshi Asheri MA, UKCP is training director and supervisor at the Chiron Centre and a visiting tutor in other psychotherapeutic organisations in the UK and Israel. She is a member of the steering committee for the UK grouping of the International Association for Relational Psychoanalysis and Psychotherapy, and has a private practice in London where she works with individuals and couples. shoshash@aol.com

Roz Carroll MA Cantab is a body psychotherapist, supervisor, trainer and author. She teaches at the Chiron Centre, the Minster Centre, the Centre for Attachment-based Psychoanalytic Psychotherapy and Terapia. She has published various chapters on neuroscience and contemporary psychotherapy, and is now working on a book – *Thinking Through the Body* – to be published by Norton. www.thinkbody.co.uk

Jane Clark has worked as a counsellor for over twenty years. She has taught counselling skills, including to GP practices, worked with drug and alcohol dependency, co-founded and run a multi-disciplinary therapies service, and co-established a youth counselling service through the NHS. She currently also practises as a body psychotherapist at the Chiron Centre, and offers therapeutic and spiritual interventions for the terminally ill.

Bernd Eiden MA, UKCP Integrative Body Psychotherapist co-founded in 1983 the Chiron Centre for Body Psychotherapy in West London and has worked there since as a trainer, supervisor and manager. He has written several articles which can be found on the Chiron website:

www.chiron.org. He has also been a member of EABP (European Association of Body Psychotherapy) for many years.

Linda Hartley MA, UKCP, SRDMP works as a transpersonal and body psychotherapist in Cambridge and North Norfolk. She is a practitioner and trainer of Body-Mind Centering® and Authentic Movement, founding director of the Institute for Integrative Bodywork & Movement Therapy, through which she runs training programmes, and is author of three books, including *Somatic Psychology: Body, Mind and Meaning*. www.lindahartley.co.uk

Morit Heitzler is an experienced integrative body psychotherapist, supervisor and trainer, with a private practice in Oxford. She teaches on various training courses. Having studied Somatic Trauma Therapy, Family Constellations and EMDR, she has developed an integrative approach to trauma work. She is a member of the Oxford Stress and Trauma Service and is interested in developmental and transgenerational trauma. www.heitzler.co.uk

Anne Marie Keary is a relational body psychotherapist (UKCP). She has a teaching background and works in private practice, runs ongoing groups for mothers, and has a special interest in working with issues around disability and sexuality. Alongside her diploma from the Chiron Centre she has qualifications in Somatic Trauma Therapy and Systemic Family Constellations. www.amkeary.net

Margaret Landale is an Integrative Body Psychotherapist (UKCP, CABP), supervisor and trainer. She has specialised in stress-related and psychosomatic disorders for many years and has developed and run a variety of professional training programmes. Until 2004 she was also a training director at the Chiron Centre. www.margaret@landale.uk.com

Alun Reynolds is a UKCP Registered Psychotherapist, Trainer and Supervisor with a private practice in Cambridge. Together with Gillian Kelly, he taught the second year Gestalt Body Psychotherapy course at Chiron. He has developed a particular interest in working with borderline and narcissistic structures, as well as in the Family Constellation work of Bert Hellinger. www.constellationsolutions.co.uk

Monika Schaible is an integrative body psychotherapist (UKCP) and supervisor, and a member of the Chiron staff. She has specialised in integrating biodynamic massage into the psychotherapeutic process. Monika has worked as a complementary therapist for a hospice for people affected by HIV and AIDS, and has been engaged with Vipassana meditation for the last 25 years. monica.schaible@ntlworld.com

Michael Soth practises integral-relational Body Psychotherapy as therapist, trainer and supervisor (UKCP). He is Training Director at the Chiron Centre and over the last 20 years has been teaching on various counselling and therapy training courses. For details of current projects, presentations and workshops, as well as all his other articles and papers, see www.soth.co.uk

Kathrin Stauffer PhD, UKCP and EAP Registered Body Psychotherapist, was born and educated in Switzerland. Originally a biochemist, she retrained at the Chiron Centre. She works in Cambridge and London as a psychotherapist and supervisor, in addition to teaching Biodynamic Massage and Holistic Anatomy & Physiology, mainly at the Cambridge Body Psychotherapy Centre. Her recent writing is available on: www.stauffer.co.uk

Tom Warnecke UKCP, EABP, IFB trained in Gestalt Therapy and subsequently with David Boadella at the International Institute for Biosynthesis. He maintains a general practice in London and integrates body psychotherapy with relational perspectives. He has worked in statutory mental health services and facilitates training workshops and seminars for various organisations. Further information is available at: www.integralbody.co.uk

John Waterston is a body psychotherapist with a private practice in Cambridge. He worked originally as a chartered surveyor before qualifying and working in various psychiatric institutions whilst pursuing psychotherapy training. He is interested in the possibilities inherent in psychotherapeutic theory to facilitate social change in small communities and is currently writing a book on the meaning and function of vengeance in groups. www.johnwaterston.co.uk

Acknowledgments

I warmly thank Roz Carroll and Bernd Eiden for inviting me to take on the role of editor of this book, and for their editorial support and ideas throughout its production. Roz must also be acknowledged for having conceived the idea of this Chiron Centre book. My thanks go also to Michael Soth for helpful theoretical clarifications, and to the Chiron Association for Body Psychotherapists for their financial support.

I am grateful to friends and colleagues for the personal and professional support I have received whilst working on the book, in particular Joan Davis, Fran Lavendel, John Waterston, and the late Sally Byford. I learnt the news of Sally's death just minutes after finishing the preparation of the manuscript, so she will always be connected in my heart to the birth of this book. I also acknowledge a great debt of gratitude to my own clients and students whose presence and commitment forms a ground for my own learning and practice to develop.

On behalf of the Chiron Centre, the contributors would like to acknowledge all past and present trainers, students and clients of the Centre, without whose contribution and presence the work could not have evolved into the form presented here.

Introduction

Linda Hartley

> The body is our sensation, our felt emotion. The body is our experience of ourselves, our temple in which the light of spirit burns. Unconscious worlds, numinous worlds, worlds with high order and worlds with no apparent order can become known within the body, because of the body.
>
> (Adler 2002: 6)

For more than two decades the Chiron Centre for Body Psychotherapy, London, provided professional training for body psychotherapists, and engaged in an active process of research, dialogue and debate to develop an embodied, integral and relational approach to psychotherapy. This book was conceived as a way to mark and honour the unique work of the Chiron Centre as founding directors Bernd Eiden and Jochen Lude move towards retirement, and the Centre brings to a close its function as a professional training organisation.

During the period since Chiron's inception in the early 1980s the discipline of body psychotherapy within the UK has moved from the margins of the psychotherapeutic profession to an established position within it. The Chiron Centre has played a central role in this process of establishment and inclusion. Interest in the findings of neuroscience in relation to attachment theory, and their application to psychotherapy and psychoanalysis have supported an increased interest in, and understanding of, the crucial role the body plays in psychological growth, distress and healing, and this has opened a doorway of interest from the mainstream psychotherapeutic community towards body psychotherapy. As Lewis, Amini and Lannon write:

> Of less renown is the reciprocal finding (provided by advanced imaging technologies) that psychotherapy alters the living brain . . . The mind-body clash has disguised the truth that psychotherapy *is* physiology. When a person starts therapy, he isn't beginning a pale conversation; he is stepping into a somatic state of relatedness. Evolution has sculpted mammals into their present form: they become attuned to one another's

evocative signals and alter the structure of one another's nervous systems. Psychotherapy's transformative power comes from engaging and directing these ancient mechanisms. Therapy is a living embodiment of limbic processes as corporeal as digestion or respiration.

(Lewis *et al.* 2000: 168)

The acceptance of the Chiron approach to body psychotherapy as a valid and invaluable contribution to the broader field has undoubtedly also occurred because of the maturing of theory and practice within body psychotherapy itself; this has been enabled through the willingness of Chiron body psychotherapists to confront their shadow, individually and collectively, courageously deconstruct their own 'cherished position', and open themselves to other approaches – integrating humanistic, psychodynamic, relational, phenomenological and characterological – in service of a deeper, broader and more inclusive perspective.

It was not always a comfortable process, but an ongoing commitment and openness to debate and grappling with the shadow of traditional body psychotherapy have enabled an approach to evolve which we believe is unique, not only in the UK, but also within the international body psychotherapy community. It is hoped that this book will offer at least a glimpse into that process and the Chiron approach to contemporary body psychotherapy which has evolved. It is hoped, too, that it will offer something to non-body-oriented counsellors, psychotherapists and psychoanalysts who are interested in expanding their own learning and practice to include awareness of embodiment, and the body's intrinsic psychological dimension.

Body, emotions, mind and spirit – a holistic approach

An earlier name for Chiron's approach was holistic body psychotherapy, before various developmental leaps necessitated a series of redefinitions (see Soth's chapter). This reflected the intention to include all dimensions of the client's process – body, emotions, mind and spirit – within the therapeutic work, and also all dimensions of process within the therapist and in the therapeutic relationship. The term 'holistic' had a precise and substantial meaning in the Reichian tradition, referring to what Reich had called 'functionalism'. This meta-psychological concept, applicable especially to the underlying 'functional' unity of body and mind, is fundamental to Chiron's work. Eiden will elaborate on this concept in Chapter 1.

Earlier formulations were included within a wider embrace as the work evolved and new perspectives were successfully integrated, so *body, emotions, mind and spirit* are all dimensions of experience that the Chiron therapist seeks to include in client work. Integration of the 'countertransference revolution' means, for body psychotherapists, that the therapist's somatically experienced responses to the client, and to the relationship between them, are considered to yield invaluable information; the Chiron therapist is trained to use their own body to attune somatically and energetically to the client's process, moment by moment.

This inclusiveness is reflected in both the style and content of the individual chapters. Each author expresses a different part of the spectrum, all of which they will each be seeking to hold and integrate within the therapeutic work. So at times you may feel invited into the present moment through remembering to attend to the breath moving through your body as you read, or through becoming aware of the sensation of gravity acting upon your body tissues, and the support of the ground beneath you. At other times the author's emotional immediacy and authenticity, as he or she engages with the client's suffering, may touch your heart and allow a resonance with the compassion expressed so lucidly through the writing. Case material presented by Asheri, Keary, Heitzler and Clark, for example, may touch you emotionally and thus bring you to a deeper appreciation of the theory and principles of the Chiron approach.

Theoretical contributions offer insight into the intellectual ground which underpins the approach, and indicate the thorough engagement with theoretical debate that has matured the work into a multi-dimensional and inclusive approach. In expanding the areas of application, core theory is also developed by Warnecke to address the borderline dynamic, a condition not always considered amenable to a traditional body psychotherapy approach. And Waterston offers a theoretical argument for the potential of body psychotherapy to act as a tool for social and political change, one of Reich's original intentions.

An explicit engagement with spirit and the transpersonal realm is touched upon lightly in some of the chapters. Awakening of the spiritual life can come about through deep work through the body, and is seen by some as a natural outcome of successful psychotherapy. In the Chiron approach it is not imposed, but allowed to flourish when the process supports it; it is enabled when the therapist holds this potential as the client works through personal material. Schaible, Reynolds and Landale also describe practices that are influenced by or derived from Eastern mindfulness meditation, which offer an essential foundation for embodied therapeutic practice, as well as a path towards acceptance, transformation and growth.

Besides these explicit inclusions, the transpersonal runs implicitly and deeply through the substrata of the book, firstly expressed in the archetype of Chiron, the Wounded Healer, after which the Centre was named. The presence of the Wounded Healer can be vividly felt in case material where the contributors bring their personal experience, wounding and the lessons learnt from their own healing journeys into the consulting room and into the heart of the work with their clients. I have also felt the presence of the Spiritual Warrior as I read these offerings; it appears throughout the book in the compassion, the wholehearted engagement, the willingness to enter humbly into the therapeutic relationship without the pretence of knowing, of being an expert, of being able to 'fix' anything; and it enters through the courageous debate, the intellectual research and deconstruction of secure and fixed positions which have enabled individuals and the community as a whole to break down resistances, go beyond familiar ground, and enter new worlds of relating within the therapeutic encounter.

Coherence and diversity – integrative body psychotherapy

Coherence and diversity are two embracing themes that have emerged as the book came into being. As all contributors are Chiron-trained therapists and/or have been Chiron trainers themselves, the content of the chapters will cohere around some shared perspectives, theories, principles and practice. For example, Carroll writes about self-regulation as a fundamental principle of body psychotherapy from its early days, and the ways in which understanding of it has continued to broaden and develop as neuroscientific and relational elements were integrated.

Alongside acknowledged differences, all Chiron therapists' work is informed by their capacity for energetic perception, attunement, somatic resonance, and right-brain to right-brain processing. A deep sensing into oneself and into the intersubjective space enables a fluid, complex and creative approach, rooted in embodied presence and awareness. Although the authors use a variety of theoretical terms and concepts drawn from different approaches, all would agree that the sense of self is rooted in the body. It is hoped that this coherence around shared principles and practice will enable the reader to gain more than just a superficial understanding of integral, relational body psychotherapy, but that he or she will be led into a deeper appreciation through viewing Chiron's work as if through a multi-faceted lens.

Beyond this, a diversity of approaches, styles of expression, and application of those common principles will be found. As the contributors may have been involved during different stages of Chiron's development, their approach may have a particular emphasis that reflects the concerns of that stage; it will also reflect their own character, interests, education and personal history.

Authors' descriptions of their work are also diverse as a result of the deep deconstruction of the stereotypes of body psychotherapy, and other models, which they have been trained to engage with. Evolving along democratic lines, and integrating many diverse theoretical and clinical approaches, Chiron has welcomed differences of opinion, practice and orientation. This will be evident within these writings where we hope to show that it was the very engagement with the rich diversity of its heritage that enabled the significant developments and paradigm leaps to occur. Central to its strength as a training organisation is its pluralistic ethos.

From the very beginning, intense debate within the training staff group around differences and contradictions provided a fruitful space for different therapeutic stances to emerge. The emphasis on 'breaking through the armour', implicit in Reich's original vegetotherapy and Lowen's bioenergetics, had been complemented by Boyesen's softer, mothering style of 'melting the armour'. Drawing from the diversity of all the Reichian schools already implied a lack of dogmatism, and prepared the ground for eventually balancing catharsis with containment. Emphasis on catharsis had been one of the most visible features of early body psychotherapy, and had led to many valid criticisms as well as prejudices against it, so the containing potential of biodynamic massage provided a helpful balance.

Another strength derived from the integration of gestalt into the Chiron approach. The contradictions between the humanistic, phenomenological approach of gestalt, and the character-analytical approach of traditional body psychotherapy, and especially biodynamic psychology, were an important source of creative tension which enabled new growth and an integrative approach to evolve.

Out of this debate the course titled Dynamics of Diversity also emerged and was included in the training syllabus. The topic widened out to include diversity in its broadest context; described in Ablack's chapter, it honours the need for psychotherapists to address difference and diversity more explicitly than is common in most psychotherapy trainings. This is also reflected in the spirit of the book where questions are explored, differing points of view put forward, and the spirit of debate continued.

For example, the controversial issue of 'to touch or not to touch' will be explored from different perspectives by Eiden, Schaible and Asheri. Also controversial is the authority given to neuroscience; whilst Carroll, Landale and Heitzler refer to its findings, Stauffer also invites us to enquire into both its usefulness and limitations for psychotherapeutic practice. In this way new levels of integration may continue to emerge through holding the creative tension between differing perspectives.

An integral-relational approach

Chiron's development has been marked by a number of 'quantum leaps', each of which has heralded in a new phase of growth, a new paradigm and a new theoretical orientation. Each phase is inclusive in as much as it has integrated what is still useful from previous phases. As a result, the contemporary approach described in this book is more than an eclectic amalgam of different techniques and theories; it is a thorough digestion and assimilation that has enabled a series of transformational leaps. Its contribution to a therapeutic field and a cultural climate interested in the embrace of ever more inclusive wholes cannot be doubted.

A particular uniqueness of Chiron's work within the body psychotherapy field is its relational approach, which has come about through a paradigm shift that Soth describes as the 'relational turn', and an understanding of the inevitability of re-enactment within the therapeutic relationship through 'parallel process'; Asheri's, Keary's and Clark's chapters offer clinical material which elucidates the theory.

Relational psychotherapy (Mitchell and Aron 1999) recognises that the sense of self develops through interpersonal relationship and is distorted through intrusive, neglectful and inconsistent early attachment experiences; neuroscience has supported this theory and psychotherapists of all persuasions agree that the quality of the therapeutic relationship is pivotal in determining the outcome of the work. As Carroll describes and Asheri demonstrates, the client begins by using the therapist as an object to facilitate self-regulation where this has not been learnt in early life; successful therapy will enable them to learn to self-regulate, and eventually appreciate and come into relationship with the therapist as subject.

In the Chiron approach this can occur through the therapist's whole-hearted and fully embodied engagement, meeting the client's woundedness through a willingness to bring their own wounded *and* wounding nature into the relationship. The humanistic orientation, which is fundamental to the Chiron approach, is informed by theory from psychoanalytic traditions – object relations, attachment theory and psychodynamic principles have influenced this phase of development.

In Part I, some of the Chiron trainers write about the *Development of core principles and theory* of the Chiron approach. In Part II, *New directions and applications*, further developments of theory and clinical application are described. The sections will be introduced throughout the book.

Into the future

Although the Chiron Centre has ended its work as a training organisation, it continues to offer a programme of professional and post-graduate workshops for those trained in or interested in body psychotherapy. It also continues to offer a clinical referral service for individuals seeking personal therapy. As the founding directors retire, it is time for the baton to be passed on to others, and a number of the contributors to this book, as well as other past and present Chiron therapists and trainers, are actively engaged in teaching and running training courses privately or through other organisations. Thus the work initiated in the crucible of the Chiron Centre will undoubtedly continue to develop and diversify through many channels.

I feel honoured to have been invited to edit this volume. I am not a Chiron psychotherapist myself – more a 'distant cousin' who has had connections over the years with some of the centre staff. It has been a great pleasure to immerse myself in the work of the Chiron Centre, and I hope the reader will gain as much from these writings as I have done.

References

Adler, J. (2002) *Offering from the Conscious Body*. Rochester, VT: Inner Traditions.
Lewis, T., Amini, F. and Lannon, R. (2000) *A General Theory of Love*. New York: Vintage Books.
Mitchell, S. A. and Aron, L. (1999) *Relational Psychoanalysis: The Emergence of a Tradition*. Lawrence, KS: The Analytic Press.

Part I

Development of core principles and theory

GROUND AND ROOTS

Linda Hartley

In *Ground and roots* the main theoretical and clinical approaches that informed Chiron's origins are introduced. Bernd Eiden will trace the Centre's development within the wider socio-political, cultural and psychotherapeutic field, and introduce the historical roots of Chiron's emergence; the earlier stages of its development, including core principles taught in the training module Body and Energy, and Reich's vegetotherapy, are described. He explores some of the conflicts and integrations that occurred between the phenomenological and character-analytical approaches, and addresses the complex issue of the use of touch and biodynamic massage in body psychotherapy.

In Chapter 2 Monika Schaible, teacher of the Biodynamic Massage course within the Chiron training, describes this practice and how it has been integrated into body psychotherapy. She addresses the history of biodynamic massage and its value as a psychotherapeutic process, exploring the dilemmas as well as the benefits of retaining this particular method of contactful touch as an approach within body psychotherapy practice.

In Chapter 3 Alun Reynolds writes about an approach to gestalt body psychotherapy that was developed at Chiron and integrated with the other modalities taught. His description brings us into the immediacy of embodiment and styles of contact, emphasising the importance of embodied presence for the psychotherapist. He describes techniques that are fundamental to the Chiron psychotherapist's practice.

During the first two years of the Basic Training, courses in Body and Energy, Biodynamic Massage, Holistic Human Biology, Gestalt Body Psychotherapy and Group Psychotherapy gave the trainee a grounding in embodied presence, energetic attunement and somatic resonance. This is drawn upon whether the relational approach being taken with a client, at any particular moment, is one of 'authentic I–Thou relating' (Buber 1958), 'treatment' through the medical model, or 'strategic relating', including working through the dynamics of the transference and countertransference. In discussing how the changing needs of clients coming to him caused his own approach to move towards working with the transference, Reynolds prepares the ground for the 'relational turn' which will be addressed in the second section of the book.

In the third year, the subtle and complex integration of modalities was deepened; alongside Gestalt Body Psychotherapy II (which evolved into Charge in the Therapeutic Relationship), a module in Massage and Psychotherapy and a series of seminars on Therapeutic Theories and Character Structures were taught. In the module Advanced Training in Body Psychotherapy, trainees were given the unique opportunity to engage in intensive practice sessions, in groups of three, under the supervision of a trainer who brought close attention to the integration of bodywork and the relational dimension. Developing upon the foundation of the first two years, and led by active dialogue within the staff group, a sophisticated integration could evolve, and a flexibility which allowed trainees to find their own individual approach. Although the structure of the training remained fairly constant throughout, within the stability it offered, change and evolution could occur.

Reference

Buber, M. (1958) *I and Thou*. Edinburgh: T. and T. Clark.

Chapter 1

The roots and the development of the Chiron approach

Bernd Eiden

Introduction

Body psychotherapy has been in existence for more than 100 years, but it is in the last twenty years that it has become organised as a discipline of its own and gained recognition. The work here at the Chiron Centre for Body Psychotherapy over the last twenty years mirrors this process. As a member organisation of UK Council for Psychotherapy (UKCP), we represent body psychotherapy in the wider professional field.

I am one of the founding members of Chiron and since the beginning have worked as a trainer and supervisor. Together with co-founder Jochen Lude, I led the organisation. As managing directors we have lived through and resolved many conflicts and instituted changes at Chiron which were crucial for the evolution of a contemporary approach to body psychotherapy. Our integrative belief requires a commitment to conflict, tension and diversity. Our leadership style was democratic and pluralistic and provided the staff with a creative space to develop their own ways of thinking and integration. Those were then shared and modified in team discussions – mostly a varied, enriching and enjoyable process. Hence the Chiron approach is a result of good team-work, which utilises the contributions each individual makes from their own personal and educational background. I would like to thank all of the members of our staff, present and past, for their invaluable contributions. I apologise for not naming you specifically in this chapter.

This discussion of the Chiron approach will begin with an overview of our heritage and the development of body psychotherapy and its application. I will illuminate the basic principles of body psychotherapy and illustrate Chiron's emphasis on the integration of the body/mind and our move away from traditional body psychotherapy approaches to a more integrative and relational one. I will present this historically, emphasising cornerstones and turning points which led to our unique approach.

Socio-political background to Chiron's foundation

Together with the other Chiron co-founders, Jochen Lude and Rainer Pervöltz, I was involved with the political left of the late 1960s and early 1970s in Berlin, Germany. This was a time of turmoil and excitement. We were all experimenting with new ways of living and working; for example, we believed in sexual liberation and enjoyed our bodies through expressive dance and nudity. Having trained as a teacher, I resisted working within the repressive school system and instead was hired by a private kindergarten project funded by the Berlin City Council. This innovative programme involved children and parents in defining and creating educational methods, drawing on the ideas of A. S. Neill in his book *Summerhill* and inspired by Wilhelm Reich's progressive attitude (Boadella 1974: 61).

Reich's theories on the effects of authoritarian oppression by society and its impact on the personality made a deep impression on us and motivated us to engage with the 'Human Potential' movement of the 1970s and participate in encounter groups. Having grown up in Germany during the Depression following World War II, we felt a deep longing for freedom, spontaneity and self-actualisation, values proclaimed by the emerging humanistic movement. Gestalt therapy and body psychotherapy were enthusiastically welcomed by the avant-garde in those years, and the movement grew and flourished. Body psychotherapy had been rediscovered after having made a rather brief shadowy appearance in the 1920s and 1930s. Its disappearance was partly due to the psychoanalytic movement's rejection of the body after Reich's and Ferenczi's expulsions from the fold and partly due to the bad reputation Reich gained through his later work subsequent to his emigration to the USA.

My colleagues and I turned towards body psychotherapy when we realised that the student political revolution did not enable the societal changes we hoped for. We read Reich and were inspired to put his theories into practice by setting up self-help groups. The decision to train as body psychotherapists expressed our hope of promoting change in individuals and groups. It also held the potential to break down rigid barriers in society and contribute to reforms through psychological approaches (Waterston's chapter will explore these ideas). In 1983 Chiron was founded in London.

The foundations of body psychotherapy

Body psychotherapy has its origins in psychoanalysis. Freud used touch in his early period of working, including massage or putting his hand on the forehead of the patient in order to facilitate free association. His pupil Ferenczi offered his patients physical holding to help them to modulate strong affects and Reich in particular focused on the bodily dimension, while he developed his concept of vegetotherapy in the 1930s and 1940s (Reich [1942] 1973). Janet also deserves to be honoured as a body psychotherapy pioneer, as he recognised well before Reich in 1885 the correlation between muscular contraction and the formation of the neurotic structure, and used massage and touch in his work (Boadella 1997).

Since the seventeenth-century philosopher Descartes, there has been a clear separation between the mental and the physical, and the processes of the mind were regarded as superior to those of the body. When psychotherapy grew into a discipline in the early years of the twentieth century, the body/ mind dualism was well cemented. Freud abandoned the body when he developed psychoanalysis, arriving at the principles of abstinence and neutrality and giving his theory of transference the greatest importance. He came to disregard the use of touch, one reason being that touch could communicate libidinous desires and in that way sexualise the analytic encounter.

Reich and Ferenczi, amongst other psychoanalysts, did not accept Freud's 'talking cure'. They resisted 'the correct' way of working by breaking the touch taboo and questioning prevailing assumptions about body/mind relationships. Both Reich and Ferenczi ended up being ostracised and were excluded from the international psychoanalytic society.

Nowadays, new paradigms are developing which include a holistic understanding of dualisms such as subject/object, body/mind, etc., acknowledging interdependence and interconnectedness (Capra 1982). The most basic manifestation of this for body psychotherapists is the interrelationship between the physical and the mental, the body and the mind. Damasio is prominent amongst those who have given neurobiological evidence that thought and reflection arise out of and follow feeling and sensation (Damasio 1994). Reich's thinking was already in line with these new paradigms.

I will summarise briefly those principles of Reich's which became fundamental to body psychotherapy and will further expand on their application and limitations when discussing the Chiron approach.

* Reich introduced an energetic model, expanding on Freud's drive and libido theory. He postulated that the energy behind a repressed situation/ conflict and the expression of the energy as a feeling was as important as remembering and talking about the situation/conflict. Those three elements together (the what, the how and the why) enable an experience to be fully integrated. The emotional expression was often neglected and needed to be discharged, hence his plea for working 'with the energy' which could lead to regression and catharsis.
* Reich's formula for the healthy energetic cycle of tension–charge–discharge–relaxation illustrated how energy was circulated and expressed through the body. This went in tandem with the functioning of the autonomic (vegetative) nervous system with its sympathetic and parasympathetic aspects (Eiden 2002: 43).
* Reich recognised that body and psyche were functionally identical, which meant that a person's beliefs and feelings manifest in physical tensions,

and conversely that energetic blockages are closely linked to emotional problems. Body and mind interact dynamically with each other and mirror each other. Reich found that physical work could reach and influence the deeper psychic level and vice versa. As a result, Reich introduced the notion of 'body armour' and 'character armour' and developed his concepts of 'character analysis' and 'vegetotherapy' as a way of working with the body's defence system (Eiden 2002).

- Reich trusted the organism's capacity for self-regulation and inner wellbeing. His therapy process aimed to reach the core, the deeper primary level, which was by nature positive, spontaneous and motivated to make contact. Reich's unconscious, unlike Freud's, was not divided in two (Eros and Thanatos) and therefore had no destructive core. Hence, Reich promised a sense of wellbeing if we could surrender to the innate 'vegetative' forces and work through the distortions and negative attitudes of the secondary layer. In her chapter in this book, Carroll will look at the theme of self-regulation as it has been developed, including the influence of attachment theory.

Characteristics of the initial Chiron approach (1983–1992)

Body oriented, holistic, humanistic and integrative

It was clear to my colleagues and me that we wanted our work at Chiron to remain anchored in the body. Having gone through training in body psychotherapy, we had experienced the changes in ourselves. We knew how significantly body psychotherapy contributes to what it is to be an embodied human being – being more alive and energetic, creative and spontaneous, more present in the here and now and more connected to sensations and feelings. It opened a deep understanding of ourselves, others and life itself, which we had never experienced before. Our training in body psychotherapy provided an invaluable understanding of the human personality on the physical, psychological and spiritual levels. I want to acknowledge the debt to our mentors, especially Gerda Boyesen, John Pierrakos, David Boadella and Jack Rosenberg who were pioneers in our professional field. Their teaching formed the foundation of the Chiron approach and became the springboard for our integrated contemporary theory of body psychotherapy.

In establishing our training programme, we aimed to create a holistic and integrative approach, while incorporating the best of various psychotherapeutic models. Our approach was 'eclectic', as we were searching for an identity, and our own version of 'integrative' work emerged over the next two decades. Twenty years ago the field of psychotherapy was disparate and divided into a multitude of factions, schools and approaches and there was little exchange and dialogue between them. This fragmentation was also tangible within the various schools of body psychotherapy. They isolated themselves with an air of exclusiveness, wanting to be special and different, each emphasising their own way of working with their own methodology and definitions.

Postmodernism has helped to change perspectives to move away from one universal truth and to respect contradicting theories as complementary.

Now, two decades after Chiron's beginning, we are supported by a creative process where new developments emerge due to a paradigm shift, fostering a tendency towards integration of different approaches and learning from each other. Psychoanalysts have become interested in being more spontaneous, immediate and inclusive of dialogue and the body. Body psychotherapists are now more aware of the need for relationship theory. Both are challenged and inspired by new research in neuroscience and attachment theory.

At Chiron, we regard our work as holistic because we do not see the psychological manifestations of human development as separate from the body or the mind. Physical symptoms have psychological meaning, emotions occur within the body, mental processes engender bodily reactions. It is in the body that our experiences live and are perceived as emotions and moods. Thought and language alone do not constitute reality. It is the body's sensations that add vitality and a felt evidence for our perceptions and memories, which makes them 'real'.

By working psychotherapeutically within a holistic framework, we cut across the dualistic thinking which perpetuates splits between body–emotion–mind–spirit, and we are able to address the inner experience of fragmentation. Motoric and sensory explorations elicit different memories, especially preverbal experiences, that words or concepts cannot reach. By teaching within this perspective we hope to contribute to a development where integration between body, mind and psyche is seen as the basis for the assimilation of different psychotherapeutic approaches.

We also subscribe to humanistic principles:

- an openness towards the possibility of equality in the therapeutic relationship
- a belief in the clients' capacity to heal themselves
- a view of the clients' potential and strengths
- a questioning of the 'medical model' and the idea that the therapist has to direct the process.

Experiential learning is highly valued in the humanistic tradition where the therapist takes on an interactive and experiential presence, sometimes using exercises, role play, dialogue work, guided imagery, etc. As body psychotherapists we tend to give priority to such a phenomenological and explorative way of working, to help the client's awareness to grow and facilitate self-regulation and self-actualisation. We hope to engender 'embodied' knowledge and 'emotional intelligence', perceiving and thinking with body and mind, which require a particular sensitivity and awareness. We therefore conduct our training in a way that helps students develop the capacity to use themselves as a body of resonance, finely attuned to the non-verbal, subliminal communication and body language of the client. This is why time must be given to learning through experience in the 'here and now'. The intention is also to encourage right brain learning informed by the left brain in such a way that therapists can develop their personal theoretical stance and style where theory is not split off from the inner felt experience.

Chiron – the wounded healer

We gave our institute the name Chiron as a symbol for our work as wounded healers. In Greek mythology Chiron was a leader and wise elder amongst the centaurs, half man – half horse, suffering from an incurable wound to his knee. For us, the image of Chiron, the centaur, symbolises the healing of the split between body and mind, between the instinctual and the spiritual. As an archetypal image Chiron, the centaur, with his body of a horse and his upper torso and head of a human being, embodies the idea of wholeness and integration and the possibility of achieving it.

Chiron teaches that our own wound is the gift we can offer to others. This transpersonal concept of the wounded healer holds a central value for our work. We bring our own woundedness as a relational commitment to the work rather than expertise or promise of a cure. Clients bring their wounds and we as therapists hope to transform them into resources helping each client to find meaning in his own. As one of our teachers said: 'It's the wound that heals, the wound that teaches, the wound that keeps us on our journey' (Somers 2002: 25).

Working with body and energy

Our understanding of working with the body is based on Reich's vegetotherapy and its further development by neo-Reichians, especially Alexander Lowen, John Pierrakos and Gerda Boyesen.

When working with the body we are aware of energy as the connecting force that links body, emotion, mind and spirit. Reich, following Freud, called it libido; neo-Reichians refer to it as 'vitality' or 'life-force'. As body psychotherapists we work with the assumption that blockages to this life-force create neuroses.

Every conflict within a person has its physical manifestation somewhere in the body, and a blocked energy flow will have implications on all levels of our being. A depressed person, for example, will have depressed energy flow, pallor, lack of vitality and joy for living, his breathing will be shallow and his concentration will be poor.

On an energetic level the body is constantly in rhythmic movement: expansion and contraction, inward and outward, charge and discharge. Many of these movements are spontaneous and involuntary; they originate on a vegetative level and are linked to the autonomic nervous system.

Body psychotherapy brings these rhythms and movements into consciousness. We are interested in how the flow of energy becomes blocked or interrupted and how we can encourage its liberation and self-regulation. Unexpressed energy creates tension and physical holding, whereas uncontained or overwhelming energy usually creates conflict with others. The familiar consequence is either a body in internal conflict with impulses habitually held back, or a body habitually driven by impulses to enact conflict with the environment.

Through bodily interventions we attend to these patterns and energetic states, attempting first to facilitate body awareness and second to unblock suppressed feelings. Our aim is to access the body's inherent life energy and dissolve the patterns of chronic muscular rigidity which Reich called muscular armouring (Reich [1942] 1973). Embodied self-awareness – through exploration of inner sensations, vegetative reactions, impulses and subtle movements – provides a clearer sense of boundaries and leads to a stronger sense of self. Tuning in to these inner sensations and feelings, which we call 'anchoring in the body', enables a deepening of contact to oneself and to others.

Examples of bodily interventions include:

- Focusing on breathing, as fuller breathing gives vitality and raises the energy level in the body.
- 'Grounding' exercises help a person gain a firmer stance and a sense of solidity. The term 'grounding' was introduced by Lowen (1975: 193) and Keleman (1975: 57) and relates to the body's gravity.
- 'Containment' is the ability to sense and to hold one's feelings with a focus on the 'centre' (middle) of the body, away from the periphery and from expression.
- 'Body awareness' can also serve as a tool for containment, for example to regulate hyperarousal. This will be explored in some of the chapters in this book, in particular Morit Heitzler's.

The intention of the therapist is crucial when working with the body. The same exercise could be used either to increase body awareness in the way described previously, or to facilitate expression of suppressed feelings. Based on Reich's model of the energetic cycle of tension–charge–discharge–relaxation, similar to Boyesen's vasomotoric cycle (Eiden 2002: 44), body psychotherapy is uniquely positioned to reduce blockages on the vegetative, muscular and cognitive-emotional levels in order to fully integrate an incomplete or suppressed experience.

Body posture encapsulates a person's characteristic attitude and can be an important focus for exploration. There are many other observations which we pay attention to, such as the emotional expression of specific parts of the body or their limited mobility, restricted breathing, the range and amplitude of emotional expression, hyper- or hypotonic muscles, signs of fragmentation, sensations of pain or numbness, vegetative symptoms like heat and coldness, tingling, uncontrolled vibrations, etc.

Lowen, a close follower of Reich, describes five basic 'holding patterns' which form in the early stages of the child's development in response to frustration and stress, leading to the formation of character patterns. 'Holding together' is a schizoid response against the fear of fragmenting and falling apart. To 'hold on' to someone is an oral response coming out of fear, when no-one is consistently present. 'Holding up' is the narcissist's mechanism against falling down into the position of being small, which equals being controlled and used. The masochist 'holds in' against the fear of exploding and letting go. 'Holding back' becomes the chronic stance of the rigid position against rejection of one's loving feelings (Cotter 1996).

These holding patterns are the 'frozen history' of a person and as Chiron psychotherapists we try to melt them and bring them to consciousness. We can address them verbally and invite the client to explore them. We might facilitate mindfulness or hypnotic relaxation to heighten self-awareness; or we might use exercises, breathing, movement or massage. It is one of our principles to use the least invasive approach, and therefore apply direct touch or manipulation of the body carefully, because in some cases it can lead to disintegration and perpetuate dependency.

Breath work can be a key to exploring these holding patterns, as shallow breathing is a very effective defence against being in touch with oneself. Breathing connects the voluntary and involuntary system and can be used as the bridge between the conscious and unconscious. The polarity of release and containment in breathing represents the polarity of holding-in or letting-go of feelings. Controlling ourselves manifests literally in the holding of the breath.

When Reich elaborated his understanding of muscular armour, he divided the body into seven segments which hold energetic/emotional patterns and can be related to the Eastern chakra system. I will only refer to the segmental work briefly; a detailed account is beyond the scope of this chapter (Rosenberg 1985).

- Working with the ocular segment, which includes eyes, forehead and skull, can release strong emotions, as eye contact can reach a very intimate level.
- The oral segment (mouth, jaw and chin) is associated with biting or sucking, nourishment and sexuality, and connects us to feelings of longing and aggression. The mouth can express a range of feelings from hurt

and contempt to disgust, for example. The skin of the face reacts more sensitively to touch as there is no connective tissue layer and the nerves are immediately under the skin.

- The neck and throat (cervical segment) offer the last chance to swallow back upsurging feelings by contracting the muscles of the neck and shoulder girdle and to not give such feelings a voice.
- The chest harbours the heart and lungs, i.e. feelings of compassion, dignity, joy, sadness or longing; it includes the arms and hands as an extension of the chest.
- The diaphragm, as the main breathing muscle, plays a vital function in holding back deeper feelings rising up from the pelvis and belly.
- The belly segment with its vital organs and colon is seen as the energy 'centre' and place of wellbeing. Holding the belly in chronic contraction has the effect of numbing stronger primal feelings such as rage, grief and terror.
- The pelvic segment (pelvic floor, genitals, uterus and ovaries, legs and feet) generates and holds our sexual feelings, erotic desires and longings, our vitality and basic trust in life.

Phenomenological and character-analytical body psychotherapy

When focusing on energetic blockages or muscular armour our therapeutic interest is twofold: to help the client to become aware of resistance to surrendering to spontaneity, and to explore how exactly she is resisting (e.g. by pulling the shoulders up, or keeping the breathing flat); and to work towards releasing the holding pattern, letting the underlying dynamic emerge. An explorative, phenomenological approach is safer, as the therapist meets the client where she is and helps to integrate the conscious material the client presents.

It is not difficult to open up strong emotional dynamics, as working with the body is very immediate and direct. It invites emotional discharge (catharsis) and regression and can take the client to a very exposed, lonely and naked place. As body psychotherapists we need to know how to get the balance right between providing safety as well as challenge in helping to let go and taking risks. Optimal balance is unique to each person. The client's ability to self-regulate is paramount and needs to be respected and supported.

The later neo-Reichian schools – Hakomi (Kurtz), biodynamic psychotherapy (Boyesen) and integrative body psychotherapy (Rosenberg) – teach mindfulness and respect for the client's defences and attend very much to the phenomenological approach. Having experienced Keleman myself, I believe his work is especially worth mentioning here as it is diametrically opposite to approaches that invite catharsis and regression (e.g. bioenergetics, Janov's primal therapy, rebirthing). Keleman lets clients explore in minute detail (over a period of twenty minutes at least) a certain holding pattern (e.g. a twisted neck) by inviting them: to be aware of the posture and sense the muscles involved; to increase the holding even more, take it to the extreme and sense its function; to let it go step by step, very, very slowly and sense how the body resonates, noticing any changes happening.

Reich's plea for 'liberating the energy' was certainly overused in the earlier neo-Reichian movement and applied too mechanically. Emotional discharge was overvalued, facilitating either ecstatic or deeply relaxed states of being, usually short-lived. Raising the energy level in the body is not enough to enable deep psychic change and growth. As body psychotherapists we know that discharge of affects can be therapeutic if it resolves fixed patterns. We also know that discharging feelings and 'getting rid of them' can be a defence. A sense of self can be restored when sensation and feelings are rediscovered and when the client is also able to regulate them internally, sometimes containing them, other times expressing them appropriately.

In addition to the more process-oriented, phenomenological approach, bodily interventions supplement the verbal psychoanalytic approach well, given that defences manifest on a physical and psychic level. This way of working is a strong focus in Chiron's teaching, which follows in the footsteps of the character-analytical tradition of body psychotherapy. The therapist is more focused on the recognition and the resolution of defences and unconscious conflicts, addressing them more directly, sometimes using interpretation and connecting them to the internalised object relations. In the character-analytical approach the psychotherapist systematically addresses the 'character' (personality traits) rather than the symptoms (e.g. anxiety or depression). 'A person's character is the ensemble of their various armourings, the complex chord created by all the various notes of repression and inhibition sounded in their history' (Totton 2003: 73). This way of working does not necessarily conflict with the phenomenological approach, but takes it a step further, in the sense of taking it beyond what the client is conscious of.

Character-analytical interventions are by nature more confrontative as they address the defences verbally as well as physically (Eiden 2002; Johnson 1994). Relevant to this is Reich's emphasis on analysing the resistance first. This has become a standard analytical principle: do not interpret the underlying impulse before the anxiety has been worked through and do not interpret the anxiety until the defence has been worked through. In his book *Character Analysis* Reich also illustrates how the resistance reveals itself in feelings of doubt, mistrust and hostility towards the analyst and how vital the uncovering of this 'negative' transference is (Reich [1945] 1990).

Bioenergetics (Lowen, Pierrakos) has revived this tradition, but bioenergetics practitioners have not given the work with the therapeutic relationship (transference and countertransference) as much importance as we do at

Chiron. We believe that Reich's energy-model needed to be re-embedded in the relational context because emotions are always in relation to an object and are directed towards that object for contact and fulfilment.

Character structures are chronic manifestations of frustration of our needs in early childhood and they protect us from painful unresolved conflicts. Character-analytical understanding is not about pathologising or boxing the client into a fixed structure, but it provides a comprehensive map of existential issues which are not met in a child. In the therapy process we revisit these developmental themes and explore the inflicted wounds with the aim of loosening the grip they still have on our ways of relating as adults in the here and now. Attachment theory informs character theory as it confirms the importance of repairing very early dysfunctional patterns through relational attunement (Schore 1994).

The distinction between 'ego weak' and 'ego strong' structures is crucial here. We need to know how to respect someone with a fragile self and how to support and not overwhelm. Ego-building work, verbally and physically, and a more phenomenological approach need to go together with the characterological work. A certain amount of confrontation is necessary in order to penetrate and destabilise the defence structure, and enable new learning. However, most clients come to therapy because of suffering. They do not need added stress or attack. Confrontation is only useful for uncovering painful traumas and conflicts from the past if some transformation and healing is possible. Increasing suffering through psychotherapy can retraumatise a client and create a secondary armour which is much harder to undo.

An initial and ongoing assessment of the client's ego strength and 'psychological mindedness' needs to confirm that the client can benefit from this way of working. Body psychotherapy works best with neurotic character structures. Body psychotherapy on its own is less suitable for clients with a fragile self structure (narcissistic and borderline structures) and may even lead to worsening of symptoms in such clients. We learned at Chiron to recognise the strengths and shortcomings of body psychotherapy and to supplement the limitations with theory and practice from disciplines external to our field (see Warnecke's chapter on working with the borderline dynamic). This process was enriching and helped to formulate our integrative approach.

Teaching and integration of other modalities

'Biodynamic Massage' and 'Holistic Human Biology' have been part of the Chiron syllabus throughout the basic training phase. Biodynamic massage is fundamental to biodynamic psychology and one cornerstone of our work. The theory and application of biodynamic massage are covered in Schaible's chapter.

The use of biodynamic massage can be an integral part of a body psychotherapeutic process with a client. I will discuss the implications of this in the next section, as it became an ongoing debate in our team discussions whether to keep the teaching of biodynamic massage within the psychotherapy training or not. The training aims to help trainee therapists to find their own integration and to determine whether or not to keep biodynamic massage as part of their style of working. More than half of our qualified body psychotherapists have chosen not to use it. Receiving and giving biodynamic massage was certainly highly valued by the students for learning a deep energetic perception of their own and other people's bodies – invaluable for a body psychotherapist.

There was never a conflict about gestalt therapy being included in the syllabus. When we separated from the Gerda Boyesen Centre where we had learned and later taught biodynamic psychotherapy for some years, we knew we wanted to teach something different. We tussled with balancing the masculine and feminine principles, as the biodynamic way of doing body psychotherapy was very feminine and midwife like. We wanted to give the therapeutic relationship more weight and gestalt offered this.

Biodynamic psychotherapy is inwardly focused and helped us to get to know the internal flow and movements of the life-force and give it expression. Gestalt is more outwardly focused, more ego-centred, concerned with being aware, making choices, being authentic and emphasising the quality of the relationship in the here and now (Buber's 'I–Thou'). At the same time gestalt is body-oriented in emphasising sensory awareness and mindfulness of inner sensations and movements, breathing, posture and embodied language, and is based on the phenomenological way of working (following whatever is, and whatever is manifesting in the client, in the therapist, and between them in the 'here and now'). In particular, heightened awareness through mindfulness enables transformation of habitual patterns and a new embodied experience. We also take the dialogic attitude from gestalt, the importance of working in the here and now, the paradoxical theory of change (change comes about only by accepting what is), a wide variety of techniques including two-chair work, and the idea of the field as an extension of the notion of the whole. Reynolds writes more on these concepts in his chapter.

Our training module 'Charge in the Therapeutic Relationship' looks in depth at oneself as the therapist, the relationship to the client, and how both client and therapist respond to the 'charge' (or the lack of it) which is created by their contact. Therapists are asked to explore their particular therapeutic style, formed by their habitual ways of relating. They are also challenged to reflect on their therapeutic impulses, thoughts and interventions, and to explore new ways to respond. New understanding and an appreciation of the transference–countertransference process, working with regression, and the importance of re-enactment and parallel process have emerged out of this. Soth elaborates on these new developments in his chapter.

'Working with Diversity' became an essential part of our work, looking at the impact of the cultural background of both therapist and client and developing a greater awareness of our values, attitudes and prejudices as psychotherapists. For more understanding I refer you to Ablack's chapter.

Regulating the profession of body psychotherapy

In 1986 Chiron joined the UKCP (UK Council for Psychotherapy) as a member of HIPS (Humanistic and Integrative Section) – an important step forward in becoming part of mainstream psychotherapy. It opened new possibilities by entering a dialogue with other training organisations who had other ways of working. Attending annual conferences, presenting our work and listening to the work of others became extremely enriching, informing us about other theories and developments in the wider field. It also helped us to develop a critical attitude to our own approach.

Besides these gains, joining UKCP meant that we also had to compromise our values at times, which could feel like a rope tightening and limiting our creativity through increasing rules and regulations.

It was also important to keep a connection to our roots through membership in the EABP (European Association of Body Psychotherapy) and to attend conferences in order to stay in touch with the development of body psychotherapy. When EABP declared Body Psychotherapy as the official name for this discipline in 1991, we changed what we called our work from holistic psychotherapy to body psychotherapy.

The integration of shadow aspects of body psychotherapy (1992–2000)

Body therapy versus body psychotherapy – the place of biodynamic massage

Most clients who come to us expect an embodied experience, i.e. to be touched, either metaphorically or physically. Biodynamic massage is a very direct way of working with the body; it is hands-on, making contact at the boundary of self and other; it is relational. We are working with the nervous system of the body, which can feel very intimate. Touch can easily be experienced as an invasion, thus confusing or even retraumatising. Not to touch can on occasions be experienced as cruel, inhuman or punitive and gives the message that the body has no place in psychotherapy.

Biodynamic massage attempts to reach the unconscious and the client is expected to verbalise arising images or sensations. It needs to be distinguished from other forms of body therapy, such as aromatherapy or the Alexander technique. Such treatments attempt to improve the client's physical and emotional wellbeing by reducing pain, diminishing fatigue or stress, relaxing muscles, etc., but the 'psyche' is not systematically addressed. The difference between body therapies and body psychotherapy is the shift to working with the therapeutic relationship, guided by and grounded in transference dynamics. The body psychotherapist actively addresses defences and works with the underlying unconscious dynamics, while body therapists tend to apply a treatment and stay within the medical model or in the role of the supportive alternative practitioner.

In order to understand the use and meaning of biodynamic massage in the psychotherapy process, it will help to widen the issue and look at the psychotherapeutic value of touch, which has become a popular theme at psychotherapy conferences in recent years. Body psychotherapy takes a fundamentally different position in relation to the use of touch in comparison to psychoanalysis (Raab 1996). The analytic position applies a 'no touch' rule and touch is explored in the patient's fantasy only, while body psychotherapy postulates that the self is embodied and experienced through and within the body. Both methods differ in their definition of the role of the body in relation to self-development and therapeutic change. Can they learn from each other?

The analytical therapist wants to ensure Freud's rule of abstinence and neutrality:

- Touch risks sexualising the therapeutic relationship. Object relations therapists provide a clearer distinction from Freud's original position between sexual and nurturing touch, which allows the conclusion that touch does not need to lead to sexual feelings. Winnicott also says that it is through touch that the infant learns to accept the body as part of the self. Object relations laid the ground for more inclusive techniques and provided a rationale for physical contact between therapist and client. However, object relation analysts usually do not use touch.
- Touch interferes with the development of the transference. The therapeutic work is based on the interpretation of the patient's transferential feelings for the analyst and the patient will repeat early relational patterns, including the projection of early oedipal feelings. Touch provides gratification and thus undermines the neutral relationship.
- Touch inhibits development of the symbolic level. The symbolic level is achieved through the process of internalisation which happens through the absence of physical touch, in order that the internal image of being held can eventually replace actual holding. Optimal frustration allows the development of internalisation, so that the infant can hold the idea of the good holding and begin to soothe himself.

The purpose of the use of touch/biodynamic massage in body psychotherapy is closely linked to the role of the body in the psychological process:

- Touch in the form of biodynamic massage can reduce body armour and lower the resistance of the client. This is based on research on muscle tension, energetic charge, the interrelationship nervous system functions such as respiration, heartbeat etc. Among the body psychotherapy theorists who have explored this are Boadella (1974), Lowen (1975) and Keleman (1989).

- Touch can also facilitate a sense of containment and safety, or nurturance, and as a 'corrective emotional experience' can help the client internalise new experiences. For some clients it is only through safe physical holding that it is possible to let themselves feel what they never had and learn to trust and reach out.
- Touch can also bridge the gap between kinaesthetic awareness and verbal expression. An exploration of physical touch can give meaning to physiological experiences, e.g. sensations of coldness can lead to feelings of anxiety. All emotional experiences are bodily based and are first recognised as sensations, which can be especially helpful in connecting with preverbal experiences. It has been our experience, with narcissistic clients for example, that words will not touch their armoured body, but touch brings awareness to sensations which can then connect them with feelings and split off parts of the body.
- Touch can also elicit body memories which have been suppressed through dissociation. Disembodiment is a common response to trauma. Touch is sometimes likely to make repressed emotional memories erupt, hence more hyperarousal may occur. Babette Rothschild teaches our therapists her model of somatic trauma therapy that is body based, focused on trauma reduction techniques, and does not include touch (Rothschild 2000). However, if applied carefully, touch can also bring aliveness to parts of the body that have been numbed, and restore a sense of embodiment.

Can psychotherapists afford not to include touch any longer? The above brief theoretical discourse provides a rationale for the possible therapeutic value of the use of touch. Biodynamic massage is a structured way of working with touch. Possible dangers when working with biodynamic massage as part of psychotherapy process are:

- It can reinforce the medical model: the therapist is doing something to the client, such as helping him to relax, or increasing the charge in the body.
- It highlights even more the imbalance of power in the therapeutic relationship: the client is lying, perhaps partially undressed, receiving, while the therapist is standing and active.
- It can keep the client in an emotionally early stage of development and foster dependency and regression. It inhibits appropriate development of separation, expression of anger, or assertive sexuality.
- It can interfere with the development of transference as it keeps the client

in the positive transference relationship. Positive transference is needed as the basis for receiving and opening up to the massage process.

- It puts an overemphasis on sensations, feelings and the vegetative level, and mental processes are less encouraged.
- It does not give enough space for the symbolic, as the physical holding provides gratification.
- Touch can easily stimulate sexual transference. When this happens it is important to create distance; sexual feelings are more easily addressed verbally.

These arguments are valid and we, as body psychotherapists, have to be aware of these tendencies when using biodynamic massage. It is the psychotherapist's skill to be alert and to assess at what stage of the process the use of biodynamic massage could be beneficial. This also compels us to reflect on the polarity between bodywork and relational work. Asheri's chapter will explore further the dilemmas we face when using touch in psychotherapeutic work.

Moving to relational body psychotherapy

After a decade of working, our team of trainers was divided between those who work more with the body and those who work more with the therapeutic relationship, and the same polarity occurred amongst our qualified psychotherapists. It appeared that those who worked primarily with the body avoided working with the relationship and transference, and vice versa. We realised that body psychotherapy on its own does not provide a comprehensive understanding of relational work and that we had to look outside our field and draw on analytical theories. This became a very important step, as we believe that the client/therapist relationship is the fundamental medium through which therapeutic change takes place.

The polarisation of bodywork versus relational work has its roots in the body–mind dilemma in western thinking that I referred to at the beginning of this chapter. Analytical psychotherapy has elevated the importance of the mind; the body is not seen as significant (except insofar as it is a useful symbolic representation of what is happening in the mind) – thus language, cognitive understanding of the client's experiences, insight and interpretation are highly valued. Body psychotherapy has prioritised the biological body, seeing it as the source of truth which has been distorted by culture and language. Body psychotherapy idealised the body, especially by overemphasising the energetic aspect. Both positions are a distortion, a cultural construct. Our aim is to develop an integrated contemporary understanding of the significance of the mind and the body that we now call relational body psychotherapy.

Analytical teaching and analytical supervision were important for us. In particular it helped us better understand how to work with fragile self structures and get a clearer map of the psychodynamics of both the border-line and narcissistic structures. We learned from psychoanalysis the import-ance of the symbolic and the containing function of the mind, to dare to frustrate the client, as well as gaining more insight into the complexities of the transference/countertransference relationship. What we also take from object relations is the importance of the 'internalised object'. The dilemma for us is that these analytical theories are perpetuating the body–mind dual-ism and see the mind as more important than the body. It has been helpful to link body psychotherapy theory and practice with recent developments within contemporary psychoanalysis and attachment theories. The concept of 'intersubjectivity' (Stolorow *et al.* 1987) shifts the focus from the mind to interaction, where psychotherapy becomes an intersubjective experience between therapist and client, and the process itself becomes more important than the content or solutions of conflicts; the analyst is interactive rather than neutral. Soth, Asheri, Carroll and Ablack have written in more detail about this last stage of integration of our approach to body psychotherapy and I refer you to their chapters in this book.

Conclusion

I have not mentioned the spiritual aspect of our work, though this deserves to be acknowledged. It has become very apparent that the embodied therapeutic journey opens many of us to an awareness of the transpersonal dimension of our existence. Working holistically necessarily includes the 'spirit'.

Some of our qualified psychotherapists move on to do further 'spiritual work' which is not the same as psychotherapy but can be closely linked. Psychotherapy helps to establish a healthy balance between the inner and the outer realities, helping people to be happier in relationships, with sexual-ity, in their work and with life itself. This also establishes a stronger 'inner core' and facilitates contentment with one's life. Spiritual teaching focuses on the 'inner dimension' and uses meditation and other practices to be more in touch with a person's essence beyond emotions and the conscious mind. As body psychotherapists we aim to work for 'embodiment', which includes an inner connectedness to oneself and to being fully present in the 'here and now'. This inner connectedness incorporates the spiritual: being connected to the world around us and feeling part of something bigger.

We always felt that spirituality is a private matter for each individual. Therefore we have been careful not to impose this dimension as part of the training. Personally I worked with a spiritual teacher (Bob Moore in Denmark) over fourteen of the years I managed Chiron. Practising his work has been a resource which enabled me to stay present and open. In addition to Bob Moore I also want to express my gratitude to the various psycho-therapists who guided me. In particular I would like to thank my Jungian analyst Dr Joseph Redfearn, with whom I worked long term.

My personal process over the years connected me to a deep joy of life and made it possible for me to experience my work at Chiron as a service. It is enormously fulfilling and allows me to give something back to society as well as make an impact on the lives of individuals.

References

Boadella, D. (1974) *Wilhelm Reich: The Evolution of his Work*. Chicago: Henry Regnery Comp.

Boadella, D. (1997) Awakening sensibility, recovering motility. *International Journal of Psychotherapy* 2(1): 45–56.

Capra, F. (1982) *The Turning Point*. New York: Simon and Schuster.

Cotter, S. (1996) Bioenergetics at Cranfield. *Journal of Management Development* 15(3): 3–76.

Damasio, A. (1994) *Descartes' Error*. New York: Putnam.

Eiden, B. (2002) Application of post-Reichian body psychotherapy: a Chiron perspective. In: Staunton, T. (ed.) *Body Psychotherapy*. London: Brunner-Routledge.

Johnson, S. (1994) *Character Styles*. New York/London: Norton.

Keleman, S. (1975) *The Human Ground. Sexuality, Self and Survival*. Palo Alto, CA: Science and Behavior Books.

Keleman, S. (1989) *Patterns of Distress. Emotional Insults and Human Form*. Berkeley: Center Press.

Lowen, A. (1975) *Bioenergetics*. New York: Coward, McCann and Geoghegan.

Raab, I. (1996) Touch in psychotherapy. Controversies and applications. Dissertation, Massachusetts School of Professional Psychology.

Reich, W. (1973) *The Function of the Orgasm*. London: Souvenir Press (copyright date 1942).

Reich, W. (1990) *Character Analysis*. New York: Noonday Press (copyright date 1945).

Rosenberg, J. (1985) *Body, Self and Soul. Sustaining Integration*. Atlanta, GA: Humanics.

Rothschild, B. (2000) *The Body Remembers. The Psychophysiology of Trauma and Trauma Treatment*. New York/London: Norton.

Schore, A. (1994) *Affect Regulation and the Origin of the Self*. Hillsdale, NJ: Erlbaum.

Somers, B. (2002) *Journey in Depth. A Transpersonal Perspective*. Marshall, H. (ed.) Cropston, Leics.: Archive Publishing.

Stolorow, R. D., Brandchaft, B. and Atwood, G. (1987) *Psychoanalytic Treatment: An Intersubjective Approach*. Hillsdale, NJ: The Analytic Press.

Totton, N. (2003) *Body Psychotherapy. An Introduction*. Maidenhead: Open University Press.

Chapter 2

Biodynamic massage as a body therapy and as a tool in body psychotherapy

Monika Schaible

Biodynamic massage, an integral part of biodynamic psychology, is a holistic form of body therapy based on the assumption that emotional, mental and physical health depends on the free flow of our life-force. The biodynamic massage therapist listens with his hands to the distressed body tissues and opens with his touch blockages that hamper the free flow of the life-force. Biodynamic massage is primarily concerned with detecting blockages that have occurred due to unexpressed and repressed emotional energy. In conjunction with or integrated into a psychotherapeutic process it can be a powerful tool for change.

Introduction

This chapter will look at the work of Gerda Boyesen, the founder of biodynamic massage and biodynamic psychology, and include some biodynamic massage techniques; I will draw attention to Walter Cannon, who investigated the interconnection of emotions and gastrointestinal movements; and David Boadella's germ layer theory and its relevance to body psychotherapy. I shall go on to discuss how biodynamic massage has been developed at the Chiron Centre and how it is used as a body therapy in its own right and as a tool in body psychotherapy. In this context I will outline some of the crucial tensions that have arisen at the Chiron Centre regarding the use of touch and the use of massage in a relational context. I will argue for the value of biodynamic massage within a psychotherapeutic process, both for pre-oedipal and oedipal developmental issues. I will conclude this chapter with an appreciation of the richness and depth of Chiron's approach to body psychotherapy.

Personally my interest and belief in body psychotherapy was stimulated by my experience with physiotherapy and Vipassana meditation. In the 1970s I trained as a physiotherapist. During my work at a hospital specialising in treating people after severe accidents, I witnessed many times the deep emotional distress in patients with severe physical injuries. Physiotherapy was administered in a mechanical way to rehabilitate the suffering body but paid attention to neither psychological factors nor trauma responses.

Vipassana meditation is the second factor which influenced me deeply in how I think about the reality of the self. It teaches insight into the nature of the mind. In meditation the meditator can become aware of the physical processes that accompany mental states. The meditator learns to differentiate between physical sense objects and mental formations and how in turn mental formations give rise to physical processes. Vipassana is a spiritual method aimed at liberation from suffering by gaining insight into the causes of suffering. Buddhist psychology states that the cause of suffering is the avoidance of pain, which is so much in line with early psychoanalytic thinking of the role of defensive and protective mechanisms which, in order to keep the pain suppressed, split and fragment the mind and thus perpetuate neurosis. Sadly, Buddhism views the body as inferior, and deeper character traits are not changed during meditation.

Having been disappointed by the limitations of physiotherapy and encouraged by experiencing the body/mind interactions in Vipassana meditation, I was keen to engage with a holistic form of psychotherapy that works with both the mind and the body. The Chiron training in body psychotherapy seemed the best choice for me as it addressed the overemphasis on and idealisation of the body, which was so prevalent in the early days of body psychotherapy.

Eiden, Lude, Pervöltz and others, who all trained with Gerda Boyesen, founded the Chiron Centre for Body Psychotherapy as they had found Boyesen's approach to body psychotherapy limiting. The new integrative approach which developed at Chiron filtered back into how biodynamic massage evolved as a therapy in its own right and as part of a psychotherapeutic process.

About the Gerda Boyesen method

Gerda Boyesen's legacy is immense. The fruits of a lifetime dedicated to creating a framework and a method of 'curing the mind through the body' (Boyesen 1980) are rich and manifold. They have not only provided the ground from which the Chiron Centre grew, but also enriched the thinking of the use of touch in psychotherapy and counselling. There is overwhelming evidence for the significance of touch in human development. Ofer Zur refers to touch as the 'mother of all senses' (Zur 2004). According to Montagu, touch is the first sense to develop in the embryo, and all other senses are derived from it. An embryo develops, within three weeks of conception, a primitive nervous system which links skin cells to a rudimentary brain. Research suggests that psychological and neurological development depend on touch (Montagu 1971). In this light I see Boyesen's work as a major contribution to the use of therapeutic touch that goes far beyond relaxation and wellbeing. Her method is especially invaluable for clients with early developmental disturbances who have been difficult to hold and work with in mainstream psychotherapy.

Biodynamic massage comprises a broad range of massage techniques for working with bone, muscle and connective tissue and more subtle forms of the human energy field, to restore the free flow of the life-force, thus encouraging the body's innate capacity for self-regulation. Biodynamic massage is based on the understanding and belief that the body reflects the totality of our life, the sum of our experience and how we relate to ourselves and to the world. Habitual ways of being determine our muscle tone and shape our posture, which in turn affect our emotional/mental states, our breath, energy levels, nervous system, health and quality of meaningful relationships. Biodynamic massage aims to undo the holding patterns that restrict free and spontaneous self-expression, and tone and strengthen frozen and collapsed tissues to make the body a stronger container for emotional charge and higher levels of energy.

The concept of a life-force which underlies the thinking of biodynamic psychology has been the subject of a rift between thinkers of different philosophical schools. On one hand, there are the vitalists who postulate that there is a life-force permeating everything, underlying every movement, thought and feeling, and on the other hand, there are the reductionists who view life in a mechanistic way. Holistic is a term that was first used by Jan Christian Smuts (1870–1950), a South African general and statesman, who introduced the idea of a holistic science paradigm to overcome the dualistic split between vitalism and mechanism (Bischof 1995).

There has been much criticism directed toward the use of 'energy' or 'life-force' within body psychotherapy, and perhaps the most constructive has come from within the ranks of body psychotherapists. Nick Totton points to the inconsistent use of the term of energy and a lack of cohesion in the theory of body psychotherapy (Totton 2002). Wilhelm Reich was the first psychoanalyst to explore Freud's term libido as a bodily reality; he formulated from his research his 'orgone theory', and laid the foundation of body psychotherapy with his vegetotherapy. Orgone is another word for life-force. It originates from the words 'organ' and 'organism' to designate its bodily origin. It is interesting that Reich's therapeutic focus shifted from behavioural patterns to working with breath and movement through the influence of his partner Elsa Lindenberg, a dancer and choreographer, who had trained in Laban movement therapy and Elsa Gindler's sensory awareness method (Boadella 2007).

Boyesen developed biodynamic massage in Norway, where she studied psychology and had been involved with Reichian analysis through Ola Raknes. Her interest in Reichian vegetotherapy led her to train as a physiotherapist, where she met Adel Buelow Hansen. Hansen, the chief physiotherapist of a psychiatric hospital in Oslo, developed a neuromuscular massage technique for psychiatric patients with predominately hypertonic musculature, which coordinates the muscular system, breathing, relaxation and emotional release (Heller 2006). Lillemor Johnson, who also trained at the

Buelow Hansen Institute, developed a successful way of toning hypotonic muscles. Those two strands of massage methods formed the basis for biodynamic massage. Boyesen continued to refine these methods and added her own discovery of psycho-peristalsis as a means of self-regulation through vegetative discharge of nervous fluids. Biodynamic psychology is the integration of her understanding of Reichian bodywork, psychology and the massage methods from the Buelow Hansen Institute (Eiden 1995).

Body armour was originally a Reichian concept that referred to the skeletal muscles; Boyesen's concept of armouring includes other body tissues and internal organs. Her dynamic methods of working with body armour follow a simple principle: provoke and dissolve/harmonise to stimulate self-regulation by deepening the equilibrium of the autonomic nervous system.

Body armour

Muscular armouring

According to Reich, muscular armour develops when the life-force stagnates or freezes in the skeletal musculature. Muscular armouring, according to Reich, is hypertonic muscle tissue (hard, stiff, contracted) and Reichian vegetotherapy often employed painful means to loosen hypertonic muscle through sustained pressure, inviting cathartic release. Too much energy held or frozen in extensor muscles deprives them of proper function and leads to hypotonic, slack muscles unable to contract and move. Both tense and slack muscle tonus interferes with posture, mobility and aliveness, and prevents the psychic contents of the life-force from becoming conscious.

Connective tissue and visceral armour

Boyesen's contribution was how to recognise and work with the distortion to the energy flow, or life-streams, in the other two organ systems. She identified armouring in the connective tissue and armouring in the viscera. Connective tissue armouring affects the fluid circulation (fluids are understood as carriers of the emotional charge), leading to oedema or dehydrated cells. Visceral armouring is expressed in tissue changes of the gastrointestinal tract, and its following dysfunction or loss of peristalsis. Peristalsis is vital not only for the digestion and elimination of food but, according to Boyesen, also for emotional energy and the stress hormones that have been released into the bloodstream to prepare for the fight or flight response. The 'closure principle' (chronic absence of peristalsis) of the viscera leads to the absorption of stress hormones in the connective tissue (Boyesen 1980).

Ongoing visceral armouring finally leads to a collapse and breakdown of connective tissue function, which now becomes a storehouse for stress hormones. This, which Boyesen (1980) termed 'somatic compromise', tricks the mind into thinking that it has dealt with the emotional charge. But according to Boyesen the emotional charge is held and encapsulated in dehydrated connective tissue cells, which now have lost their ability to exercise their many functions of vegetative self-regulation. Biodynamic massage works with the underlying muscular tension to restore muscle function, thus increasing fluid circulation. Once collapsed connective tissue is rehydrated, the calcified components of the original charge can be reactivated, released and digested via vegetative discharge.

Working with the vegetative discharge is a gentle process, and the content of the emotional charge is not always conscious. Incomplete vegetative discharges can recycle older emotional material which may impinge upon consciousness via involuntary movements, emotional expressions, or through the client's dream life. Here it is important to give space for the impulses to become conscious and be integrated.

Principle of the vasomotoric cycle

The vasomotoric cycle is a useful concept for understanding the flow of emotional energy. In biodynamic psychology emotional energy is understood to follow a cycle that is governed by the autonomic nervous system. Stimulation and emotional charge are supported by arousal of the sympathetic nervous system (SNS) flowing upward, seeking emotional expression or action (discharge), which stimulates the parasympathetic nervous system (PNS) that governs relaxation digestion, and promotes a downward flow of the life-force; these are described by Reich and later by Boyesen as pleasurable streaming. Emotional blocks due to developmental injuries can occur at any stage within the vasomotoric cycle. A body psychotherapist can identify the blocks within the vasomotoric cycle and support the client through verbal or non-verbal contact, touch, imagery or movement to recognise underlying conflicts and work towards integration of repressed impulses. Anger, rage, fear and joy are understood to be supported by SNS arousal; sadness, depression and despair by PNS dominance.

Biodynamic massage techniques

Emptying

Boyesen developed a massage technique called *emptying* that can release the build-up of emotionally charged fluids in the cells. This very gentle form of bodywork exploits the fact that a relaxation response activates the parasympathetic branch of the autonomic nervous system, which supports peristalsis. Peristalsis is monitored by the therapist with a stethoscope that amplifies the peristaltic sounds. These sounds vary dramatically in pitch and speed, and offer feedback as to how emotional charge held in the body tissues is released and digested. A deeper homeostatic equilibrium is restored and the intensity of the pressure of unmanageable feelings is reduced.

Energy distribution technique

Energy distribution is another biodynamic massage technique that aims to restore the free flow of the life-force in the body. This method has a close resemblance to Boadella's concept of the three life streams originating from the three embryonic germ layers, on which I will elaborate later. The therapist manipulates through touch the downward flow and expansion of the life-force through the three energy circulation systems, encouraging a sense of pleasurable energy streaming and thus an interconnection of thinking, acting and feeling. For this the therapist focuses, with his developed kinaesthetic sense of energetic perception of the bodily layers, on bones, muscles and connective tissue, and the aura, the energetic field that goes beyond the physical boundaries of the body. He draws and guides with his touch the energy flow along the three primary embryonic energy pathways. Physical and emotional tensions, stemming as far back as prenatal development, are reduced.

According to Boyesen, the free flow of the life-force is intrinsically pleasurable, and clients experience an independent sense of wellbeing. The assumption is that when people experience this independent sense of wellbeing they are less likely to search for symbolic substitutes, and develop healthier styles of relating to themselves and others. The energy distribution massage can give rise to spiritual experiences, in which the mind is neither asleep nor awake, and the inner psychic life is illuminated.

Deep draining

Central to all forms of body psychotherapies is the role of breath. Breath is understood as an intersection between conscious and unconscious processes, as it can be either under voluntary or involuntary control. Socialisation and injuries to the self lead to repression and, in biodynamic terms, a somatic compromise and the development of a secondary personality. Physically it is expressed in a distortion of muscle tone and the interplay of flexor and extensor muscles. Emotionally it shows as alienation from self and environment with all the internal states of the absence of wellbeing and ability for self-regulation. Breath mirrors intimately and immediately our emotional states. Under emotional stress or physical threat we stop on our in-breath. This is considered a normal physiological process which prepares the person for the fight or flight response. When emotional expression or physical action takes place, the body returns to equilibrium. Incomplete emotional cycles result in 'startle reflex' patterns. A hostile or abusive family climate prevents the child from finding a healthy balance of arousal and calm. Chronic hyperarousal in childhood is today seen as a stronger contributing factor to psychological and mental health problems than single stressful events.

According to neo-Reichian therapists and Boyesen, a neurotic person develops a breathing block. A breathing block is the result of incomplete emotional cycles, where emotional expression was not allowed or possible; it results in dysfunctional breathing patterns and loss of mobility of the thorax due to degeneration of the muscles involved in the breathing process. Muscle tissue of the primary and secondary breathing muscles can become frozen or rigid (hypertonic) and create a barrier to free breathing. With neurosis there is often a disposition to contract on the in-breath. Neurotic breathing patterns lead to a lack of oxygen in the blood and decreased energy levels. Another important aim of biodynamic massage is to restore free, spontaneous breathing.

Boyesen modified Hansen's neuromuscular massage technique to what is today known as *deep draining*. Hansen's method, although often successful in softening muscular armouring and releasing emotional tension, led to strong vegetative reactions like diarrhoea, vomiting or shivering. Those reactions subside within a few days. More problematic, especially with psychiatric patients, was that the inner up-drift of emotional charge was sometimes too strong and could not be contained or integrated. Deep draining is a muscular technique that works directly with the breath. A cross-fibre shock impulse is applied to primary and secondary breathing muscles, timed with the moment just before the client reaches the breathing block in the phase of the inspiration. Through the shock impulse the client's in-breath overrides the habitual breathing barrier and the breathing muscles become activated. This initiates a biodynamic process in which the neurotic equilibrium is interrupted and repressed emotional material surfaces. Like no other technique, deep draining reaches beyond the ego defences and needs to be used only within clear guidelines of indications and contraindications. Ethically, deep draining requires the agreement of the client to enter into a deeper biodynamic process, and proper timing as to when to challenge the defences is essential.

David Boadella's germ layer theory and its implications for biodynamic massage and body psychotherapy

David Boadella, a Reichian psychotherapist and founder of biosynthesis, who was a guest trainer at the Gerda Boyesen Institute in London, made a major contribution to an embodied psychology with his theory derived from embryonic development. Seven days after gestation, embryonic tissue divides into three germ layers, the endoderm, mesoderm and ectoderm, which further differentiate into nerves, muscles, connective tissue, etc. (Boadella 1987). According to Reichian psychotherapists, the three organ systems represent the energy reservoir or energy streams in which Reich's postulated orgone energy circulates (Bischof 1995). Boadella views the body as three interconnected tubes derived from the three germ layers.

The following is a simplified presentation of Boadella's theory and psychotherapeutic use of the germ layer theory. Active from the beginning of embryonic development is the ectoderm which lies on the outside, and differentiates into skin, sense organs and nervous system, including the brain. This organ system regulates the relationship between self and environment and is related to thinking. The mesoderm, the middle germ layer, builds the skeletal musculature and bones, and relates to heart and circulation, fluids, muscle tone; relating to the movement function, it becomes more active close to birth. The endoderm is the innermost tube and forms the gastrointestinal tract and glands. This is the most passive organ system in embryonic development and is activated after birth. The endoderm is related to the feeling function. Boadella postulated that psychological health could be understood as a congruence and integration of thinking, acting and feeling, and depends on optimal prenatal development.

The discovery of peristalsis as a means of self-regulation

Since the seventeenth century, science and philosophy embraced Descartes' separation of mind and body and dismissed the idea that the immaterial mind could affect a material body. The body is now seen as a cultural representation constructed through language, reflecting values and taboos of respective cultures. The body can be understood through physical drives and relational needs, and a cultural control of those drives and needs (Cavallaro 1997). Freud and Reich were pioneer thinkers in understanding the body in terms of functionality as opposed to physicalism, which tries to understand the world primarily in terms of its physical laws. As today, psychotherapeutic thinking leaned on structural scientific advances in biology and physiology.

Heller (2006), in his article 'The golden age of body psychotherapy in Oslo', traces the development of Walter B. Cannon's work on psychoperistalsis and self-regulatory systems. Cannon was a leading authority on the subject of physiology. During World War I, Cannon spent time in Paris where he came in contact with the work of Claude Bernard, a nineteenth-century French biologist and physiologist. Bernard showed that all living organisms, including plants, are membranes that contain fluids which must be regulated by a physiological system.

On his return to the US, Cannon continued working and researching physiological regulation systems. In his book, *The Wisdom of the Body* (1932), he developed a vision in which behaviour, thought and feelings are viewed as organismic functions; they evolved to participate in homeostatic regulation in the form of organic structures such as nerves, hormones, muscles. He came to the conclusion that emotions play a central part in the body's self-regulatory system. (Self-regulation will be explored further in Carroll's chapter.) Cannon continued to research the complex interactions between emotions and gastrointestinal movements, and found that emotions can increase or decrease peristaltic movement. Anxiety reduces peristaltic mobility and blind rage stops it (Heller 2006).

In *The Way of an Investigator* (1945) Cannon writes about his interest in the peristaltic waves and his desire to learn about their effects. He observed that in the absence of peristaltic waves there was perturbation, and with restored serenity the waves returned. The inhibition of digestive activity by emotional excitement, he thought, made sense in an emergency situation, where supply of blood was needed elsewhere (Heller 2006).

The notion that all living organisms could be characterised as embodied fluid had a deep influence on Reich while he worked in Scandinavia, and later influenced the thinking of Boyesen and Stanley Keleman (Keleman 1985).

Cannon's vision of intestinal movement and emotion was almost forgotten after 1945, and was replaced by the generally accepted assumption that the brain was the only physiological support of the mind (Heller 2006). It took nearly another fifty years before Michael Gershon, a neuroscientist, stepped into the scientific arena with his publication *Your Gut Has a Mind of Its Own: The Second Brain* (1998). He showed that the gut contains a nervous system, which he called the enteric nervous system, that could, separated from the central nervous system and outside of the body, function independently; it contains more neuron-receptors for serotonin than the brain. Serotonin is a neurotransmitter involved in mood and impulse control (Aldridge 2000). Gershon also showed that more impulses travel from the enteric nervous system to the central nervous system than vice versa.

Psycho-peristalsis and its implications for body psychotherapy

Boyesen continued to reflect on Cannon's theory and its implications for psychotherapy. She coined the term 'psycho-peristalsis' to designate the psychological functions of the gut and pursued the idea of 'repairing the self-regulatory system' within a psychotherapeutic framework (Heller 2006). She observed that patients she was treating with neuromuscular techniques at the Adel Bulow Hansen Institute showed greater emotional improvement when they showed peristaltic movement, which was audible as gut rumblings. She further observed that patients had spontaneous gut rumblings at moments of deep emotional insight. Based on Cannon's theory and her own observations of the relationship between emotional excitement and peristaltic behaviour, she developed and refined massage techniques to regulate the emotional charge and to restore the physiological self-regulatory system.

How biodynamic massage has developed at the Chiron Centre

Chiron offers training in biodynamic massage both as a body therapy in its own right and as a method that can be integrated into a psychotherapeutic process. The teaching has stayed close to Boyesen's original concepts and techniques but draws a clearer distinction between body therapy and body psychotherapy. The main difference here is that as body therapy, biodynamic massage works within the protective resistance with the intention of melting the defensive bodily layers. In a psychotherapeutic context defensive patterns are gradually brought to consciousness, explored and worked through.

Body psychotherapy in general and biodynamic psychology specifically have held an idealised view of the body and paid no attention to working with the relationship. It was all about the client's process and the therapist was reduced to the role of a facilitator. Perhaps the most significant change in how biodynamic massage has evolved at the Chiron Centre is recognition that injuries to the self arise in relationship and need to be worked with within the therapeutic relationship in order to resolve developmental fix- ations and self-defeating patterns of relating. Chiron has harnessed psycho- analytic and psychodynamic thinking around working with transference and countertransference, parallel process and the potency of re-enactment as a prerequisite for change. (This will be explored further in Soth's chapter.)

Integrating biodynamic massage into a psychotherapeutic approach

The aim of Chiron's approach to body psychotherapy that integrates biody- namic massage could be summarised as: sustaining wellbeing in the body during the process of emotional transformation and maturation.

Chiron attributes great value and significance to touch as a psycho- therapeutic tool. Body and body processes are the foundation of psycho- logical states and self-structure (Caldwell 1997). Touch has also been proven to increase the therapeutic alliance, one of the most influential factors for therapeutic outcome. Through touch, deeper parts of the self-structure can be accessed, and by bringing them into consciousness they become available for working through.

However, there are limitations and potential harm in the use of touch. Touch that is sexualised, cold, hostile or punitive is naturally harmful and indicative of unreflective countertransference. The client also constructs the meaning of touch in the light of his early experience; a client can perceive touch as hostile, intrusive, controlling and punitive. These transference responses to ethical and therapeutic touch can be understood as re-enactment in the here and now, and by bringing them into consciousness they can be worked with. Great caution needs to be given to using touch when working with clients who have experienced physical or sexual abuse. Contraindications for touch, apart from medical considerations, are given for clients who show hysteria, paranoia, high levels of hostility or aggression, are highly sexualised or demand touch (Zur 2004).

At Chiron, a body psychotherapeutic approach that incorporates bio-dynamic massage aims to integrate three major psychotherapeutic approaches: working with the theory of drives and the objects of a person's inner world; working through a relational model that explores relational needs and parallel process; and working with the self-regulatory vegetative system. This requires great flexibility from the body psychotherapist and a capacity to hold and integrate three major, different, but complementary approaches to psychotherapeutic theory and practice in working with a client's process. It challenges the psychotherapist to work integratively and holistically, moving between relating and treating, learning from the client and educating him, working with mental and vegetative processes (Soth's chapter will reflect further on this challenge).

When a person comes to the Chiron Centre for body psychotherapy and expresses an interest in working with biodynamic massage he is assessed by one of the clinical directors for his suitability for this method and then referred to a psychotherapist. The initial interview, as rigorous as it would be in any type of psychotherapy, aims to learn about the reasons for seeking psychotherapy, to gain information about the primary scenario and to get a felt sense of the early relational distortions that are brought into the therapeutic encounter. At least to begin with, there must be a strong enough positive transference and countertransference in order to work with touch. To begin with I often use *basic touch* as a means for establishing non-invasive contact and *diagnostic touch* to build up a picture of how the client is functioning in biodynamic terms. I pay attention to the breathing pattern, sounds or lack of peristalsis, the quality of the body tissues, responses from the vegetative system (such as changes in the breathing and temperature, sweating, shivering, goose pimples) and to my own somatic resonance (embodied countertransference).

Somatic resonance is a term used in body psychotherapy for embodied empathy. Such sensations are the basis for reflecting on how the client is impacting on me. Gradually over many sessions I form an assessment of the client's relational and developmental needs and how his life-force functions. Cold in the body often suggests fear and resignation, heat indicates arousal of anger and rage. Breath is the most immediate mirror of how we handle our emotional charge. Sudden shallowing of the breath is for me an indicator as to when the client's defences are activated or they are dissociating from their experience. I believe that the most crucial aspect in working directly with the body is to know when the client's defences are activated to help him manage his process. Melting of defensive layers is desirable at any stage of the process, but challenging the defences successfully requires proper timing to avoid a premature ending of the therapy. And sometimes clients need containment, which requires leaving the protective resistance intact.

It is my experience that sensitive use of biodynamic massage fosters trust in the therapeutic alliance, which is a prerequisite for allowing transference and parallel process to ripen. Some clients need and benefit from actively going into emotional expression within this work; others need to learn to surrender more deeply into themselves, depending on where they are habitually stuck within the vasomotoric cycle. My therapeutic intention is to bring involuntary movements, which occur in the melting process, to the client's consciousness; by inviting them to amplify the impulses, I help the client to identify and own repressed infantile impulses (e.g. sucking, kicking, biting, spitting) and thus build up a stronger ego structure. According to Reich, the melting of a resistance brings up earlier and more primitive defences in the client, and each defensive layer needs to be worked through. It is here that I see the value in using biodynamic massage also with more highly developed ego structures.

But biodynamic massage can also help to build up and to sustain embodied feelings of wellbeing. The work towards a deeper homeostatic equilibrium brings the client in touch with mental and physical states that have been out of reach. Biodynamic massage can give rise to spontaneous and powerful images and metaphors that can be explored and grounded in the therapeutic relationship. I recall one client with a low-functioning borderline structure. As I massaged her hand (this was where she could tolerate touch), she said she felt like 'being in God's hands'. With this metaphor she communicated to me for the first time, after months of distrust and sustained attacks, her growing trust in the process and her desire to feel whole.

There is no fixed structure to this process; each process is unique, as is each person's life story and character. Depending on the developmental stage of the client, the work can move from the massage table to the chair or to working on a mattress to allow space for negativity and separation. I find that the theory of character structures provides me with a map of developmental conflicts, body structures and relational styles (Johnson 1994), which helps me to make sense of what is happening and what is avoided in the process.

Crucial tension in Chiron's work regarding the use of biodynamic massage in a psychotherapeutic process

The process of alignment with the requirements of UKCP proved to be a critical time for biodynamic massage and its survival as a core part of the body psychotherapy training at Chiron. This resulted in a polarisation among the trainers and the students. For many, 'touching the body' had become the shadow and consequently biodynamic massage became marginalised. It is to Roz Carroll's credit that she brought together findings from neuroscience in the context of body psychotherapy and biodynamic massage and related its relevance to the psycho-physiological development of the infant. However, not all Chiron psychotherapists use biodynamic massage or touch in their approach. Students and therapists choose their own integration of body psychotherapy.

Criticisms expressed towards this form of body psychotherapy are that it: invites regression; sets up an unequal power dynamic in the therapeutic relationship; creates transference and countertransference that are impossible to work with; gratifies the client; and, perhaps worst of all, does not provide the client with the necessary frustration and rage he needs in order to be able to work through infantile dependency, grief and rage. This, according to the critics of biodynamic massage within a psychotherapeutic process, would leave the client with a deluded view of reality and perpetuate neurotic and immature behaviour.

In particular, the archetype of the 'good mother' has been associated with body psychotherapy and biodynamic massage. The identification with the 'good mother' archetype can block awareness of the complexity of transference and countertransference. It is my experience that working hands-on directly with the body actually deepens my experience of the countertransference and often helps me to sense what is hidden.

However, the principles of a psychodynamic or psychoanalytical model cannot be compared with the biodynamic model, and the two evaluated solely on their differences, based on the assumptions of their own school. All approaches to psychotherapy have in common that they seek to alleviate emotional suffering and promote the overcoming of developmental arrests. The difference lies in the method, and each method needs to follow its inherent dynamics to achieve its goals. The real challenge is in how successfully the integration of different approaches can be achieved.

Conclusion

Writing this chapter has been for me a process of rediscovery and appreciation of the roots of body psychotherapy. An incredible richness of scientific and metaphysical thinking and knowledge of the psyche and the body have informed and shaped body psychotherapy as it is practised and taught at the Chiron Centre today, since the beginnings of body psychotherapy with Wilhelm Reich. It is almost impossible within this framework to validate all the influences and contributions from the many different fields such as psychoanalysis, object relations theories, body and movement therapies, sensory awareness method, biology, psychophysiology, physics, chemistry, neuroscience, western and eastern philosophy. They all have contributed and still are contributing to deepen our understanding and vision of a person whose mind and body are intrinsically linked with their emotional life, and physiological and cultural processes. The growing view of the body is that of a body evolving through consciousness.

The quality of touch or the lack of it is for everybody such a fundamental experience; touch can broaden and deepen the therapeutic experience and meet developmental needs which often cannot be worked with in models that exclude touch. There still remains the task of working towards a more cohesive theory. We need to accept and bear the flaws of a therapeutic method that has developed empirically and does not always fit neatly into scientific categories. Today, body psychotherapy and biodynamic massage receive validation and new impulses from advances in neuroscience of the brain and the gut. In my experience biodynamic massage has proven to be invaluable, particularly for clients with very early disturbances and fragile self-structures who cannot benefit from more verbally oriented models. Biodynamic massage can feel magical to receive. Conscious contact with one's life-force enables self-actualisation and integration. However, it is by no means a magical method that provides a shortcut to psychological health. Deep and lasting change requires the cultivation of a reflective self and acceptance of the consequences of one's own actions and pain as a part of our human condition.

References

Aldridge, S. (2000) *Seeing Red & Feeling Blue: The New Understanding of Mood and Emotion.* London: Arrow.

Bischof, M. (1995) Biophotonen: *Das Licht in unseren Zellen.* Frankfurt: Zweitausendeins.

Boadella, D. (1987) *Lifestreams: An Introduction to Biosynthesis.* London: Routledge and Kegan Paul.

Boadella, D. (2007) *Wilhelm Reich: from Psychoanalysis to Energy Medicine.* Online publication. Retrieved from http://www.biossintese.psc.br/WilhelmReich.htm.

Boyesen, M. L. (1980) Psychoperistalsis: the abdominal discharge of nervous tension. *Collected Papers of Biodynamic Psychology, Volumes 1 and 2.* London: Biodynamic Psychology Publications.

Caldwell, C. (1997) *Getting in Touch: The Guide To New Body-Centered Therapies.* Wheaton, IL: Quest Books.

Cannon, W. (1932) *The Wisdom of the Body.* New York: Norton, 1960.

Cannon, W. (1945) *The Way of an Investigator.* New York: Hafner, 1968.

Cavallaro, D. (1997) *The Body for Beginners.* New York: A Writers and Readers Documentary Comic Book.

Eiden, B. (1995) The history of biodynamic massage. *Association of Holistic Biodynamic Massage Therapists Newsletter,* No 3.

Gershon, M. D. (1998) *Your Gut Has a Mind of Its Own: The Second Brain.* New York: Harper Collins.

Heller, M. C. (2006) *The Golden Age of Body Psychotherapy in Oslo.* Online publication. Retrieved from http://www.vegetotherapyorg/modules/articles/article.php?id=14.

Johnson, S. M. (1994) Characterstyles. New York/London: W. W. Norton & Company.

Keleman, S. (1985) *Emotional Anatomy*. Berkeley: Center Press.

Montagu, A. (1971) *Touching: The Human Significance of the Skin*. New York: Columbia University Press.

Totton, N. (2002) The future for body psychotherapy. In: Staunton, T. (ed.) *Body Psychotherapy*. Hove: Brunner-Routledge.

Zur, O. (2004) *To Touch or Not To Touch: Rethinking the Prohibition on Touch in Psychotherapy and Counseling*. Online publication. Retrieved from http://www.drzur.com/touchintherapy.html.

Chapter 3

Gestalt body psychotherapy

Alun Reynolds

The history

Gestalt Body Psychotherapy was a second year module in the Body Psycho-therapy training at Chiron, following the first year modules in Body and Energy work and Biodynamic Massage, alongside their second year sequels. Gestalt Body and its own third year sequel, Charge, were both originally formulated and taught by Rainer Pervöltz, influenced in particular by Jack Rosenberg (1985). When Pervöltz left, Gestalt Body was then developed by Gillian Kelly and Alun Reynolds whilst Charge developed separately under Michael Soth (see Soth's chapter).

Pervöltz's version of gestalt was very exciting, experimental and embodied, emphasising a real meeting in the here and now between client and therapist. Kelly not only added to this a more rigorous theoretical background but also brought a more spiritual strand of gestalt (I–Thou relating of Martin Buber [1923] 1958) that she had learned from Robert Resnick (1995) and others at the Gestalt Therapy Institute of Los Angeles summer schools. Having originally trained more in the Fritz Perls style of gestalt under Helen McLean (1996), Ischa Bloomberg (Hemming 1993) and Joseph Zinker (1977), Reynolds also brought a new focus on an embodied spirituality in gestalt, using ancient practices such as meditation and sensing, 'mindfulness' and 'bare attention' as a basis for working in the here and now. He was influenced by Robert Hall (1975) of the Lomi school and other colleagues who had broken away from Fritz Perls such as Ron Kurtz (1990) and Claudio Naranjo (1993).

Even though it had more theory than before, Gestalt Body remained one of the most experiential modules on the training so this chapter is faithful to that.

Sensing as a starting point for awareness practice

The starting point for my day as a therapist is sensory awareness.

So join me now in placing the soles of both your feet on the ground and bring your attention to the contact your feet are making with it. Just bracket any ideas or ideals you may have about how your feet should be feeling and feel them exactly as they are. Then gradually add sensing your legs, hands and arms and make them the objects of your concentration.

As you attempt to focus your consciousness on sensing, you quickly become aware of how difficult it is to do this simple task. Our habitual ways of not being present 'here and now' arise, often known as resistances or hindrances or demons. You may find you have soon wandered off, either attracted to something else or grappling with the opposite demon of repulsion and aversion which may take the form of anger, fear or judgement. You may be experiencing doubt about whether this is a good thing to do. Or you may just experience sleepiness and find it difficult to stay awake. Or you may conversely feel restless.

Even if you accept that sensory awareness is a good thing, it is easy to fall into the trap of wanting to get rid of the hindrances that appear to be in the way: this leads rapidly to feeling stuck, arising from an internal fight between the desire for awareness and its resistance.

The gestalt solution, rooted in more ancient spiritual practices such as bare attention, is to bring the process of awareness itself to everything, including the hindrances and the reactive self, not just locating awareness in some ideal of a self-aware, fully embodied, conscious, authentic self. So the most skilful way of dealing with these hindrances is to sense them and name them as they arise (Kornfield 1993) and bring your awareness back to sensing your objects of concentration, your arms and legs. The practice of concentrating on sensing naturally leads us to the phenomenological method.

Phenomenological method

Phenomenological inquiry is a bit of a mouthful but it simply means experiencing whatever is emerging here and now. In this, we describe and investigate the what-and-how of our experience, putting to one side our beliefs, assumptions and explanations in the interest of allowing novelty to emerge. The phenomenological data include our body sensations, our breathing, our images, our behaviour, our feelings and the meaning we make of it. The aim is not to change our experience but to inhabit it more fully and to investigate it with an attitude of curiosity and inquiry. This means facing our life exactly as it is, rather than how we would wish it to be. This embraces whatever is happening including states of confusion, emptiness, wanting something else to happen and, most importantly, nothing ostensibly happening (Almaas 2002).

Phenomenological inquiry involves describing rather than explaining, bracketing previous assumptions, assuming anything in the field may be of importance and an attitude of curiosity (Mackewn 1997). The inquiry could be into the inner zone (body sensations, breathing, inner feelings), middle zone (thoughts, memories, expectations) or the outer zone (seeing, hearing, touching, smelling, tasting) of our here and now experiencing. An alternative way of classifying experience is Peter Levine's SIBAM: body sensations (S), images (I), current behaviour (B), affect (A) and meaning (M). An integrated experience will involve each of Levine's five elements whereas character formation or traumatic experience will result in one or more of these five elements going missing (Levine 2006).

So not only is sensing important as an often neglected part of our phenom-enological field but also sensing, meditation and bare attention practices help us to be more anchored, centred and focused to experience more depth and richness in our inquiry.

The intrinsic power and beauty of phenomenological inquiry is based on a hugely significant principle: the paradoxical theory of change.

Paradoxical theory of change

The paradoxical theory of change is attributed to Beisser (1970) and gestalt but of course is rooted much more deeply in ancient spiritual traditions. Change occurs by being more what we fundamentally are, not by aiming at becoming what we are not. It involves feeling and living the truth of our existence, rather than trying to fix and meddle with things. Life in all its forms is inherently dynamic so that deep and lasting change unfolds from within, not from an imposed agenda from outside. So in terms of my earlier example, paradoxically by naming the hindrances and bringing them into conscious awareness, they start to lose some of their power rather as Rumpelstiltskin does when named in the old Grimm's fairy tale (Grimm [1812] 2004). In other words, change occurs from being fully present with whatever is happening, fully experiencing it, naming it and investigating it as it is without trying to change it. As you do this, whatever you are experiencing gives way to a deeper reality or you are already at the deepest reality so that change is organic or dynamically part of whatever it is you are experiencing. It happens as part of your full engagement with the experience rather than you making it happen.

Embodied therapeutic presence

So let us return to sensing. Whilst you read, see if you can keep at least 50% of your attention on sensing your feet, your hands and your sitting-bones.

Another reason why sensing and your senses are so important is because one of the key aspects of being a psychotherapist is therapeutic presence. Traditionally gestalt talked about the importance of the therapist and client being in the here and now but said precious little about how to do it. It was implied that it was a matter of intention, all one had to do was to resolutely bring oneself into the present. In the late 1960s, some eminent colleagues of Fritz Perls at Esalen such as Hall (1975), Kurtz (1990) and Naranjo (1993) started to address more seriously how to be present and noticed how much of gestalt was not new but rooted in ancient spiritual practices. The principle of embodied therapeutic presence became a vital element of Gestalt Body and indeed the Chiron approach, being present in your belly and heart as well as in your head (Kepner 2003).

Fritz Perls went too far in saying 'lose your mind and come to your senses' but what he may essentially have been trying to do was to reduce the importance given to the intellect. There are three main areas of experience: the head centre, the heart centre and the belly centre. All are important. The head centre is to do with thinking and the intellect and is well developed in many people in the west. The heart centre is to do with feeling and emotions and is less developed in general, leading to a high rate of heart disease in the west. The belly centre (also known as the hara or kath centre) is the sensing or power centre of the body and is the least developed area for most people in the west.

Another form of sensing is to concentrate your attention on the hara centre. Usually it helps most people to focus on the breathing in this area. For some it helps to count in-breaths and out-breaths up to ten and then begin again. After a count of one or two, many find their attention has wandered, in which case begin again. Every time you return to your breath counts.

One of the aims is to be able to centre and locate oneself in the present, here and now. It can help us feel more solid, stable and grounded when we have our feet on the ground, with a better connection to both the earth and reality. Or this may initially show up our lack of these things which, whilst painful at first, can be helpful. The arms and legs are the less emotional parts of the body so they can be a good place to start to reclaim your embodied awareness. With our legs and feet, we make contact with the ground and the earth; with our arms and hands, we reach out and contact others in the world. Sensing our limbs therefore helps us integrate our inner journey with our life outside.

Movement and energising

One of the pitfalls with some sensing and awareness practices is a lack of movement so I like to use more movement in my sensory practice.

A more mobile sensing practice is to lift, move and place your feet almost as if walking in slow motion. The aim is presence and sensory awareness whilst building your powers of concentration, keeping your mind focused in one direction. Lift, move and place. Lift, move and place. Continue for ten or twenty minutes.

An alternative is one of the grounding or energising exercises pioneered by Lowen and Lowen (1977). Stand and have your knees bent and your feet shoulder distance apart with the outer edges of your feet parallel. Have the weight on the balls of your feet. Bend forward so that your head is hanging down. Soften your head, neck and your breathing and put all of your weight into the balls of your feet. Experiment with varying the bend in your knees so that your legs start to shake. Put your hands on the floor to balance but keeping all your weight on your feet. Allow the vibrations to happen as your life-force flows down into the ground. If your legs do not shake, that is OK too; just stay with your experience exactly as it is.

Alternatively, stretch your body in any direction it wants to go in and support this with your breathing and by letting a sound out to the end of your breath as you do this. Move around the room: slow then fast, forward, back and then sideways, first on tiptoe then on your heels. Jump up and down several times.

Stand with feet shoulder distance apart. Take a deep breath as you raise your hands and arms above your head. Then holding your breath, bring your hands down, massaging the front of your body all the way from head to toe five times. Then with a cutting motion downwards with both arms, shout 'Hape' (pronounced Har-pay). Just take a few deep breaths and notice any change in the quality of your energy. Say one word to describe it, for example burning, heat, alive, refreshed, or if your experience is less pleasant or uncomfortable, say whatever is happening: irritated, discomfort, numbness.

Self-regulation

Embodied presence supports phenomenological enquiry, which in turn leads to the unfolding of a reality that is inherently dynamic. The more we investigate and have a felt experience of reality as it is, the more we align ourselves with its inherent dynamism. As we enquire, deeper and deeper layers are revealed, each layer giving way to another part of the truth, to move us closer to our true nature which wants to reveal itself and know itself. This process of unfolding dynamism leads us to another key Chiron principle of self-regulation or self-organisation (see Carroll's chapter for further discussion). In other words, we have the inbuilt capacity and tendency to unfold and become our deepest nature, although of course factors such as inertia, character structure and traumatic events can block this self-regulating tendency.

The contact cycle and styles of contact

Gestalt therapy puts an emphasis on the development of self through contact and awareness which occurs in a self-environmental field in which the emerging foreground (figure) always occurs in relation to a background (ground). Figure–ground or gestalt formation and destruction occurs in cycles of sensation, awareness, mobilising energy, taking action, contact, integrating and digesting, and then withdrawing again. A gestalt is a pattern in which the figure that is foreground is always connected to the background against which it stands out. The natural order of reality is flux and flow so that inherently built into reality is the dynamism of change. One response to this is to try and control the change and its impact on us by rigidifying our habitual patterns, which become fixed gestalts that trap and imprison our natural flow and vitality. One of the themes of early body psychotherapy (Soth 2006) was to find methods of releasing us from our fixed patterns, which of course get embodied in muscular and other bodily tensions (Lowen and Lowen 1977). This can indeed be liberating but it is not enough on its own as it sides with one half of an internal conflict, creating another conflict between the other part of us and the therapist. We need to also enquire into the restriction and resistance itself so we can understand why it is in place (Reynolds 2000).

Early gestalt theorists talked about projection, retroflection, introjection, confluence, desensitisation, egotism, deflection and reaction formation as being 'bad' interruptions to an otherwise 'good' free-flowing contact cycle. More recently, Wheeler (1991) and Melnick and Nevis (1992) have emphasised how people do not actually interrupt their contact but instead they have styles of contact which modify the flow of contact along a series of bipolar continua. So confluence is neither intrinsically good nor bad but is part of a contact style along a continuum of confluence, separateness and isolation (Mackewn 1997). Similarly, projection is along a continuum of projecting–imagining–owning, whilst introjection is part of introjecting–chewing–rejecting, and retroflection is part of retroflection–expression–aggression. Whether a particular contact style is appropriate or not depends on the individual and the situation or 'field conditions'.

In the Gestalt Body module at Chiron, we were really able to integrate the gestalt cycle with the biodynamic cycle (see Schaible's chapter), which gave trainees a powerful tool in their work with clients. Gestalt therapists were often taught to turn 'It' into 'I', but the advantage of biodynamic therapy is that it has a subtle and inviting method of working with the 'it' or id energy, allowing it to emerge and grow spontaneously. Biodynamic work can also be particularly appropriate in supporting digestion and integration within the whole body–mind. So there was a good fit between what was done in the Body and Energy and Biodynamic Massage modules and what was taught in the Gestalt Body module on the Chiron training.

Being an object in the first person

Let us explore one of these contact styles with a few exercises that we used at Chiron. Our teaching method was to start with experiencing, which would form the ground for later explanation of theory.

For the first exercise, get some pen and paper and then find an object in your immediate environment which has some interest to you. Then stretch your imagination to see if you can feel what it is like to be that object. Then start to describe yourself as that object in the first person, for example, 'I am a sea-shell etc.'

I am a precious blue stone. I am strong electric blue with darker lines running across me. I am spectacular. I am an object of great beauty and fascination. I am sensuous and very smooth to touch. I am heavy and substantial and appear to be made of stone but if you turn me over there is an entrance that shows that I am made of glass inside. I appear hard and tough at first but I am also sensitive and vulnerable. I have been fashioned out of fire and heat. As you look, some of my glow remains inside reminding me of my origins. If you hold me up to the light, the fire from which I was formed shines forth in a deep, unfathomable mystery, the coolness of the blue impregnated with glorious amber. I am not a regular shape. I am unusual and unique. I stand out in a crowd. I am not mass-produced. I have been shaped and formed by a craftsman or artist who has created me out of love and passion for his craft. I am a valuable object to my keeper and owner.

The famous empty chair or internal dialogue

For the second exercise, think of three people you have some connection with. You could choose people with whom you have a lot of charge like your mother, father, siblings or life partner. Or you could choose relationships that may or may not be less charged such as colleagues, friends, neighbours or acquaintances. Take four chairs or cushions or pieces of paper. Use one to represent yourself, with the other three a short distance away next to each other facing you. Sit on the first chair and imagine becoming the first of the people you chose. See if you can feel what it is like to be them and describe yourself in the first person. Then speak as that person back to the empty chair representing you for about seven minutes. When you have finished come and sit in your own chair and hear what has been said to you. You can reply briefly with one sentence if you wish. Then do the same for the other two people you have chosen.

For some, gestalt therapy is synonymous with the empty chair technique (even though it originated from the founder of psychodrama: Moreno 1987), with hitting a cushion to express rage towards mother, or with other variants of an essentially internal dialogue between different parts of oneself, including our projections on to other people. Others have reacted to this gross over-simplification by emphasising a completely different form of dialogue, that of the live dialogic relationship between the therapist and the client, which includes both strategic and authentic relating. I will say more on this later.

But for now, let us focus on skilful use of internal dialogue. Internal dialogue can be between different people in your life as in the above example, between different sub-personalities (such as the classic topdog–underdog), between different parts of a dream, or between different parts of your body (such as one hand speaking to the other or your belly speaking to your head).

There are a number of key parts of a fruitful internal dialogue.

1 Make sure it is in the form of a dialogue between the parts and that they talk to each other in the form of I–You. A common mistake is to let the client talk into the air or carpet or to move into third person description.
2 Make sure the two parts are clear at the beginning. Choose the parts with the most energy or interest.
3 It is often helpful to set up a third meta-position for observing the dialogue.
4 Give time for the client to feel each role and to separate when the client switches from one role to the other.
5 Sometimes it can help to exaggerate one of the roles.
6 Make sure the client switches to the other role. A common mistake is to allow the client to speak from only one part which is often the habitual position.

There are some contraindications against using internal dialogue. First, the empty chair and other such techniques often do not work well with narcissistically wounded clients (Greenberg 1996). Those who are highly compliant will do it but as a performance or to please you, the therapist, rather than as a genuine voyage of discovery. The internal dialogue then lacks energy and does not go anywhere because the compliance is sitting on top of it. Or the client will not want to do it at all out of a fear of being vulnerable or exposed or not in control. The obvious therapeutic move instead is to focus on the compliance or fear itself and work more in the transference/countertransference relationship. Secondly, the empty chair does not work well with highly divided clients such as borderline clients who have deeply split object relations (Yontef 1993). In this case the experiment of internal dialogue makes the client feel more intensely and worse, without resolution. Again, the therapist has to focus instead on the material arising in the therapeutic relationship, and there is usually plenty of that. With the increasing prevalence of narcissistic and borderline disorders in our consulting rooms, there are good reasons why the empty chair technique is used less, even though in the right circumstances it is very useful.

Projection–imagining–owning

The two exercises above, of being an object in the first person and the empty chair technique, both illustrate the phenomenon of projection. Projection occurs when what is actually part of oneself is located in other people or even in objects. For example, our disowned anger may be experienced by us as anger of others towards us.

Originally Fritz Perls (1973: 37) talked of projection only in its negative aspects but there may be positive aspects to this style of contact. One positive aspect of projection is that it can be the basis for empathy, being able to project oneself into another's shoes and imagine what it is like to be that person. The gestalt term for this is inclusion, in the sense that the therapist includes herself into the world of the client. Great artists project themselves into their writing, painting or music, hopefully without suffering from confusion of identity.

An obvious negative effect of projection is a considerable loss of energy and vitality within the self as well as a loss of reality. There may be irritation towards the outside world which carries the projection. Neurotic or unaware projection leads to a lot of misunderstanding or conflict. An example of this is an unfriendly person who always complains others are rejecting him. And projection is at the heart of much paranoia and prejudice.

Projection is a strong characteristic of the narcissistic structure where those elements that do not fit in with one's self-image are disowned. This supports the 'me-superior, others-inferior' illusion of the narcissistic structure.

Proflection takes projection one step further into action by doing to others what you hope they will do to you. An example would be hugging others or being kind to others, with the underlying wish that others will hug you or be kind to you.

An important task of therapy is to re-own these projections, to take responsibility and not be just a hapless victim. Often there is a grain of truth in the projection so acknowledgment of this helps the disengagement. As you experienced above, one way of working with projections is to make use of the classic gestalt experiment of the empty chair in which one dialogues between oneself and the disowned parts. Dreams can be seen as projections, so that a dialogue between different elements in the dream in the first and second person can be a way of working with this. One can also look out for which people and what behaviours most annoy us and then reflect on how we might also be like that. Perls also insisted on clients using 'I' language, not 'you' or 'it' language. For example, instead of 'it's a nuisance' say 'I don't want to do that' or instead of 'it's miserable weather today', say 'I'm miserable today'. Re-owning unfelt projections can be supported by exaggeration ('I'm livid with you' rather than 'I'm feeling a bit angry'). Awareness of projections may also increase with reversal, so if you suspect someone is rejecting you, then reverse the process and see on what grounds you are rejecting them.

Desensitisation–sensitisation

A common way of avoiding awareness is to desensitise so that we do not feel what is really going on in our deeper layers but only feel the surface. At some level we realise this, feel dead, and respond by increasing the stimuli (often several at once, e.g. eating breakfast with the radio on whilst talking, looking at the newspaper and getting ready for work). Or this may initially show up as being oversensitive to our internal and external world, leading to hysterical responses and ultimate withdrawal to be able to cope. Sensing and meditation practices, such as those mentioned earlier, help restore the ground for being present with our here and now experience, whatever that is.

Introjection–chewing–rejection and the superego

As we inquire into anything, one of the unhelpful forces that tends to come up is the inner critic or superego that wants to keep things stable and restore things to how they have always been, not because that is the optimum way of being but because there is some sort of safety and security in the familiar, however horrible and dysfunctional it may be. In gestalt terms, the parental voice that tells us things should be done a particular way is introjected or swallowed whole. Byron Brown (1999) points to three ways in which we engage with the superego (by trying to reason with it in our head, by crumpling in our heart, or by wrestling with it in our belly) and gives many different ways of disidentifying from it (e.g. by indignation, truth, humour, exaggeration, disinterest, changing the subject, or compassion).

Introjects can also be loosened using the empty chair, allowing the topdog inner critic to dialogue with our underdog soul child. Another way is through the Fritz Perls eating exercises, to encourage healthy chewing and spitting out rather than swallowing whole from others, not just food but ideas, feelings and sensations (Perls *et al.* [1951] 1972). And of course there is always phe-nomenological inquiry; especially inquiring into ways in which we are a harsh critic to others or ourselves, as well as inquiring into what we think is right, good or strong about doing so.

If you have a rejecting style of contact with the world or with yourself, then the rejecting object relation may need exploring from both sides. You may identify more with the part that rejects or the part that is rejected or with both. Similar methods of dialogue and internal inquiry can be used.

Retroflection–expression–aggression

Retroflection involves turning sharply back against oneself and doing to yourself either what you want to do to the other (e.g. biting your fingernails instead of making biting comments) or what you want them to do to you (e.g. stroking your own body). Like all contact styles, retroflection has some very positive aspects, for instance preventing you hitting other road users or your children or your clients when you feel severely provoked. The negative aspects may show up bodily in tight muscles, limited breathing, and psycho-somatic symptoms like headaches, stomach upsets and arthritis, as well as emotional and behavioural symptoms such as self-harm and self-torment through a harsh inner critic. Undoing harmful retroflections involves facilitating expression of feeling and healthy aggression. Awareness can be directed towards non-verbal gestures and other bodily signs of retroflection. These can be exaggerated or taken over (Kurtz 1990). We can do ego motoric work such as the Lowen exercises (Lowen and Lowen 1977). Using the empty chair, we can dialogue between the topdog repressor and the underdog repressed parts of ourselves. We can inquire into the intelligence behind the retroflection and the ways in which we repress. The classic Fritz Perls method was to reverse retroflections: guilt was changed into statements of I resent, complaints into expressions of I want and so on.

Confluence–contact–isolation

Confluence is a flowing together of you and I into a we. We may experience healthy confluence as a fetus in our mother's womb or as a baby at our mother's breast. Or later in life, we may experience a melting with our sexual partner or oneness with the universe. Unhealthy confluence or dysfunctional closeness and/or isolation occur when the mother or caretaking figure rewards clinging and punishes independence at the rapprochement stage of individuation in child development, about the age of eighteen months or the 'terrible twos'. In extreme cases, this gives us the split object relations of the borderline personality (Masterson 1976, 2000), but given that our upbringing is never perfect, all of us to some extent experience something of the same dilemma when negotiating a healthy balance between closeness and independence.

Sensing, breathing, movement and other body awareness exercises help support the ground for healthy separation, for therapists as well as their clients. Often unhealthy confluence has a sticky or superficial niceness or sleepiness which masks hidden negativity. Encouraging that negativity to surface, to be felt and to find safe expression enables, more and more, the unspeakable to be spoken and healthy difference to be tolerated and eventually celebrated.

Egotism–spontaneity–impulsivity

Egotism blocks spontaneity with control, thereby stepping outside oneself and becoming a spectator or commentator on oneself and one's relationship with the environment. A positive use of egotism is when you as a therapist or client use your observing ego in a therapy session, or when anyone constrains impulsivity with a big purchase like buying a house or a new car. With unhealthy egotism, we try to control the uncontrollable or surprising aspects of life, leading to a deadness and dullness so that we are lacklustre, lacking true spontaneity. Again, we can inquire into the ways we block spontaneity and the beliefs behind the blocking. And, we can connect more with our here and now sensations, feelings and thoughts so that our talking becomes rooted in our here and now experience.

Reaction formation–responsiveness

Reaction formation occurs when we do the opposite of the inner impulse, so that our secondary reaction replaces the original primary feeling. For example, hate can mask love, rage or self-pity can cover grief, compliance can be a substitute for anger, guilt avoids resentment, and aggression can hide fear or anxiety. A common trap is to be diverted by the expression of secondary feelings, which is circular and self-defeating. Resolution is found in the expression of primary feelings, leading to action and completion.

Deflection–focusing–bluntness

Deflection is a style of contact that avoids sensation or meaningful impact. Healthy deflection may enable traumatised clients to deflect from the trauma and to find a safe space (Levine 2006). However, deflection can lead to super- ficiality and avoidance, not only excluding trauma and criticism but also keeping out appreciation and love. One way of working with it is to bring the deflection itself to the client's attention and explore what happened at the point where the deflection was made. Another is to deflect the deflection, gently insisting on going back to the original material. And anchoring in body sensations, breathing, and here and now primary feelings can help the client to focus on what really matters.

I–Thou gestalt

Another aspect of our work that gestalt sheds light on is the therapist–client relationship. Influenced by the work of Martin Buber ([1923] 1958), gestalt therapy distinguishes between I–It relating and I–Thou relating. Both are part of therapy, but according to Buber, it is I–Thou relating that is the more important for healing and becoming a full person.

Strategic or I–It relating is about us trying to *get* somewhere or trying to *do* something. Even if the client is coming in order to learn to be more authentic, that is still in the context of a strategic relationship. We relate strategically to clients right from the start in establishing the therapeutic alliance, when either we as therapists or our clients have aims, when we are working with the transference and countertransference, when we are taking a back-seat or eagle-eye view, or when we are thinking about clients or taking them to supervision.

Authentic or I–Thou relating between the therapist and the client is about us *being* together in the room, in a person to person dialogue, without strategy or aim. The more the therapist is present, the more the therapist is able to stand in the client's shoes and confirm that to the client, and the more the therapist can communicate genuinely in the service of the client, the better the conditions are for authentic relating to occur. Despite its importance, authentic relating cannot be made to happen: it happens by grace not by aiming at it.

However, the I–Thou relationship calls on the client to see the therapist as another real person rather than through the veil of their own transference. Therefore I–Thou relating is contraindicated when working with those with strongly habitual characterological patterns such as those with masochistic, borderline or narcissistic tendencies for which a more transferential understanding and way of working is more needed. This was recognised in the third year courses which over time increasingly brought a more psychodynamic way of working into the training (see chapters by Soth and Asheri).

Conclusion

It has not been possible to do justice to what we taught in Gestalt Body in one chapter, for instance the practical and experiential teaching of the many bodily interventions available, though I trust that I have nevertheless given some flavour of its dynamism, spontaneity, aliveness and vibrancy. I give my heartfelt thanks to all those who contributed to its development, especially to all my teachers, to my colleagues Rainer Pervöltz and Gillian Kelly and to all our students. And above all, I give thanks to my own parents and ancestors whose presence in my heart enables me to do the work I love so much.

References

Almaas, A.H. (2002) *Spacecruiser Inquiry: True Guidance for the Inner Journey.* Boston and London: Shambala.

Beisser, A. R. (1970) The paradoxical theory of change. In: Fagan, J. and Shepherd, I. L. (eds) *Gestalt Therapy Now.* Palo Alto, CA: Science and Behavior Books.

Brown B. (1999) *Soul Without Shame: A Guide to Liberating Yourself from the Judge Within.* Boston: Shambala.

Buber, M. (1958) *I and Thou.* Edinburgh: T and T Clark. (First published 1923.)

Greenberg, E. (1996) When insight hurts. *British Gestalt Journal* 5(2): 113–120.

Grimm J., Grimm W. and Byatt A. S. (2004) *The Annotated Brothers Grimm Fairy Tales.* New York: Norton. (First published 1812.)

Hall, R. K. (1975) My life measured out in abandoned words. In: Stevens, J. O. (ed.) *Gestalt Is.* Moab, UT: Real People Press.

Hemming, J. (1993) Beyond right and wrong: an interview with Marianne Fry. *British Gestalt Journal* 2(2): 77.

Kepner, J. (1987) *Body Process: A Gestalt Approach to Working with the Body in Psychotherapy.* New York: Gardner.

Kepner, J. (2003) The embodied field. *British Gestalt Journal* 12(1): 6–14.

Kornfield, J. (1993) *A Path with Heart: A Guide through the Perils and Promises of Spiritual Life*. New York: Bantam Books.

Kurtz, R. (1990) *Body-Centred Psychotherapy: The Hakomi Method*. Mendocino, CA: LifeRhythm.

Levine, P. (2006) *Trauma through a Child's Eyes: Awakening the Ordinary Miracle of Healing*. Berkeley, CA: North Atlantic Books.

Lowen, A. and Lowen, L. (1977) *The Way to Vibrant Health: A Manual of Bioenergetic Exercises*. New York: Harper and Row.

Mackewn, J. (1997) *Developing Gestalt Counselling*. London: Sage.

McLean, H. (1996) Ischa Bloomberg 1930–1995: Personal reflections and tributes. *British Gestalt Journal* 5(2): 79–83.

Masterson, J. F. (1976) Psychotherapy *of the Borderline Adult: A Developmental Approach*. New York: Brunner/Mazel.

Masterson, J. F. (2000) *The Personality Disorders*. Phoenix: Zeig-Tucker.

Melnick, J. and Nevis, S. (1992) Diagnosis: the struggle for meaningful paradigm. In: Nevis, E. C. (ed.) *Gestalt Therapy*. New York: Gestalt Institute of Cleveland and Gardner Press.

Moreno, J. (1987) *The Essential Moreno: Writings on Psychodrama, Group Method, and Spontaneity*. New York: Springer Publishing.

Naranjo, C. (1993) *Gestalt Therapy: The Attitude and Practice of an Atheoretical Experientialism*. Nevada: Gateways Publishing.

Perls, F.S. (1973) *The Gestalt Approach and Eyewitness to Therapy*. New York: Science and Behaviour Books

Perls, F., Hefferline, R. and Goodman, P. (1972) *Gestalt Therapy: Excitement and Growth in the Human Personality*. London: Souvenir Press. (First published 1951.)

Resnick, R. (1995) Interviewed by Malcolm Parlett – Gestalt therapy: principles, prisms and perspectives. *British Gestalt Journal* 4(1): 3–13.

Reynolds, S. (2000) Working with resistance in dance movement therapy. *E-Motion: Association of Dance Movement Therapy (ADMT) UK Quarterly* XII(3): 18–24.

Rosenberg, J. L. (1985) *Body, Self and Soul: Sustaining Integration*. Atlanta: Humanics.

Soth, M. (2006) What therapeutic hope for a subjective mind in an objectified body? In: Corrigall, J., Payne, H. and Wilkinson, H. (eds) *About a Body*. London: Routledge.

Wheeler, G. (1991) Gestalt *Reconsidered: A New Approach to Contact and Resistance*. New York: Gardner.

Yontef, G. (1993) *Awareness, Dialogue and Process*. New York: Gestalt Journal Press.

Zinker, J. (1977) *Creative Process in Gestalt Therapy*. New York: Vantage Books.

THE CRUCIBLE

Linda Hartley

The training programme at Chiron, and the shared exploration that took place in service of its development within a core staff group which remained stable over a period of about ten years, formed a 'crucible' where theory and practice were intensely debated. The constant presence of directors Bernd Eiden and Jochen Lude, who together held the Centre through many tensions and conflicts, created a unique opportunity within which Chiron's work could grow. Within this crucible the transformatory processes of evolution could occur, sourced in those approaches that formed its foundations, and informed by the grounded, rich and divergent positions of the different trainers.

In *The crucible*, Soth, Carroll, Asheri and Ablack share aspects of their work, exploring the development of core principles of the Chiron approach from their individual perspectives. (Other trainers who were part of the core staff group and made significant contributions to this process, not represented here, include Jochen Lude, Rainer Pervöltz, Werner Prall, Kristiane Preisinger, Michaela Boening, Susan Law, Gillian Kelly, Tree Staunton and Margaret Landale.) The leap from a holistic to an integrative approach is outlined, then the evolution of Chiron's contemporary integral, relational and pluralistic approach explored more fully. Although a more or less linear path of development can be extrapolated in retrospect, as Soth outlines, he also acknowledges that the process of evolution was more spirallic in nature – a weaving and interweaving of many threads of theory and practice forms the rich, complex, and sophisticated tapestry that evolved.

A training director since 1993, Michael Soth took over the third year gestalt module, Charge, from Rainer Pervöltz, and initiated a process of challenge which enabled some major theoretical developments to take place. The notion of working with 'charge' as attending to 'body-emotion-mind in the here-and-now, within the relationship' had been established by Pervöltz, who had trained with Jack Rosenberg. With its attention to 'the relationship', this notion was the origin of and precursor to the focus on the relational dimension which was to develop in the following years. Drawing on character formation and Rosenberg's 'primary scenario' (developmental notions originally deriving from psychoanalysis (Rosenberg 1985)), as well as gestalt (more allied to Buber's 'I–Thou' relating (Buber 1958)), as described by Reynolds, Charge prepared the ground for another creative tension between dialogical –authentic and transference–countertransference relating. Allied with the gestalt principle regarding the paradoxical nature of change, Pervöltz's teaching inevitably drew attention to the therapist's habitual stance and efforts to 'be a good therapist' or 'fix the client'. The phenomenology of the therapeutic relationship came into the foreground through his suggestion that, as therapists, we are 'relating to others as we are relating to ourselves'.

Soth acknowledges the enormous influence that Pervöltz's contribution had upon his own thinking, and Chiron's work in general, as he challenged himself and his colleagues to embrace the relational dimension more fully. In Chapter 4 he outlines Chiron's history from a theoretical perspective, focusing in particular on two major leaps which he calls the 'integrative project' and the 'relational turn'. He addresses this both from a broad theoretical overview and from the personal experience of undergoing a process of deconstruction, a dismantling of held beliefs and a 'habitual position' as a body psychotherapist. Recognition of the inevitability of re-enactment within the therapeutic relationship, and questions as to how to surrender to and relate from within it, led him to the theory of the 'fractal self' and parallel process.

A central aim of psychotherapy is the development of self-regulation, the capacity to monitor internal processes of the bodymind and orient the whole organism towards balanced function; this is ideally learnt in infancy through responsive parenting. Roz Carroll continues in Chapter 5 with a discussion of this core principle from her perspective as a Chiron therapist. She weaves together ideas from attachment theory, neuroscience and physiology, integrating them with Chiron's evolving model of body psychotherapy which incorporates the complexities of intersubjectivity and parallel process. Her descriptions of interaction and attunement between infant and carer offer a developmental understanding of the roots of the subtle client–therapist interactions described in chapters by Asheri and others. Self-regulation and interactive regulation between client and therapist, the therapist's own self-regulation, contact and the function of imagery, are some of the themes explored.

In Chapter 6 Shoshi Asheri, also a training director, further explores 'the paradoxical tension of the intersubjective engagement' through the question of whether to use touch in body psychotherapy, and if so, when and how to touch. In the contemporary Chiron approach it is a complex, multidimensional question where touch is perceived to be a relational event; consideration is given to the multiple self-states and changing developmental needs of the client, as well as the therapist's multi-layered engagement. Asheri addresses the issue within the integral relational model introduced in Soth's chapter, bringing theory to life through case material and personal story which highlight the transformatory potential that can be realised when conflict, paradox and charge within the relationship are embodied and fully engaged with.

In 'The dynamics of diversity' Carmen Joanne Ablack describes her experience of confronting and working with different identities of function and form, as well as social definition, in psychotherapeutic practice. She argues passionately for awareness of cultural diversity in all its expressions, for 'conscious relationship', to be an integral part of psychotherapy training, acknowledging that our woundedness, and that of our clients, includes prejudice and discrimination, often unconscious, around personal, social and cultural diversity. When this dimension of experience is consciously explored within the therapeutic relationship, it enriches the multi-layered nature of integral relational psychotherapy and reveals another level of truth. Chiron's engagement, from the very beginning, with different, often contradictory, theories and modalities has enabled a creative attitude towards diversity of all forms to be fostered.

References

Buber, M. (1958) *I and Thou*. Edinburgh: T. and T. Clark.

Rosenberg, J. (1985) *Body, Self and Soul – Sustaining Integration*. Atlanta, GA: Humanics.

Chapter 4

From humanistic holism via the 'integrative project' towards integral-relational body psychotherapy

Michael Soth

Caveat: beyond linearity

Although for the sake of brevity and clarity I will present the development of my work as a sequence of theoretical shifts, it is important to remember that this is a linear abstraction imposed on the messiness of the actual developmental process. A journey has been made, and in looking back on the path we identify particular stations along the way which we can now connect in our mind as if the route had been there all along. However, as the poet Antonio Machado (1912) reminds us: 'You traveller – there are no paths, only wind trails on the sea!'

With hindsight we may realise that certain stations were necessary preparations for what was to follow. But there is a difference between recognising an overall meaningful unfolding (thus encouraging a teleological faith in the process) and the presumption that a map of the process enables us to predict, manage and control it.

How my notions of 'development' have developed

My own notions of development have themselves developed, from a fairly idealised linear conception imaged as a journey up the mountain of 'truth' to some pinnacle of self-realisation, to the less predictable, multi-dimensional, contextual-relational and paradoxical view I have of the process now.[1] This parallels in many ways the evolution of Wilber's integral meta-model over the last three decades.[2]

As this constitutes a whole theme in its own right, I will here only briefly make explicit some basic assumptions regarding an integral notion of 'development'. Development:

- is not simply linear progression; a closer geometric metaphor: spirallic
- occurs both incrementally *and* in sudden leaps (both continuous *and* discontinuous)
- is multi-modal and multi-dimensional; in complex systems (Maturana

and Varela 1980, Gleick 1987), has aspects of both chaos *and* order

- proceeds in overall 'holarchic' fashion, with ever more complex, embracing and qualitatively 'higher' systems emerging from and through the structures of previously established ones (epigenetically building on prior evolution) where each new level brings something qualitatively new and unforeseen which both *transcends and includes* prior levels
- can often be recognised with hindsight as following an overall dialectic (Hegel's thesis–antithesis–synthesis), which *can* be reductively interpreted as linearity
- involves transformational thresholds where the breakdown or death of an old, partial and previously exclusive and dogmatic identity allows the emergence of a new more complex and embracing sense of self
- is, therefore, a painful, messy affair (one step forward, two steps back); each new level presenting potentialities and dangers ('with great power comes great responsibility')
- is not always unambiguously positive: there is regression as well as progression, and regression in the service of progression
- can be pathological: e.g. 'dissociate and repress' instead of 'transcend and include'.

These principles inform both my therapeutic thinking about my clients' changes as well as my own, and in this chapter I am aiming to present some reflections on my professional development in such a way as to be consistent with these principles.

An integral perspective suggests that development occurs incrementally within an established level or structure (via 'translation', Wilber 1980), until forces both from within and from without the system push towards a breakdown of that structure. At that point development occurs in more radical fashion (via 'transformation', ibid.), and an emergent process *may* allow a new structure to organise itself – in terms of human identity: a more embracing sense of self.

Whenever a previous identity is challenged and eventually transcended, an experience of loss and death occurs – this is a necessary ingredient in transformation. Certain cherished assumptions and identifications will need to be shed: the new identity recognises these – with the benefit of hindsight – as manifestations of an outgrown partiality. From the perspective of the original identity, however, these losses may appear as betrayals and compromises, as a 'watering down' of essential principles.

These 'identity issues' pose emotionally charged questions in any developing organisation:

- What belongs 'inside' our shared collective identity – who is 'in' or 'out'?
- How do we understand and frame that identity in any stable, coherent

sense as well as remaining open to its evolution and possibly radical revision?

Both as a community of practitioners and as a training organisation we had to struggle with these questions.

Principles in reflecting on past development

Because a detailed enquiry into transformative process often reveals some degree of swinging from one extreme to another[3] (as the old identity is increasingly opposed and breaks down), I use a third term 'contradiction' alongside 'translation' and 'transformation' to characterise that particular conflictual phase of the process. These terms may be clarified by their resemblance to Hegel's thesis–antithesis–synthesis.

As in an individual's journey, in reflecting on past developments, I look for turning points and crises which punctuate and structure the process. In evaluating these, I wonder:

- Are these crises translations, contradictions or transformations?
- How thoroughly are earlier positions revised or deconstructed?
- To what extent are earlier positions *included* in any transcending synthesis (or fudged, ignored or forgotten)?[4]

The phases of Chiron's development

In preparing this chapter I have applied these ideas to the last twenty-five years' development since the founding of Chiron, and a sequence of four phases and three major quantum leaps (with a possible fourth on the horizon) suggests itself to me, interspersed with expansive periods of translation, followed by phases of contradiction which then ushered in the next transformation (Fig. 4.2).

This distinction is debatable, as in some ways we may view each phase as just a further incremental extension of the previous one. However, this would fail to take into account the radical discontinuities involved in each shift. I am proposing to think in terms of three such quantum leaps, as each time a thorough deconstruction and contradiction of previously held principles was necessary, involving painful struggles and shedding of once precious beliefs. I explain the apparent incremental continuity through the fact that in each transformation the previous identity was indeed *included*, not only *transcended*.

However, in spite of the apparently seamless evolution of core concepts, one of the challenges for the reader of this book will be that – although the same terms may be used throughout the chapters – they have acquired profoundly different meanings and contexts in the various phases. One example

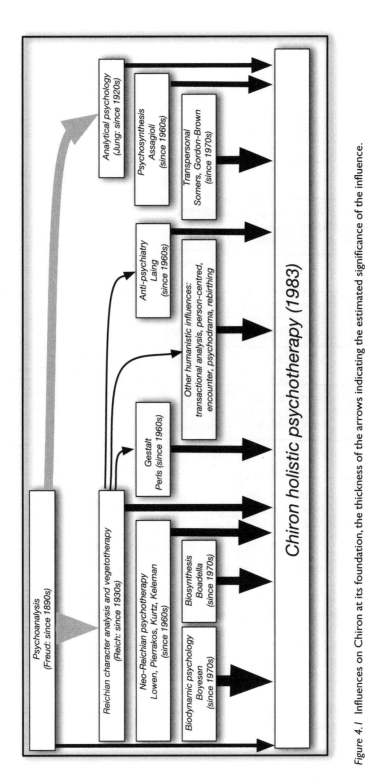

Figure 4.1 Influences on Chiron at its foundation, the thickness of the arrows indicating the estimated significance of the influence.

Psychoanalysis
(Freud: since 1890s)

Reichian character analysis and vegetotherapy
(Reich: since 1930s)

Analytical psychology
(Jung: since 1920s)

Psychosynthesis
Assagioli
(since 1960s)

Transpersonal
Somers, Gordon-Brown
(since 1970s)

Anti-psychiatry
Laing
(since 1960s)

Other humanistic influences:
transactional analysis, person-centred,
encounter, psychodrama, rebirthing

Gestalt
Perls (since 1960s)

Neo-Reichian psychotherapy
Lowen, Pierrakos, Kurtz, Keleman
(since 1960s)

Biosynthesis
Boadella
(since 1970s)

Biodynamic psychology
Boyesen
(since 1970s)

Chiron holistic psychotherapy (1983)

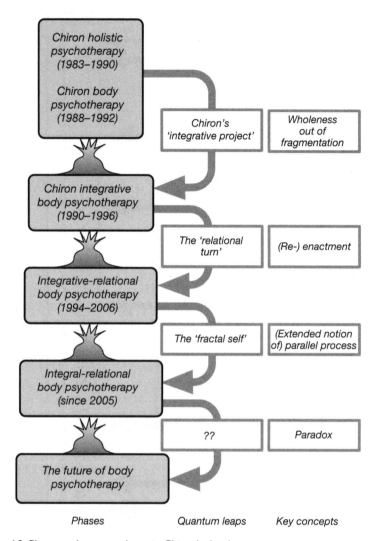

Figure 4.2 Phases and quantum leaps in Chiron's development.

that I will later touch upon is the notion of 'ego': initially understood as a static, defensive structure opposed to the body's aliveness, the notion became more complex and paradoxical with each quantum leap, resulting eventually in my 'parallel process' formulation of the 'conflicted ego in conflict with a spontaneous conflict' (Soth 2005a). But the same point applies to apparently more simple and innocuous terms like 'attunement', 'self-regulation' (see Carroll's chapter), 'containment', 'somatic resonance' and even more so to complex terms like 'transference' and 'countertransference'. One identifiable difference in meanings arises through the shift from 'one-person psychology' to a 'two-and-many persons' perspective. Although the term 'countertransference', for example, was used and recognised in its broad meaning all along, the 'countertransference revolution' (Samuels 1993; Soth 2005a) fills it with profoundly new meanings that not only transcend prior ones, but in some ways reverse them.

Other shifts in meaning have to do with the deconstruction of 'medical model' notions and with understanding the therapeutic relationship as a whole system.

Purpose and scope of chapter

A detailed outline across all four phases to date, both of the many theoretical influences from other approaches and how they were – step by step – partly integrated, partly rejected, is beyond the scope of this chapter (but see Fig. 4.3). Space will not permit a comprehensive presentation of the substance of these developments, which would involve detailed discussion of the struggles between competing models, how established concepts were found to be insufficient, how they were complemented and opposed by others, leading to eventual revision.

Rather, after a brief overview, I will present a highly subjective and incomplete series of 'snapshots': turning points significant to my own personal–professional development, with no claim to comprehensiveness, balance or impartiality. Especially the discussion of what I call the 'integrative project' at Chiron is sketchy in this chapter (but see Soth 2007d), as here I focus primarily on the developmentally later 'relational turn': how it transformed my outlook and work and the theoretical re-formulations which made this visible.

Rather than offering the reader the illusion of a final worked-out product, I want to convey the flavour of the process, with both its agony and conflict as well as its transformations and quantum leaps. In order to get across the 'spirit' of Chiron as the 'wounded healer', I want to evoke the process rather than the outcome, the atmosphere of 'transcend and include' rather than merely the latest, up-to-date soundbite.

Brief outline of Chiron's development

From humanistic-holistic towards integrative

In broad terms, we could say that – true to the original principles we were pursuing (wholeness, the 'wounded healer') – we first went through a phase of *consequently applying the principles of our own therapy to ourselves*, both as people and as practitioners. The continuing connection with our own wounds and conflicts had to eventually confront us with the limitations of our own 'character' (our habitual positions and shared identity as a community

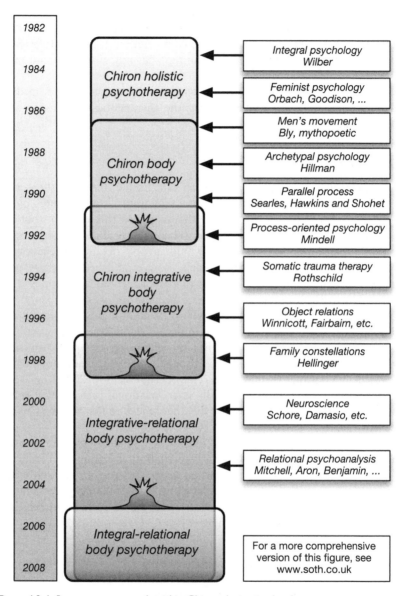

Figure 4.3 Influences on my work within Chiron during its development.

of practitioners – Soth 2007c), including its idealisations, limitations and denials.

In *engaging with our own shadow aspects, as individuals and as a subculture,* we had to painfully recognise that our initial identity excluded – to our own and our clients' detriment – areas of therapeutic sensitivity and expertise which other approaches took for granted and which we had been oblivious of.

This was the beginning of the integrative impulse, based on the recognition that the fragmentation of the psychotherapeutic field reflects and mirrors the condition of our clients' – and our own – *psyche*. If we ourselves cling to a particular therapeutic identity (glorifying and only identifying with a small sliver of a vast rainbow of diversity), using it as a defensive shield with the same fixity as our clients (trapped in *their* habitual protection mechanisms), we are hardly in a position to facilitate or contain their process. The validity we had been ignoring in (or denying) other therapeutic approaches reflected areas of wounding, denial and insensitivity in ourselves.

Chiron's integrative project

Our own principles of inclusiveness helped us challenge within ourselves unconsciously-held omnipotent self-images of idealised 'perfection' which excluded and dismissed other perspectives. Through thus questioning our habitual humanistic-holistic stance and its dogmatism, we began to recognise our own approach as partial (considerably less 'whole' than intended and proclaimed) and discovered its limitations and counter-therapeutic aspects. We needed help and thus had to reach beyond our 'comfort zone', becoming curious about other approaches and perspectives. Slowly then, we *began turning the principles of other therapies upon ourselves*, exposing us to severe and radical critique by other approaches (psychodynamic, Jungian, existential etc.) as well as their inherent richness. The *integrative project* significantly expanded our range of theory, technique and especially relational flexibility. However, it also enhanced our awareness of the underlying fragmentation, both in the field and in ourselves, to the point where both students and trainers often felt confused by piecemeal *eclecticism*, buffeted between contradictory principles and paradigms, *all* of which were now recognised as valid (Soth 2007d).

The question then becomes: what holds the pieces together? what constitutes the 'glue', the pattern that ties the fertile chaos into a complex whole?

The disavowed, but pervasive hidden 'medical model'

In terms of our subcultural background, we were committed to humanistic values of equality, transparency, authenticity, and were opposed to power-over, imposed authority and hierarchy. We were influenced by anti-psychiatry, and like Laing (1970; Laing and Esterson 1970) questioned pathologising labels and diagnosis altogether, being more interested in growth and transformation than – as we saw it at the time – pessimism and illness.

However, the Reichian tradition – we began to realise – had always had a strong bias towards the therapist as expert-doctor, and had followed standard medical procedure in terms of diagnosis, application of theory and treatment.

Our everyday practice *was pervaded by 'medical model' implications and interventions*, even whilst we were forcefully opposed to any notion of therapy as 'treatment' on a philosophical level. These contradictory paradigms co-existed side by side, but split off from each other, in the background,[5] communicating themselves as subliminal double-messages to our clients.

In pursuing the integrative project I had come across incisive critiques of these *hidden 'medical model' assumptions* (Gadamer *et al.* 1996; Hillman 1972, 1983; Hyman 1999; Laing 1998; Ricoeur 1970; Soth 1998; Szasz 1965, 1984). But whilst some aspects of my identity had been deconstructed through integration, the 'medical model' had remained a secure, albeit ambiguous, pillar of my habitual stance. On the contrary: to some extent every new theory and technique I was learning about and integrating was feeding into my 'expert' knowledge and skill, thus enhancing my omnipotent 'doctor' status, making it more comprehensive and thus more compelling.

The 'relational turn'

Ultimately it was through engagement in the relationship – with clients and with each other – that these habitual constructions of the therapeutic position were confronted and thus revealed their limiting consequences. In practice, we were holding on to attitudes and beliefs which were not commensurate with the depth characterological work we were professing to offer, and actually undermined and restricted the relational space necessary for such work to occur.

I locate the *'relational turn'* at *Chiron* in the mid-1990s, although it took another ten years before I published a coherent account (Soth 2006). With hindsight it is apparent that we were part of a wider movement and that similar ideas (e.g. the 'countertransference revolution', Samuels 1993) informed the cutting edge in other approaches. There were advantages to remaining relatively undisturbed and unpublicised: we were exploring the relational dynamics through our inherited bodymind perspective and were coming at it fresh, without the often confusing historical baggage and dualistic terminology, and could thus develop *a holistic phenomenology of the therapeutic relationship* from the ground up.

The nineteenth-century legacy: dualistic conception of doctor–patient and body–mind relationship

As I have suggested elsewhere (Soth 2005b, 2007a), we were thus beginning to address – in a two-pronged approach – what I see as the two main dualisms pervading the last 100 years of psychotherapy, restricting our practice and theorising: the doctor–patient and the body–mind dualism (Fig. 4.4). As in our clients, underneath the bewildering surface fragmentation of the psychotherapeutic field lies a continual avoidance of painful and unresolved legacies,

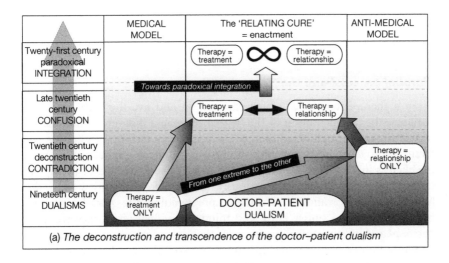

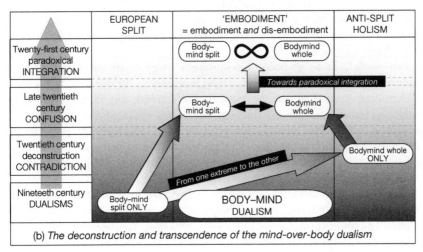

Figure 4.4 The deconstruction and transcendence of nineteenth-century dualisms. (a) The deconstruction and transcendence of the doctor–patient dualism. (b) The deconstruction and transcendence of the body–mind dualism.

reaching all the way back to the origins of the profession in the dualistic, positivist, reductionist *zeitgeist* of the late nineteenth century. I have called this the *'birth trauma' of psychotherapy* (Soth 2005b).

It is only when we transcend these dualisms[6] that some of the paradoxes inherent in psychotherapeutic work can be embraced as necessary and creative. Much of the dogmatism and tribal parochialism pervading psychotherapy theory and training is structured by an avoidance of *the paradox at the heart of therapy*: that the helping relationship we aim to provide involves both the healing as well as the *replication of the client's wounding in and through therapy*, what we call *enactment*, or – if we think in developmental terms – *re-enactment*.[7]

'Parallel process' and the 'fractal self'

From a therapeutic stance which can sustain and live the embrace of this paradox, the fragmentation of the field appears in a different light: when we recognise that our conflicted therapeutic impulses – feeling torn between different approaches and principles moment-to-moment – reflect and parallel the client's inner world, we are inclined to take the multitude of therapeutic theories and techniques less seriously and are less identified with their literal 'truth' or validity.[8] Through apprehending the *parallel processes* between inner and outer, body and mind, individual and collective, interpersonal and intrapsychic dimensions as they get communicated, externalised and internalised in relationship, we appreciate the wholeness underlying (and co-existing with) the reality of fragmentation, in the client, in ourselves and the field we belong to. Parallel process is the 'glue' which turns a heap into an integral whole, allowing a glimpse into what I have called the 'fractal self'[9] (Soth 2006).

Our work calls us to become relationally involved in many scenarios of complementarity (Benjamin 1995, 1998), not only in the dualistic battlefields of feminine–masculine, doctor–patient, body–mind, but in a multitude of polarised issues. Recognising the relativity of *any* amongst a vast diversity of positions (rather than seeing each position as an absolute), prepares us for attending to relational context. We then rely on our capacity to look *through* beliefs and philosophical assumptions *psychologically* (Hillman 1972) in order to recognise both archetypal dynamics and parallel process organising the co-existence of multiple and contradictory 'truths' in *all* human conflict. An awareness of parallel process helps us stay connected with how multi-layered and multi-dimensional polarised issues hang together and reflect each other across all the levels from the biological to the emotional, psychological and mental, and beyond the intrapsychic into the interpersonal and collective domains. It thus helps us to engage in an 'integral' intersubjective manner which does not take refuge in privileging or absolutising certain domains at the expense of others (which only ever leads to one-sided, biased and unworkable solutions). Through parallel process we begin to understand how pathology maintains itself, both individually and collectively: how patterns of uncontained conflict and denied pain replicate themselves through being enacted, internalised and externalised from one person to the next, across all our relationships and down the generations like falling dominoes, in the hope of finally finding containment *somewhere*.

Without a recognition that the supposedly 'helping relationship' *needs to* be 'unhelpful', that it *needs to* involve re-enactment of the client's wounding, and that the practitioner needs at times to be helplessly available to participating in these patterns so they can transform themselves, therapists and their profession are part of the problem of such blind replication.[10]

The future: containing parallel process through resting in paradox

Through encouraging us to keep experientially participating in enactments and to surrender to them, the integral view of 'fractal self' facilitates an experience of *a priori* passionate relatedness (Spinelli 2007) from which a potential 'third position' beyond polarisation and fragmentation can arise, *whatever* the particular conflict or issue. Beyond the specific paradoxes central to our profession, it thus opens the door to inhabiting a fundamental sense of paradox in *all* existential struggles and relational contexts. From such a perspective, we glimpse also how the pathologies of our profession maintain themselves. This may give us some ideas how to engage with the established splits and fault lines running through psychotherapy as we know it.

Idealisation and disappointment

The above brief and abstract overview over the last twenty-five years' development provides a framework in which I can reflect on my own participation in these adventures.

I first addressed the emotional aspects of these developmental issues in 1999 (Soth 2000), where I phrased them in terms of our initial idealisation of the body, and subsequent disappointments and disillusionment. In applying these notions, derived from Kleinian thought, to our own development both as a community of practitioners and as a therapy organisation, I was drawing on models and assumptions in many ways antagonistic to Chiron culture in order to highlight aspects of our shadow. In Klein's view the crucial developmental shift is from an omnipotent position based on fusion with an 'ideal object' versus splitting off the 'bad object' (paranoid-schizoid) to the maturity of the 'depressive position' which is characterised by the capacity to sustain difference and ambivalence. Certainly for myself, this was a much needed perspective, but one which I had neglected and avoided precisely because it derived from a therapeutic model alien and threateningly 'opposite' to my habitual identity.[11] It raised important questions: does our practice and our belief system as Chiron therapists – both individually and collectively – shore up a defensive identity,[12] perpetuating a hidden grandiosity and requiring constant feeding through idealisation[13] from colleagues and clients? Or do we at some point react against the pain and disappointed longing inherent in this addiction to idealisation, and make ourselves a home in a determined, yet bitter, refutation of it?

As I hinted in 2000, I believe a third position – beyond idealisation and resignation – is both desirable and achievable,[14] and I will aim towards this elusive possibility throughout this chapter.

The 'habitual position'

The implicit relational stance underlying theory and technique

When we characterise a particular psychotherapeutic approach, traditionally we tend to define it in terms of its theory and technique. However, closer inspection reveals that this convention harks back to psychotherapy's nineteenth-century origins (Soth 2007c). It implies the assumption that – like doctors – therapists base their interventions (their technique) in dealing with a particular 'case' on a quasi-scientific application of established general principles (theory), translating what are presumed to be objective perceptions and understandings of reality as 'out there'[15] into diagnosis and appropriate 'treatment plan'.[16]

However, what significantly influences the way theory and technique arrive on the client's end of the therapeutic relationship is a third factor: the therapist's underlying or implicit relational stance. This stance, although rationalised through the practitioner's models and beliefs, is often taken for granted and outside awareness, both intrapsychically and in its impact on the client (Fig. 4.5).[17]

As 'wounded healers' and 'reflective practitioners', we turn our psychological theories upon *ourselves*, not only in the sense that every therapist

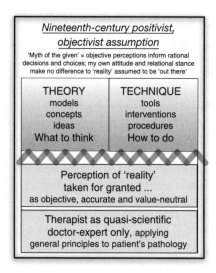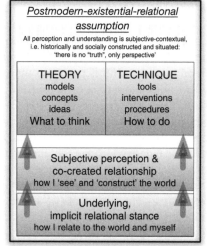

Figure 4.5 The implicit relational stance underlying theory and technique.

is also a client, but to reflect on how we function *within our therapeutic role when at work*. It is in regard to our implicit relational stance as therapists that Reich's holistic characterological understanding of habitual positions and their developmental origins can make a profound contribution.

A characterological understanding of the therapist's relational stance and 'habitual position'

In Reich's understanding, rigidly held positions, on all bodymind levels from muscular to cognitive, indicate the presence of defensive character armour which has both repressive and protective functions. He sees *all* perceiving and thinking as arising in the context of character and the emotional wounding at its root. Beliefs, assumptions and world views of all kinds arise *through* a personal, subjective history and are conditioned by it.[18] Our current view of reality, however convincing it appears to us, carries the scars of that emotional history, all the more so if denied and unconscious.

The five steps of character formation[19] (Johnson 1994), as an adaptation to internalised developmental wounding, can be seen to inform a therapist's implicit relational stance and 'habitual position'.[20] Thus body psychotherapy, following in Reich's footsteps, provides tools needed to apprehend the defensive uses of our own theory and practice, manifesting in habitual patterns of relating to ourselves and other practitioners and contributing to the rigid dogmatisms maintaining the schisms within the psychotherapeutic field.

Deconstruction of my 'habitual position'

The rest of this chapter will illustrate Chiron's general development as outlined so far through the description of more specific episodes, personal to me. Each quantum leap challenged within me a deeper taken-for-granted layer of my own habitual position, starting from a layer of more personal and idiosyncratic wounds and leading to more collective issues, shared by the field and the culture.

I will only focus here on the first two leaps[21] and how they transformed some cherished models and assumptions; beyond cursory indication, space does not permit detailed discussion of the theoretical revisions and new concepts which needed formulating (but see Fig. 4.6). These resulted in a new bodymind language for the moment-to-moment phenomenology of the 'wounded healer' involved in the relational dynamics that unfold within the therapeutic encounter (Soth 2005a).

Expanding beyond humanistic-holistic idealism

The shift from the humanistic-holistic towards an integrative perspective has to some extent been described in Eiden's chapter. For myself, this involved

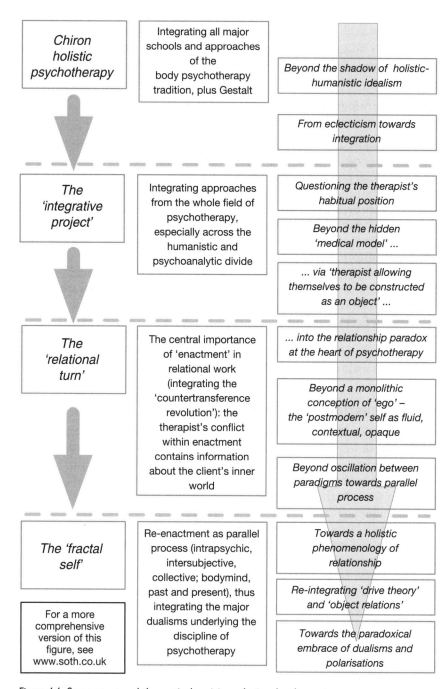

Figure 4.6 Some steps and theoretical revisions during development.

increasing awareness of the extent to which I was projecting aspects of my own history and *psyche* into my perception of what was 'wrong' with the world and my concomitant defensive idealisations as to what therapy might enable me to do about it.

At the time I understood western social reality in terms of hierarchical dualisms imposed by patriarchy (Dodson-Gray 1982; Kaschak 1992), and – underestimating investment in my own privilege – I both idealised 'the oppressed' and fancied myself as their champion. In this context I saw 'the ego' as an agent of male oppression, injuring and curtailing the healthy, spontaneous aliveness of the body which it was my therapeutic task to liberate.

Eventually I understood that my attack on all manifestations of patriarchal power was not free from identification with my mother against my father: I was seeing him and – by extension – everything male (including myself) through *her* eyes only. Recognising that I felt implicated like a pawn in my parents' marriage and torn between them,[22] released me from a whole complex set of mutually reinforcing idealisations which had circumscribed my therapeutic thinking.

I relied on several gross oversimplifications: I equated the repressed and neglected body with the gifted, but wounded child (Miller 1983), the core, the self, the unconscious and the oppressed feminine over and against the repressive force of the 'ego'. The 'ego' also was oversimplified, as I presumed it to be identical with the conscious, male mind, Reich's facade as well as the superego and wounding 'bad' parent.[23] Therapy was supposed to be a heroic process of freeing the former from the latter – a retro-romantic fantasy of reconstituting the 'noble savage'. Having assumed Reich's 'core' to be identical with Jung's 'Self', I then realised that these two models were also profoundly contradictory. This led me to Hillman's (1983) critique of the Great Mother archetype as dominant in the humanistic growth movement and a beginning appreciation of the soul's 'pathologising'.

Having previously dismissed Klein's theories as 'blaming the child', I now appreciated her understanding of primitive modes of contact and communication, increasingly recognising states of merger and fusion in my relationships with clients. By idealising expression and catharsis, I had contributed to an underlying lack of containment and implicit re-traumatisation, both in myself and my work. Klein – having represented the antithesis of everything I believed in – now became a source of support. Theoretically, this was reflected in understanding habitual positions in the tension between merger and differentiation which later led to my current model of the therapeutic position in the paradoxical forcefield between colluding and objectifying (Fig. 4.6).

In recognising the 'ego' as a collective fantasy (Hillman 1983), I became aware of my particular projections onto the concept: far from the homogeneous impenetrably fortified castle I had imagined, it made sense to consider the ego as split (Fairbairn 1974). In fighting against the disconnected, inhibiting rationalising mind, I had underestimated the significance of fantasy, imagination and symbolisation and the containing function of the mind. As a result I had been trapped in literalism, with an understanding of the body only as concrete and physical. The integration of literal and symbolic perspectives prepared the way for a more differentiated response: I recognised more deeply the objectification of the body, not only as a pervasive problem in the culture but also as exacerbated through my own therapeutic approach to it (Soth 1999, 2006).

The simplistic notion that in any given situation there was *one* specific feeling that was identifiably blocked and needed to be released from the singular grip of an inhibiting ego proved misleading and untenable, along with some basic principles of character structure theory. In questioning Reich's own habitual therapeutic position, inconsistencies and weaknesses of his theory seemed more apparent; in particular, the internalisation of the parent (so central in object relations theory) seemed insufficiently conceptualised (along with the rest of the inner world and the unconscious mind).

Most of these developments can be seen as a process of losing my idealised notions, discovering the shadow aspects hidden beneath them and opening up to other approaches better suited to naming and dealing with these areas traditionally neglected by body psychotherapy. As a culmination of these revolutions and revisions – all still in the context of the 'integrative project' of the mid-1990s – I could not persist in habitually constructing my therapeutic role as an enemy of the client's ego. What replaced this, years later, was the integral notion of the conflicted ego in conflict with an internalised spontaneous conflict (Soth 2005a).

My experience of the 'relational turn'

A discussion of the blessings and pitfalls inherent in the 'integrative project' goes beyond the scope of this chapter (see Soth 2007d), but although aspects of relational thinking had long been gestating during the 1980s, the radical impact of the 'relational turn' was surprising and profound. For a long time, the integrative project still co-existed within me next to unquestioned medical model assumptions: I continued to see myself as the bodymind expert 'operating' – albeit in a highly attuned and empathic fashion – on the client's patterns and pathology. I constructed my role as an enemy of the client's ego precisely because their defences were unconscious and seemed to require an expert to bring them into awareness. I was siding with *my idea* of the client's body against *my idea* of the client's mind, thereby enacting relationally the very real body–mind conflict which the client was trapped in. I admired Reich's concerted and systematic attack on the client's character structure which gave way layer after layer to his quasi-medical treatment. There was no doubt in my mind that essentially I was being paid to deliver doctor-like interventions.

At the same time I saw myself as available to authentic relating and offering the possibility of 'real' I–Thou contact. It never occurred to me that the client might receive these two sets of responses (the 'doctor' and the 'person') as conflicting, as I was assuming that *both* my well-intentioned helpful interventions as well as my genuine human presence were being recognised and received for what they were. I thought, therefore, that my intention *behind the intervention* was paramount, and that as long as I was sincere, everything would be fine. Implicitly I subscribed to established notions of the working alliance, based on a bond between those aspects of the client's and my own personal–professional ego which could be considered 'healthy' and 'realistic' (Clarkson 1995).

All these assumptions and beliefs I now consider partial and flawed, recognising their defensive and protective functions. I see nothing wrong with me wanting to protect myself in what is in many respects a painful and impossible job. But the problem was that these protections operated in habitual and unconscious ways which I was largely oblivious of. They did not actually serve to protect me against specific threats with specific clients, as they were in place indiscriminately as soon as I stepped into the therapeutic position. With hindsight I do not doubt that during these years I did much useful work for many clients from within and in spite of my habitual position. But I now question whether the work actually delivered what at the time I claimed to provide: a therapeutic space in which the deep characterological patterns at the root of my clients' distress could be addressed and transformed.

One of Reich's criticisms of psychoanalysis in the 1920s had been how patients readily divined their analysts' intentions, assumptions and agendas and how their ego therefore easily subverted or avoided the therapeutic process (Reich [1942] 1983: 117–130). I now realised that the same also applied to body psychotherapy as I was practising it. Reich had intended to develop a systematic bodymind therapy that would overcome the ego's resistance. Although I recognised my clients' body–mind conflicts and ego defences, and threw my concerted Reichian toolbox at them, I had to admit that their ego more often than not *did* manage to usurp the process after all. With every breakthrough I contrived to engineer, further weaknesses in their armour were exposed, only for the defences to be strengthened and to become more impenetrable next time.

How unconscious is 'unconscious'? How pervasive is the transference?

One important thing I noticed, however: clients did not perceive my attack on their ego 'correctly' or realistically. On the contrary: they seemed to perceive and experience my interventions in the light of their early 'primary scenario' (Rosenberg 1985). A typical example might be a client consistently (mis-)hearing my challenge of their *lack* of feeling as a 'new edition or fac-simile'[24] of the father chiding the client for the *presence* of feeling, e.g. tears.

Whilst as a therapist I had always had a working notion of transference, this seemed to indicate a whole different degree or dimension of transferential pervasiveness. The more we approached regressive states, the more consuming the client's immersion in the transference would become. It dawned on me that in these moments of intense transference, *my* intentions, *my* feelings, *my* reality were no longer clear and transparent to the client.

Previously I had assumed that transference and working alliance were clearly distinguishable and that transference was like a lake of irrationality in the otherwise solid territory of the alliance; that at least the therapist – if not the client – could reliably monitor the therapeutic path when it descended and led through that lake of projections and misperceptions. I never doubted that my reflective self-awareness as therapist, if communicated appropriately, would enable the client to become aware of their transference reactions and thereby put them into perspective.

These are common assumptions amongst humanistic practitioners who do take account of the transference. In the literature, this is referred to as the client's capacity for 'dual awareness' or for recognising the 'as if' nature of the therapeutic relationship. These notions imply the client's capacity to observe and reflect on their transference reactions as well as communicate about them.

But how strong, really, is that capacity, and how easily recoverable when lost?

Searching through the analytic traditions, I found a wide divergence of assumptions regarding these questions. Whilst analysts really do think of the client as thoroughly unconscious of the transference, more so than humanistic therapists, there is very mixed opinion as to how recoverable the client's reflective awareness is. Ultimately, of course, most classical analysis relies on the analyst's capacity to engender such awareness in the patient through mutative interpretations (Strachey 1934), thereby making the unconscious conscious.

But that begs the question as to the therapist's own grip on the unconscious dynamics in the relationship, and to what extent their unwavering meta-position serenely hovers above these dynamics, or – at the other end of the spectrum – to what degree they are involved, lost and unconscious, too.

I increasingly doubted the archetypal metaphors underlying my practice and wondered whether they were not self-protective wishful fantasies, the products of an ego fancying itself as having much more awareness, insight and agency than was actually the case. What if the underlying power distribution between unconscious and conscious was reversed? What if the working alliance was like a frequently vanishing isle in an otherwise pervasive sea of transference which for prolonged periods drowns out both the client's and the therapist's reflective meta-position?[25]

Allowing oneself to be constructed as an object by the client's unconscious

My experience in practice indicated that – both in terms of the client's and my own position – we were much more at the mercy of unconscious patterns than I had previously allowed myself to notice.

Often I went out of my way to counteract what I perceived as a dangerous, destructive enactment. For example: a client with a history of indoctrination kept asking me for help in the form of advice and instruction. 'This client has been disempowered', I thought, 'and near-brainwashed – I *must not* play into this. He needs to rediscover faith in his own judgement, rather than further introject – now from me as the new authority.' Knowing better (so I thought), I refused to give advice, only to be perceived as indoctrinating him with principles of self-reliance.

The more I enquired into my practice through this perspective, the more obvious it became to me that these were not isolated incidents, but that *layers and layers of pervasive enactment* are the norm – they constitute the territory we work within. I formulated the following principle (Soth 2006):

> It is impossible to pursue a therapeutic agenda of breaking through the armour or undercutting the ego's resistance without enacting in the transference the person against whom the armour/resistance was first developed.

The 'relational turn' helped me recognise that the developmental origins of the client's patterns were *always already* in the room and that I was implicated in them via the transference; that I *am* the 'bad object' and as such inescapably involved with the client's pain; that enactment is inevitable because meeting the client where they are requires entering *their* world and relational logic. The necessity of attunement opens me to an enmeshment on the level of unconscious communication which I no longer imagined my therapeutic ego to be separate from. This led me to the notion: 'the client's conflict becomes the therapist's conflict' (Fig. 4.7). If I can embrace the fact that many of my therapeutic responses are an unconscious acting-out of the countertransference, I am more free to attend to *how* enactment happens *via* intervention. My internal conflicts in the countertransference can then be seen to reflect the client's conflict via parallel process. Taking *any* habitual position as a therapist can, therefore, be seen as a defence against the – inexorably pervasive – pressures of being constructed as an object by the client's unconscious.

I grew less invested in my position as a therapist, and less threatened by the swirling cauldron which I more and more recognised as a fairly perennial feature in the underworld of the therapeutic relationship. This culminated in questions such as how to surrender to enactment, how to apprehend it in all

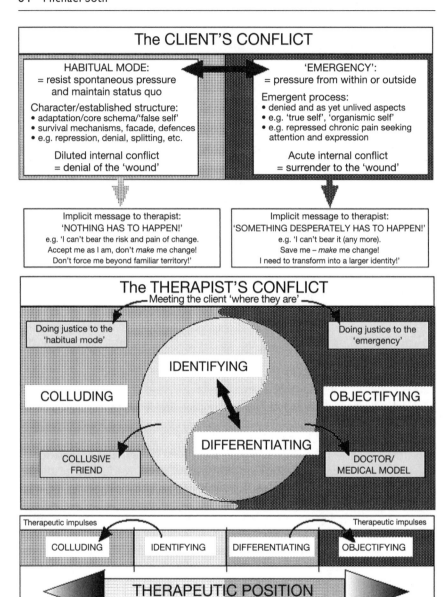

Figure 4.7 The therapeutic position between the extremes of colluding and objectifying.

its bodymind detail and how to relate from *within* it. With hindsight, some of these questions required the next quantum leap into the 'fractal self' and parallel process to find satisfying answers.[26] Whilst not minimising the dangers and counter-therapeutic implications of enactment, we can nevertheless appreciate its paradoxical power as an ingredient in profound transformation.

Notes

1 In our practice we find that initially most people's horizon is restricted to a *dualistic-linear* conception of development, consistent with a scientific worldview of evolution and history as well as notions of rational, goal-oriented individual consciousness. Whilst as therapists we do not argue with the validity claims of these views on a philosophical level, from our perspective they are at best partial accounts of the much more complex phenomenon of development. We frequently find that such beliefs turn out to operate in a defensive fashion, to deny, compensate and rationalise other emotional 'truths'. A discussion contrasting linear, cyclic and holistic notions of development and their integration is beyond the scope of this chapter.

2 The beginnings of Chiron (see Fig. 4.1) coincided with the publication of Wilber's first books in the early 1980s (Wilber 1977, 1980). His meta-model concerning the evolution of the Kosmos – itself developing approximately throughout the same timespan as Chiron's existence – influenced our own thinking, and articulated and reflected many of the concurrent changes in our own evolving philosophy. It is now well recognised that Wilber's theories can be divided into five phases (Wilber 2000; Reynolds 2006). Although I have misgivings about Wilber's model even in its current form, it offers undoubtedly the most comprehensive and well-established language articulating integral thinking. Whilst systemic-integral ideas can be applied to all kinds of inanimate and living systems, I focus here on *psychological* development.

3 Jung's 'enantiodromia': process by which powerful unconscious counterpositions build up, which first inhibit, then oppose and subsequently break through conscious control. (Jung 1971, para. 709).

4 Along the lines of Campbell's statement: 'Throughout history the gods of the defeated become the devils of the victors' (Campbell and Moyers 1988).

5 One symptom of this conflict was our perennial unease about the pathologising terms the Reichian tradition had borrowed from psychiatry to describe the 'character structures'.

6 Rather than fight *against* them through a decidedly holistic anti-dualistic philosophy; for the process by which a dualism that one is initially unwittingly caught in is transcended, see Soth (2007b).

7 For the client the equivalent subjective experience is that the transformation of the pain they both seek and avoid (often largely unconsciously) *can* occur through the whole bodymind's surrender *to it* in this relationship here and now.

8 In Wilber's (2000) terms: we can then take a step from integrative pluralism (with its attendant dangers of relativism) into a second-tier integral perspective.

9 Thus extending into the relational domain and beyond the notion of 'wholeness' implicit in Reich's original impulse and bodymind functionalism.

10 These ideas will be elucidated in some of the case material to follow; see chapters by Asheri, Keary and Clark.

11 This 'blindspot' is manifest on a theoretical level in the Reichian developmental schema in the gap between the oral and masochistic character structures – exactly where Klein locates the crucial developmental hiatus of rapprochement (Almaas 1996: 286).

12 By functioning essentially as a narcissistic self-object.

13 E.g. as the 'transformative object' (Bollas 1987) capable of bringing about 'bodymind integration'.

14 When I accept Klein's developmental view and embrace disappointment not only as unavoidable but beneficial to maturation, both in therapy and especially in psychotherapy *training*, the important question is: to what extent is that kind of disappointment actually 'worked through'? What happens to the initial idealisation that drives our investment in therapy or therapy training? Does 'working through' lead to an embracing both of that 'original impulse' as well as the wounding it arose out of? Unless both the unbearability of the underlying wounding and the need for defensive idealisation which arises from it can be felt and lovingly inhabited, we cannot understand in an embodied way why it is impossible to have the 'original impulse' fulfilled within the terms originally imagined and idealised and therefore cannot relinquish it. Here an understanding of the internalised object as bodymind process becomes essential.

15 What postmodern epistemology calls the 'myth of the given'.

16 The absence of any self-reflexivity in this assumption means that psychotherapy has been prone to generalising its models as universally valid and self-evident. Postmodernism (and 'standpoint theory' Hartsock 1999) has deconstructed this fallacy and recognised that it usually betrays a disavowed investment in a normative power position which is implicitly oppressive as it nonchalantly denies other realities and subjectivities. We are less likely to presume our theories as taken-for-granted consensual reality if we recognise that reality as socially and subjectively constructed rather than simply and objectively given. The irony is, of course, that as a discipline psychotherapy is ideally suited to champion subjectivity and to corroborate abstract postmodernist philosophy by grounding it in psychological depth: we have the theoretical and practical tools to perceive and understand the postulated subjective construction of reality in actual experiential detail.

17 The socio-cultural and historical-political implications of the underlying relational stance will be further explored in chapters by Ablack and Waterston. How the implicit relational stance communicates itself subliminally from right-brain to right-brain has been elucidated amply by neuroscience (Schore 1994).

18 The concept of 'character', therefore, goes much further than CBT's 'schema' or Stern's (1985) RIGs (representations (of relational experiences and configurations) which have been Internalised and Generalised).

19 There are certain theoretical inconsistencies and weaknesses in character structure theory which I cannot address here, but see www.soth.co.uk.

20 The term is *not* meant to imply a static, singular position – I think of the 'habitual position' as a relationship system with at least two poles, like Masterson's 'relational units', or more accurately sets of interrelated stances or a matrix of attractors in a complex system (Soth 2007c).

21 For the third one, see Soth (2005a); for the fourth, see Soth (2003); Pizer (1998).

22 Formulated in general theoretical terms in 1993 in a presentation on 'Parental identification'.

23 This simplistic binary schema, of course, cannot but exacerbate the underlying dualisms which consciously I was battling against.

24 Freud's (1901) original definition of 'transference'.

25 Some Jungian, archetypal and psychoanalytic perspectives suggested to me that such a reversal of my habitual assumptions was more realistic and therefore ultimately more helpful to the therapeutic endeavour; see Mitchell's (2002) postmodern psychoanalytic view of self as 'fluid, opaque, shifting, de-centered, multiple and contextual'.

26 A detailed discussion is beyond the scope of this chapter, but see 'the three kinds of contact' (Soth 2005a) for an indication of how I conceptualise the tides of

enactment as one of the central features and conundrums of the therapeutic relationship.

References

Almaas, A. H. (1996) *The Pearl Beyond Price: Integration of Personality into Being – an Object Relations Approach*. Berkeley, CA: Diamond Books.

Benjamin, J. (1995) *Like Subjects, Love Objects: Essays on Recognition and Sexual Difference*. New Haven, CT: Yale University Press.

Benjamin, J. (1998) *Shadow of the Other: Intersubjectivity and Gender in Psychoanalysis*. New York: Routledge.

Bollas, C. (1987) *The Shadow of the Object: Psychoanalysis of the Unthought Known*. New York: Columbia University Press.

Campbell, J. and Moyers, B. (1988) *The Power of Myth*. New York: Doubleday.

Clarkson, P. (1995) *The Therapeutic Relationship*. London: Whurr.

Dodson-Gray, E. (1982) *Patriarchy as a Conceptual Trap*. Wellesley, MA: Roundtable.

Fairbairn, W. (1974) *Psychoanalytic Studies of the Personality*. New York: Routledge, Chapman & Hall.

Freud, S. (1901) *Fragment of an Analysis of a Case of Hysteria*. Standard Edition, 7. London Hogarth Press.

Gadamer, H.-G., Walker, N. and Geiger, J. (1996) *Enigma of Health: The Art of Healing in a Scientific Age*. Stanford, CA: Stanford University Press.

Gleick, J. (1987) *Chaos*. Abacus: London.

Hartsock, N. (1999) *Postmodernism and Political Change*. London: Routledge.

Hillman, J. (1972). *Re-visioning Psychology*. New York: HarperCollins.

Hillman, J. (1983). *Healing Fiction*. Dallas: Spring.

Hyman, M (1999) *Why Psychoanalysis is Not a Health Care Profession*. In: Kaley, H., Eagle, M. N. and Wolitzky, D. L. (eds) *Psychoanalytic Therapy as Health Care: Effectiveness and Economics in the 21st Century*. Hillsdale, NJ: Analytic Press.

Johnson, S. (1994) *Character Styles*. New York: W.W. Norton.

Jung, C. G. (1971) *Psychological Types*. Vol XI Collected Works. Bollingen.

Kaschak, E. (1992) *Engendered Lives – A New Psychology of Women's Experience*. New York: Basic Books.

Laing, R. D. (1970) *The Divided Self*. Pelican

Laing, R. D. (1998) *The Politics of the Family and Other Essays*. London: Routledge.

Laing, R. D and Esterson, A. (1970) *Sanity, Madness and the Family*. Pelican.

Machado, A. (1912) *Campos de Castilla*.

Masterson, J. (1985) *The Real Self: A Developmental, Self and Object Relations Approach*. New York: Brunner/Mazel.

Maturana, H. and Varela, F. (1980) *Autopoiesis and Cognition*. Dordrecht, Holland: D. Reidel.

Miller, A. (1983) *The Drama of the Gifted Child: The Search for the True Self*. New York: Basic Books.

Mitchell, S. (2002) *Can Love Last? The Fate of Romance over Time*. New York: W.W. Norton.

Pizer, S. A. (1998) *Building Bridges: Negotiation of Paradox in Psychoanalysis*. Hillsdale, NJ: The Analytic Press.

Reich, W. (1983) *The Function of the Orgasm*. London: Souvenir Press.

Reynolds, B. (2006) *Where's Wilber At? – Ken Wilber's Integral Vision in the New Millennium*. St Paul, MN: Paragon House Publishers.

Ricoeur, P. (1970) *Freud and Philosophy: An Essay on Interpretation*. New Haven, CT: Yale University Press.

Rosenberg, J. (1985) *Body, Self and Soul – Sustaining Integration*. Atlanta, GA: Humanics.

Samuels, A. (1993) *The Political Psyche*. London: Routledge.

Schore, A. (1994) *Affect Regulation and the Origin of Self*. Hillsdale, NJ. Lawrence Erlbaum Associates.

Soth, M. (1998) Collective mothering and the medical model. *AChP Newsletter* 1998.

Soth, M. (1999) Relating to and with the objectified body. *Self & Society* 27(1): 32–38.

Soth, M. (2000) The integrated body/mind's view on body/mind integration. *AChP Newsletter* 2000.

Soth, M. (2003) Psychotherapy: paradoxes, pitfalls and potential. *Self & Society* 30(6): 34–44.

Soth, M. (2005a) Embodied countertransference. In: Totton, N. (ed.) *New Dimensions in Body Psychotherapy*. Maidenhead: OUP.

Soth, M. (2005b) Body psychotherapy today – an integral-relational approach. *Therapy Today*, 16(9).

Soth, M. (2006) What therapeutic hope for a subjective mind in an objectified body? *Journal for Body, Movement and Dance in Psychotherapy* 1 and 2 (June & September).

Soth, M. (2007a) How 'the wound' enters the room and the relationship. *CABP Journal* No 34, February.

Soth, M. (2007b) *No 'Relating Cure' without Embodiment*. Unpublished manuscript.

Soth, M. (2007c) The implicit relational stance and habitual positions. *CABP Journal* No 35, July.

Soth, M. (2007d) The 'integrative project' as a phase within the development of Body Psychotherapy. *UKAPI Journal* October.

Spinelli, E. (2007) The therapeutic relationship: a view from existential psychotherapy. *Therapy Today* February.

Stern, D. N. (1985) *Interpersonal World of the Infant: A View from Psychoanalysis and Development Psychology*. London: Karnac Books.

Strachey, J. (1934) The nature of the therapeutic action of psycho-analysis. *International Journal of Psycho-Analysis* 15.

Szasz, T. (1965) *The Ethics of Psychoanalysis – The Theory and Method of Autonomous Psychotherapy*. Syracuse, NY: Syracuse University Press.

Szasz, T. (1984) *Myth of Mental Illness: Foundations of a Theory of Personal Contact*. New York: Harper.

Wilber, K. (1977) *The Spectrum of Consciousness*. Wheaton, IL: Quest.

Wilber, K. (1980) *The Atman Project: A Transpersonal View of Human Development*. Wheaton, IL: Quest.

Wilber, K. (2000) *Integral Psychology*. Boston: Shambala.

Chapter 5

Self-regulation – an evolving concept at the heart of body psychotherapy

Roz Carroll

Appealing to the body as some sort of absolute ground, immune to the demands of relativism, is tempting but unhelpful . . . However, bodies in relationship can generate an authenticity of contact that carries its own authority, and that grounds psychotherapy in ways which allow creative transformation.

(Totton 2005: 24)

Self-regulation: regulation, control, or direction by or of oneself (itself) (OED)[1]

Self-regulation: a key component of Chiron holistic psychotherapy

The historical context

In the field of psychotherapy self-regulation is a term widely used term to describe the ability of an individual or system to maintain, or recover, equilibrium. Despite variations in the theory of how self-regulation is achieved, it is generally perceived to be an attribute of a dynamic ongoing organismic process – a movement towards balance, self-expression and health.

The seeds of a scientific model of self-regulation were based on the concept of homeostasis. This principle of biology was first observed by the founder of modern experimental medicine Claude Bernard, then developed by the physiologist W. B. Cannon, and summed up in the title of the latter's famous book *The Wisdom of the Body* (1932).[2] Bernard's discovery about how each organism maintains stability of its internal environment influenced Cannon's own research (Heller 2007). Cannon coined the term 'homeostasis' which is still used today to refer to the body's capacity to maintain dynamic equilibrium within a range of variables, managed by the autonomic nervous system. These include heart rate, body temperature, breathing, blood pressure, and metabolism and must be kept within a certain range for physical well-being, and indeed for survival. 'Fight or flight', Cannon's phrase for the action of the sympathetic nervous system, refers to an organism's stress response. The complementary function of the parasympathetic nervous system is associated with rest, digestion and relaxation (Carroll 2005a).

Homeostasis is the prototype for the broader term of self-regulation which is now used in a range of contexts (psychotherapy, child development, education, sports psychology) to describe the internal rules of a system, including learning styles and how individuals manage feelings, impulses and bodily states. It is a concept that has been influenced by science, philosophy, and by many theorists of psychotherapy, often with different emphases and meanings (Carroll 2003; Heller 2007; Jung 1921; Reich 1972; Schore 2003).

Europe in the 1920s–1930s was the birthplace of a modern wave of ideas about emotion and the relationship between mind and body. Discoveries in physiology, medicine, neurology and psychology created excitement amongst intellectuals in Paris, Berlin, Vienna, Oslo and London (Heller 2007). Many were inspired with the idea that the principles of living systems had been grasped, and could be taken and applied therapeutically. Cannon himself was not a psychotherapist, but his felicitous phrase 'the wisdom of the body' seemed to sum up the quest for a whole generation of therapists who were exploring the intrinsic mechanisms for repair and self-healing of the body-mind. Among these figures were Mesmer, Jung, Reich, Ferenczi and Perls. As each of these pioneers drew on his own experience, pathology and creativity, new systems of therapy were created, and their influence still ricochets around the ever-broadening field of body psychotherapy.

Self-regulation as a spontaneous process of self-healing

In this early era of body psychotherapy the concept of self-regulation gathered around a sense that the bodymind has an intrinsic momentum towards health beyond any rational, cognitive or even reflective process. For Jung, symptoms and dreams reflected an important aspect of self-regulation showing how what was repressed was bound to emerge elsewhere as an unconscious compensation (Jung 1921). For Reich, the 'elsewhere' was more specifically focused on the body. Reich considered that restriction of breathing was the prototypical defence against feeling, at the root of character armour. By undoing character defences in the form of muscular tension, he believed that energy – in the form of changes in breathing, involuntary movement and sound, changes in skin colour, temperature, sensations – could be 'liberated' and allowed to flow more freely (Reich 1972). The idea that unblocked flow regulates itself quite naturally is a core belief of the early body psychotherapists. Perls used the term 'organismic self-regulation' to describe the capacity of the individual to know or to sense through the body what he or she needs (Perls et al. 1972). This included a model of the cycle of experience which contained the important idea that incomplete processes (the expression of feelings, or thwarted attempts to get needs met) would re-present themselves, given the opportunity, for resolution, thereby grounding Freud's descriptive notion of 'repetition compulsion' in a purposeful, self-regulatory context (1920).

At Chiron these influences – including Boyesen's tellingly named 'midwife' approach – shaped the basic idea of self-regulation. The key element in all these approaches was *trust* – trust that if as a therapist you can be present, attend to the phenomena of the body, without interpretation, without urgency, the client's own spontaneous bodily response will contain the seeds of a movement towards health.

I remember as a first year trainee doing a practice vegetotherapy session with another student. 'Kerry' was a very anxious woman, and I sat patiently near her, quietly inviting her to feel her body on the mattress and notice what was happening. After a while her legs started to twitch and I encouraged her to stay with the feeling in them. Her anxiety was increasing and I was concerned that she was becoming 'ungrounded'. Following an impulse I moved to her feet and took hold of them gently, and after a few minutes, found myself saying firmly without quite knowing why, 'these are your feet'. This provoked a dramatic reaction: she started kicking into my hands, writhing and yelling, 'get off me, get off me you bastard'. I supported this process by giving some resistance to her feet as she pushed them alternately into my hands, and by asking her to make eye contact and direct her verbal tirade at me. Later she talked about what she was feeling and thinking as this process had unfolded. She had been sexually abused as a child, and my words had triggered a rage which she had not previously been able to identify and link so clearly and immediately with that abuse.

This session fitted well with what I had grasped so far about self-regulation in body psychotherapy, fitting into the phase that Soth in his chapter categorises as 'Chiron holistic psychotherapy'. I had allowed the body to lead, supported the spontaneous expression (the kicking of the 'abuser'), and provided a new healing context of understanding and acceptance. Kerry and I were both pleased that she had been able to feel and show her anger. She was able to breathe more freely, and feel her legs as more alive and connected to the ground.

This trust in the process, and in paying close attention to the body, remains central to the Chiron approach. However, Rothschild taught us that trauma is equivalent to a loss of regulation and that sometimes more structured techniques are needed to help the client re-establish self-regulation, as the clinical material in chapters by Heitzler, Stauffer and Landale show (Rothschild 2000). Even so, structured techniques are not used in isolation – the therapist's embodied understanding of unconscious processes is crucial to her ability to contain quite complex information and shifts between levels.

Self-regulation incorporates defences and has its own internal logic

As a student at Chiron I gained an experiential knowledge of body processes and particularly how certain core experiences of fear, rage, longing or excitement move and enliven the body when it feels safe to surrender to them. Yet at Chiron there was also a strong emphasis both on grasping the transference, and on deconstructing and updating the frameworks of the body psychotherapy tradition (see chapters by Eiden and Soth). With the integration of ideas from object relations into the frame, right at the beginning of Soth's 'integrative body psychotherapy' phase, 'self-regulation' started to become a more complex, qualified notion. There was a focus on understanding and getting a bodily sense of internalised relationships and the way in which unconscious structures are perpetuated.

> In my third year of training I had another key learning experience. The assistant role-played a difficult client and trainees took turns to work as therapist with her. The 'client' was unwilling to engage with what the therapist had to offer and sabotaged proposed experiments, rejected all interpretations, gave one word answers to questions and sat back whilst the student therapists alternately battled or squirmed. The exercise was designed to get us to focus on what was actually going on between client and therapist. Jumping into the therapist role, I invited the 'client' to become aware of her body; this was dismissed with a rolling of her eyes, and an expression of contempt. Letting go of my usual inviting, supportive interventions, and improvising in an attempt to make some kind of contact with this frustrating client, I said 'you're not very impressed with the show so far, are you?'

As with all therapeutic approaches, body psychotherapy attracts clients who both want what it appears to offer (a more connected relationship with the body) and fear that at the same time. Some clients easily identify with the idea of getting in touch with their body and letting it speak, others gradually come to appreciate the potential of listening to their body. In this case self-regulation can be developed and invited through both client and therapist paying close attention to sensation, breathing, imagery and movement (Landale

2002). Awareness of the body creates the conditions for spontaneous processes to emerge directly, and some clients find this experience quite profound and revelatory.

For others this way of working poses a considerable challenge to their normal mode of managing and thinking. Far from spontaneous, it feels artificial, frightening and weird. Body psychotherapists learn to engage relationally and use their understanding and awareness of the client to gauge both content and mode of exploration. The point is always, however, to understand the logic of the client's behaviour whether it is a flight *to* or *from* the body; or, more confusingly, both at the same time on different levels. In the course of therapy the client's relationship to their own body is revealed in all its complexity. The body may be idealised (as a source of wisdom, power or pleasure) or denigrated (evoking a range of feelings including disgust, suspicion and hatred). The body may be experienced as a self-object or as an alien 'other'.

With the 'difficult' client in the role play the therapeutic task would not be to convert her to the potential of bodywork, but to understand the function of her response, and to be prepared to address the relational imperative implied by it. Is this deflection protecting her from shame? Whom do I represent from within this client's inner world? Is she unable to feel her body or does she feel too much?

Self-creation, self-protection: imagery and narrative

> [T]he body is actively and continuously involved in any imaging process.
>
> (Landale 2002: 118)

In any exploration with a client my curiosity is directed at getting a sense of the conscious and unconscious regulators shaping their life – beliefs, images, needs, secrets, fantasies, obsessions. There will inevitably be tangled layers of impulse, defence, contradiction and creative adaptation to circumstances, family and cultural systems. Self-regulation is a capacity related to self-structure and these structures are made up of impulse, affect, image and role which often hide out in fragments of our awareness (see Reynolds' chapter). Often the clue to what sustains a particular way of being is contained in a phrase or image which holds a powerful meaning.

'Sean' struggled with directly feeling and sensing his own body because anxiety and fear of judgement interfered with simply attending to his experience. I found that the best way into a more spontaneous exploration of a process with him was through drawing his attention to the imagery embedded in his narrative. He felt safe with words and poetry and began to reveal his awareness, and his vulnerability. We started to address his narcissistic wounds when I picked up on his reference to 'brooding' and his obsessiveness 'like picking a scab'. He was reminded of the saying 'to nurse a grievance' and remembered being a little boy described as a 'sulker' and called a 'baby', not being taken seriously. Brooding was a way of managing difficult feelings, holding onto the baby part of himself, not giving up something important. (Significantly, around this time, he had a dream of a tiny fragile baby.) Then we were able to explore on a body-sensory level his way of holding inside both what was precious, and what was dangerous (rage); and the fear of being humiliated.

The term 'self-regulation' also means self-direction.[3] This takes us deeper into the paradox at the heart of the concept of self-regulation which may stem from a fundamental tension in human nature between the need for relationship, including sharing feelings and meaning with others, and the desire for autonomy and self-definition. Shame has a particularly distorting effect on the self-regulation process because it fuels a dread of spontaneity, a horror at the self's needs, and a deep distrust of self and other. This in turn may feed the urge to self-invention and omnipotence (Schwartz-Salant 1982).

Working with imagery creates the opportunity to explore micro and macro aspects of the client's self-regulation, as Landale's chapter illustrates so well. Images gather into themselves concentrated information about one's bodily state, inner relationships, and fantasy. Sometimes images coalesce around figures or archetypes that represent core self-structures and splits.[4] Sometimes an image captures the nuance of a moment, sometimes a long-standing encapsulated aspect of self. Like many aspects of Chiron psychotherapy described here, the richness and depth of exploring body phenomenology and verbal language/imagery in a relational context could characterise the work of any therapist at any time. This approach owes a particular debt to the Jungian stream but still remains within the 'holistic' or 'integrative' psychotherapy phase.

The perspective of attachment theory and neuroscience

Regulatory theory and attachment: a synthesis of body and relationship

> [A]ttachment can be defined as the interactive regulation of biological synchronicity between organisms.
>
> (Schore 2003: 39)

In 2001, as a member of the conference organising committee for the UKCP, I interviewed neuropsychoanalyst Allan Schore. This was a major turning point, crystallising my interest in neuroscience, and propelling me to explore its potential to offer a fresh injection of theories and data from recent decades of interdisciplinary research. When I asked Schore what was the organising principle of his work, he replied:

> Regulation is the cardinal principle, which is now being used in all of the sciences, from neurochemistry and developmental biology through psychology and sociology . . . highlight[ing] self-regulation as a major goal of human development.
>
> (Schore 2001)

The essence of Schore's dense, detailed and complex argument is that the function of attachment between mother and child is to enable and enhance regulation of biological and behavioural systems (Schore 1994; 2003).

Many interrelated physiological phenomena are involved in a psychobiologically attuned interaction between a mother and infant: nuances of facial expression, rhythmic coordination of sound and movement, gazing and touching, all of which have a direct impact on the nervous system. The mere perception of emotion on the mother's face or in her voice can generate a resonant emotional state in her son or daughter (Beebe & Lachmann 2002: 37). The attuned mother adjusts the mode, amount, variability and timing of her stimulation to the child's temperament and capabilities; this 'demonstrates her sensitivity not so much to the child's overt behaviour but to his or her internal state' (Schore 2003: 39). As well as learning to soothe her infant, the mother is involved in

> Face to face interactions . . . [which] are affect-laden, short interpersonal events . . . To regulate the high positive arousal, mothers and infants . . . *synchronize* the intensity of their affective behaviour within lags of split seconds.
>
> (Feldman, *et al.* 1999: 223, quoted in Schore 2003: 38)

This interactive resonance enables the infant to experience feelings which are co-regulated with an adult in a meaningful way. Repeated interactions, attuned and non-attuned, pleasurable, frightening, or calming, become internalised, with a multiplicity of implications for the 'body–mind–brain' (Schore 2003). This builds the intersubjective sense of self derived from mapping motor-sensory elements of the body-engaged-with-another (Trevarthen and Aitken 2001). These implicit early prototypes of relationship are structured into the infant's body at every level – motor, autonomic, hormonal and sensory – underpinning the pervasive tenacious unconscious expectancies that clients and therapists bring to the therapeutic encounter (see the section 'How unconscious is "unconscious"?' in Soth's chapter).

It is the calibration by the parent of degrees of feeling, of change, of engagement according to the infant's spontaneous self-regulating that teaches and conveys how to relate. There are obviously huge variations in parents' capacity to respond to their child – depending on their own state, their history and the context – and infants are also able to spontaneously regulate their own level of arousal by turning away, interrupting eye contact, gesturing, crying, and so on. Infants and children may also be used by the parents for their own regulation via projections into the child. When the infant is left alone, or responses are persistently inconsistent and unattuned, self-regulation gets tilted towards auto-regulation (Schore 2003). This involves substitute contacts, such as thumb sucking, which may develop into elaborate and compulsive modes of caretaking and control in relation to the self or the other (Winnicott 1972). These modes of 'management' come into therapy as defences and re-enactments, which are sometimes very subtle and encapsulated. In her chapter, Asheri gives an example of working with a client who longs for touch to meet an inner need: 'What I really want is to be held so that I can really let go.' Asheri observes that 'although she expressed a deep longing to be held, her body and her current life situation expressed the many layers of defence against such contact'. This calls for the therapist to engage in a delicate negotiation which is attuned to the multi-level communication of the client.

Schore's updated, neurobiologically informed attachment model places an emphasis on *complex modes of regulating intensity*. The infant's sensitivity to qualities of contact generates continuous adaptations, from the micro (breaking eye contact) to the macro (grabbing, reaching) to the temporary or prolonged emergency defence of dissociation. The developmental process continues through different stages which reflect the child's growing emotional and cognitive capacity. But in each phase the caregiver's failure to respond to her child's feelings, and to interact with him in an attuned way, underlies the difficulty for the child and later adult in managing feelings (see chapters by Heitzler, Landale and Stauffer). Chronic difficulties in early relationships, including abuse and neglect, restrict the growth of flexibility, robustness and awareness in self-regulation. Interactive processes in early attachment are fundamental to the development of self-reflexivity and the capacity to symbolise (Bateman and Fonagy 2004: 75).

The ability to self-regulate is critical to a sense of agency, healthy narcissism and social confidence. When self-regulation is unsupported, the infant, child or adult may be exposed to intolerable feelings of loss, shame, fear, rage and impotence.

Warnecke's chapter on borderline clients describes in more detail how early persistent failures in attunement impact upon an individual's capacity to tolerate affect, and build flexible self-structures.

Differentiating self-regulation and interactive regulation in psychotherapy

> *Relating . . . requires that one have more or less continuous feedback about the state of the other.*
>
> (Beebe and Lachmann 2002: 99)

All theories of self-regulation depend on a systemic view. In neo-Reichian theories self-regulation is seen as an intra-psychic, intra-organismic event in response to the environment (characterising the early holistic model of Chiron therapy). In contemporary attachment theory the emphasis is on mother and baby as a *mutually regulating system*. Two parallel strands of intersubjective theorising, one clearly linked to infant observation, the other to psychoanalysis, focused on the reciprocal, co-constructing nature of the client–therapist relationship. This developing area of theory, summarised and illustrated in Asheri's chapter, marked for us at Chiron, and many in the field, 'the relational turn', a re-thinking of the intrinsic structure of psychotherapy.

What I found exciting in the work of Beebe and Lachmann, two psychoanalysts combining infant research and adult treatment, was a valuable, thoroughly grounded distinction between 'interactive regulation' and 'self-regulation'. Even though these are *intricately interrelated* processes, they provided a model that held the tension between self-regulating and the importance of the intersubjective. Coming from an infant development perspective, they describe how:

> Self-regulation refers to the management of arousal . . . and the capacity to inhibit behavioural expression . . . [including] readiness to respond and . . . clarity of cues . . . and strategies that dampen arousal
>
> (Beebe and Lachmann 2002: 28)

They argue that, across the life span, self-regulation is a critical component of the capacity to engage with others. For adult clients this means 'access to, articulation of, regard for, and capacity to use inner states, including fantasy' (ibid.: 29). Interestingly, however, what is missing from this conceptualisation is a more genuinely holistic formulation which is precisely what is emphasised in the body psychotherapy model. In our view, self-regulation includes the capacity of the body *to re-organise* through expressive movement, reflexes and other involuntary processes such as shaking, crying, laughing; or indirectly through symptoms; or to defend itself by such means as restricting the breath (Totton 1998). Indeed, through all the stages of development at Chiron, self-regulation has always been conceptualised as a bodymind process across all levels (Soth 2005).

Beebe and Lachmann show how interactive regulation, on the other hand, involves a finely-tuned subliminal level of *coordination between two people*, involving split second responsivity of face, gaze and head orientation. This complex and continuous communication, paralleled in mother–infant and therapist–client relationships, has come to be recognised as a result of micro-analyses of interactions between human beings in many contexts. The rapid, non-conscious, implicit and coordinated exchanges between pairs reveal how much relating is based on anticipation of the other, adjusting, and responding. Whilst Schore calls this 'synchronisation' and Trevarthen 'proto-conversation', others use terms such as 'tracking', 'accommodation' and 'resonance' (Beebe and Lachmann 2002: 152). Beebe and Lachmann's concept of interactive regulation is a term which describes the process of coordination between self and other across a range of possibilities from the extreme of non-coordination (disconnection) to very high coordination (vigilant or merged). Operating continually at either end of the spectrum – very high or low coordination – correlates with defensiveness. Mid-range coordination is less constrained, leaving more 'space' for affective interaction (ibid.).

When I attuned to 'James' fully, matching his rhythm, responding to the intonations in his voice, accurately empathising, I was 'rewarded' with greater openness from him. However, if I misattuned or deliberately differentiated my position, verbally and non-verbally failing to match him, then our interactions could become quite staccato, with abrupt shifts of movement and eye contact.

Beebe and Lachmann comment that:

Simultaneously with the exchanges on the verbal level, patient and analyst are continually altering each other's timing, spatial organisation, affect and arousal, on a moment-to-moment basis.

(Beebe and Lachmann 2002: 33)

Experientially, this can mean that either or both parties in an exchange can feel controlled by the other. To connect to the other is to be affected. No-go areas get demarcated through powerful covert signals. The therapist strives to maintain awareness of the tension between many levels of communication. To do this, however, requires some freedom of movement across the range of coordination, to be able to step back from the 'dance' of reciprocal interaction, as well as into it.

I find Beebe and Lachmann's description of interactive regulation and self-regulation helpful precisely because it confirms and clarifies an equivalent set of terms used at Chiron. 'Vertical' self-regulation refers to the organismic regulation of self, such as through breathing or involuntary movement. 'Horizontal' regulation refers to interpersonal interaction – communicating, negotiating and being with another. The focus of the client's or therapist's attention may be on either of these interlocking aspects. With Kerry, for example, my interventions were predominantly aimed at supporting her self-regulation, in terms of bringing her to awareness of her body; with the role-played client, I was forced to deal with the 'horizontal' relational aspect. Alternating between aspects and indeed *addressing both simultaneously* has been central to Chiron's pioneering synthesis of ideas. This was the greatest challenge – Asheri calls it our 'hot potato' – that spurred the intensive thinking and debate in the Chiron staff group through the 1990s. (See Soth's chapter for an overview of this process, and Asheri's for a clinical example of working with the tension between the vertical and the horizontal.)

The web of affect: pulling some threads together

'Energetic perception' and 'contact' revisited

Whilst neuroscience has studied specific measurable elements of the complex exchanges that occur between people, body psychotherapists have focused on the subjective means for processing the data exchanged between bodies. 'Energetic perception' is the name given at Chiron to the capacity to hold an awareness *at a bodily level* of the client's multiple micro-signals. Information is too rapid and too various to be processed consciously in all its detail, but it does appear to synthesise into a felt sense through the process of resonating with the other.[5] Whilst this is an intrinsic human skill, body psychotherapists develop a particular receptivity to their own and others' bodily states. To do this effectively requires a paradoxical capacity to resonate with the other, whilst maintaining some continuity of contact with oneself.

Energetic perception heightens the therapist's sensitivity to the client's capacity for contact, and the congruence – or lack of it – between verbal and body language. Spatial-relational signals from the client may prompt the therapist to sit back and wait for the client to initiate, or alternatively, the therapist senses the importance of going forward to meet the client, or improvising to 'join in' or respond appropriately. When I work with clients I am often conscious of a basic impulse to 'go forward' or 'sit back'. This may be a response to the sense that 'something is brewing' – in other words the client is following some internal thread that requires me to 'hold the space'. Or I may have an impulse to challenge a defensive manoeuvre that keeps the client out of contact with himself and with me. At other times, it is the client's anxious search for connection and holding that may prompt me to engage in a direct and immediate way with their struggle.

Gauging the right degree of contact minimises defensiveness. At other times a carefully calibrated risk of challenging the implicit limit may also pay off (Carroll 2005b). Indeed transformation in contact may occur either through the therapist's empathic acceptance of the client's self-protection, or, at the other end of the scale, by the therapist's refusal to be warded off and their persistent attempt to 'find' or get through to the client (Winnicott 1972). Relating is based on energetic perception, which includes a capacity to detect intentional states in the other and oneself. It involves at least a subliminal level of awareness, as well as the ability to consciously slow down and reflect on the implicit unfolding dynamic between oneself and another.

Gaie Houston, reflecting on the history of the term 'contact' in gestalt therapy, defines it as 'the intersubjective . . . as outwardly-directed activity . . . in the here and now' (Houston 2003: 20). As she points out, 'the contact boundary' may be a 'constant, richly informative play of approach and retreat, of fear or warmth or other feeling, of changing pace, mirroring and much else' (ibid.: 20).[6] This description of contact shows its closeness to the more recent term interactive regulation and the two terms can describe the same phenomena: the rhythms of the exchange (pacing of speech, pauses, breaking eye contact), facial expression and matching of postural shifts or tone of voice. Ablack's account of a first meeting with a client conveys some of the therapist's nuance of regulating and inviting contact.

What, then, is the difference between all these terms apart from their invention by different theorists? What I find useful is to think of 'energetic perception' as the *perceptual act*, contact as the relational *event/process*, and interactive regulation as describing *function*. The close overlap between terms is itself significant – the processes of perceiving, feeling, responding, understanding, guessing, pre-empting, coordinating and so on are rapid, interwoven and multi-faceted. One of the themes of this chapter is the range of possible therapeutic responses that can be incorporated under the heading of supporting 'self-regulation' or 'interactive regulation'.

As a Chiron-trained psychotherapist my moment-by-moment attention is as engaged in monitoring shifts in intensity and state between myself and the client as it is in making sense of it. Whilst I may well enquire, comment or speculate on the motivation behind or meaning of what is being presented, I am fascinated by the regulatory process itself. For example, if I bring the client's awareness to the phenomenology of their experience, and to the mode of engagement, will this enhance their sense of how they are managing contact with me? Occasionally it is quite productive to ask a client not to talk but to be aware of the pressure to talk and what lies behind it.

Aaron's talking was unrelenting, although not without insight. A need to impress, flatter, control, and pre-empt my possible response stifled any chance of spontaneous exchange between us. So I asked him to notice what was happening in his body, or what he saw on my face while he was speaking. Then I suggested he tried pausing between statements. Aaron found this extremely difficult and I had to be persistent in this approach over quite a number of sessions. Eventually he became curious about what would happen between us if he was not controlling the space all the time by anticipating my reaction and 'talking for both of us'. This facilitated a huge shift in our work together because it brought his feeling into the foreground, especially the burning question: do you really care?

Regulating intensity of affect and staying in contact

> *The more realms of experience patients can bring into our relationship, the more resilient, cohesive and integrated their self-regulatory capacities.*
>
> (Jacobs 1992)

Not many clients will leave therapy and say to themselves or others 'my self-regulation has significantly improved'. But many might say or feel 'I can be myself' or 'I am more at ease with my feelings' or 'I'm more confident about saying what I think or feel'. Central to self-regulation is the capacity to accept the reality of one's feelings – the range of feelings, the variations in intensity (from a mild stirring, to being in the full throes of it), and the fact that emotions are felt with others, provoked by others, and ultimately given meaning by their relational context. For many clients, a key turning point in therapy will be when they express or show feelings that they have generally kept buried; and a further turning point comes when they can explore them in the here-and-now as they are evoked by and in the therapeutic relationship.

The body psychotherapy tradition has always emphasised the potential of a fully expressive body, and with it 'the integration of affect into the organization of self-experience' (Jacobs 1992). However, both the extremes and limits on expression or sharing of feeling which the client experienced in their early attachments will be re-lived in the transference. At Chiron the term 'charge' is used to describe the intensity of affect on a bodily level and its manifestation in a relational and transferential context. For example, Soth refers to 'the relational charge arising from the subjective spontaneous and inherent meaningfulness of the contact, internally or externally, or both' (Soth 2005: 46).

The therapist plays a critical role in influencing the intensity that the client is encouraged to experience, and the form in which that affect is expressed (Carroll 2003). Avoidance of difficult feelings, including avoidance of conflict, limits self-regulation. Arguments, for example, are often critical events in therapy. They can be prompted by erotic impulses, intolerance of difference or over-excitement about difference, as well attempts to maintain control. They may be used to protect the self against feeling loss, shame and failure. Precisely because of this – and because arguments may touch both the client's and the therapist's own weaknesses and wounds – the capacity of client and therapist to argue with each other can be vital to deep therapeutic work (Carroll 2005b). A good argument requires the capacity to stay aware of one's own feelings and views (self-regulation) whilst being able to recognise those of another, with both parties able to make adjustments (interactive regulation).[7]

The therapist's self-regulation

The therapist's self-regulatory capacity within the relational context of psychotherapy is critical to their ability to consciously and non-defensively calibrate interventions (Schore 2003). How much to say, show, feel, how far to penetrate, how much to risk disturbing a pattern, are all judgements influenced in part by the therapist's trust in their ability to regulate their own feelings.

The ability to regulate intense affect depends upon the therapist being anchored within their own body, able to bear and attend to sensation, and allow spontaneous autonomic shifts to occur. I notice, for example, how my breathing functions as an anchor. A bigger breath moving like a wave through my body is a barometer of the intensity of affect present at that moment and an indication that I am adjusting (self-regulating) and literally making space in my body to take it in. Self-regulation does not mean being totally contained; however, it is a finely-tuned flexibility in relation to oneself and another. Keary's example of crying with her client, of being 'deeply affected, raw and unable to hide', and on another occasion, revealing her deep exhaustion, 'I can't do it', are, to my mind, examples of a therapist being truly self-regulating.

The therapist's spontaneous response must be available to her in some form – whether as a sensation, feeling, image or impulse. Body awareness enhances the therapist's subjectivity which is an important factor in holding a sense of the multi-layered process between herself and the client (Soth 2005). If this underlying self-regulation is there, then the therapist can also allow herself to be knocked off balance, controlled, or confused in the process with the client. At times her job may be to survive the intensity of her own and the client's feelings, staying with the process and with the client at the border between chaos and order (Carroll 2003).

Countertransference: the self-regulation of the therapeutic couple as a system

Energetic perception enables the therapist to 'see' the layers of history in the client's body, as well as heightening sensitivity to the client's current readiness to engage. Countertransference, a phenomenon which follows inevitably from such a resonant engagement, is a process whereby the therapist becomes affected by the client, pulled in, and increasingly defined through, with and by the other.

The principles that apply in individual self-regulation also apply to the therapeutic pair as a couple. The two-person system is a dynamic balancing act, with the level of feeling often fluctuating as the interaction between client and therapist is managed both implicitly (through self-regulation and inter-active regulation) and explicitly (as far as these processes are the subject of verbal exploration). As therapist and client get to know each other, and the defences against interactive regulation begin to melt, new patterns emerge like new dance steps, new experiments in being-with-another. A comment or look may lead to a subtle shift, or a new cycle (Carroll 2005b).

Sometimes, though, these transformative shifts occur in more radical or dramatic ways. The countertransference is generated by a deep encounter between therapist and client, and an intense charge may build as certain elements remain fixed or hidden or unacknowledged over a period of time. What is not self-regulated by the therapist and by the client, and between them, starts to form its own 'demand' for regulation. Powerful unregulated affect pulls or pushes the therapist into an action that re-orients the system by bringing to the surface what has been suppressed.

Nested regulatory systems and ever shifting levels

Self-regulation is not a singular process, but occurs in a kaleidoscopic way because it is a function of a complex system with many layers (the bodymind) interrelating with a complex human environment. Shifting back and forth between layers, disentangling old patterns of self-regulation and establishing new ones, is a distinctly non-linear process which the term 'self-organisation' (which incorporates dis-organisation-and re-organisation) more fully captures (Carroll 2003, 2005b). Rather than detail insights from the extensive body of research on self-regulation, attachment, and neurobiology, I have concentrated on a set of conceptual distinctions which reflects and extends the developments in theory and practice at Chiron. Ultimately, however, in body psychotherapy, self-regulation is more than a set of theories; it is 'a way of perceiving and knowing and understanding', a way of thinking through the body.[8]

Notes

1 The word 'self-regulation' dates back to 1693 with the meaning of 'control or direction of oneself'. It was first used in biology in 1896.
2 I remember the emphatic support among the Body Mind Centering training group for the title *Wisdom of the Body Moving* when the editor, Linda Hartley, proposed it as the title for her forthcoming book (Hartley 1995).
3 German editions of Reich's books show that he occasionally used the term 'Selbststeuerung' (more like self-direction) as well as 'Selbstregulierung' (Soth, personal communication). My thanks to Michael for valuable comments on the final draft.
4 Jungian thinking has also richly informed the work of Chiron therapists (particularly Hillman 1991; Kalsched 1996; Schwartz-Salant 1982).
5 Schore suggests that the orbito-frontal cortex may be involved in detecting 'somatic markers' which provide information about self and others (Schore 2003: 105).
6 Contemporary gestalt has further contributed to the idea of self-regulation and the associated concept of field theory. See Hycner and Jacobs (1995), Jacobs (1992) and Parlett (1991).
7 Cf. discussion in Altman (2005: 33–40).
8 to borrow Parlett's phrase about field theory (1991: 1).

References

Altman, N. (2005) Relational perspectives on the therapeutic action of psychoanalysis. In: Ryan, J. (ed.) *How Does Psychotherapy Work?* London: Karnac, pp. 15–50.

Aposhyan, S. (2004) *Body-Mind Psychotherapy: Principles, Techniques and Practical Applications.* New York: Norton.

Bateman, A. and Fonagy, P. (2004) *Psychotherapy for Borderline Personality Disorder: Mentalization-based Treatment.* Oxford: Oxford University Press.

Beebe, B. and Lachmann, F. (2002) *Infant Research and Adult Treatment: Co-constructing Interactions.* Hillsdale, NJ: Analytic Press.

Cannon, W. B. (1932) *The Wisdom of the Body.* New York: Norton.

Carroll, R. (2003) On the border between chaos and order: neuroscience and psychotherapy. In: Corrigall, J. and Wilkinson, H. (eds) *Revolutionary Connections: Psychotherapy and Neuroscience.* London: Karnac.

Carroll, R. (2005a) Neuroscience and the therapeutic relationship. In: Totton, N. (ed.) *New Dimensions in Body Psychotherapy.* Maidenhead: Open University Press.

Carroll, R. (2005b) Rhythm, re-orientation and reversal: deep re-organisation of the self in psychotherapy. In: Ryan, J. (ed.) *How Does Psychotherapy Work?* London: Karnac, pp. 85–112.

Damasio, A. (1994) *Descartes' Error: Emotion, Reason, and the Human Brain.* London: Putnam.

Feldman, R., Greenbaum, C. W. and Yirmiya, N. (1999) Mother-infant affect synchrony as an antecedent of the emergence of self-control. *Developmental Psychology* 35(1): 223–231.

Freud, S. (1920) *Beyond the Pleasure Principle.* SE 18: 7–64.

Hartley, L. (1995) *Wisdom of the Body Moving.* Berkeley, CA: North Atlantic Books.

Heller, M. (2007) The golden age of body psychotherapy in Oslo 1: from gymnastics to psychoanalysis. *Body, Movement and Dance in Psychotherapy* 2(1): 5–16.

Hilman, J. (1991) *The Blue Fire*. New York: Harper Collins.

Houston, G. (2003) *Brief Gestalt Therapy*. London: Sage.

Hycner, R. and Jacobs, L. (1995) *The Healing Relationship in Gestalt: A Dialogic Self-psychology Approach*. Highland, NY: Gestalt Journal Press.

Jacobs, L. (1992) Insights from psychoanalytic self psychology and intersubjectivity theory for gestalt therapists. Online: http://www.gestalttherapy.org/publications/self_psychology_and_intersubjectivity.html (accessed 14 May 2007).

Jung, C. G. (1921) Psychological types and the self-regulating psyche. In: Storr, S. (ed.) *The Essential Jung*. Princeton University Press, 1983.

Kalsched, D. (1996) *The Inner World of Trauma*. London: Routledge.

Landale, M. (2002) The use of imagery in body psychotherapy. In: Staunton, T. (ed.) *Body Psychotherapy*. Hove: Brunner-Routledge.

Parlett, M. (1991) Reflections on field theory. *The British Gestalt Journal* 1: 68–91.

Perls, F., Hefferline, R. and Goodman, P. (1972) *Gestalt Therapy: Excitement and Growth in the Human Personality*. London: Souvenir Press. (Originally published in 1951.)

Reich, W. (1972) *Character Analysis*. Reprinted Farrar, Strauss and Giroux, New York, 1990.

Rothschild, B. (2000) *The Body Remembers: The Psychophysiology of Trauma and Trauma Treatment*. London: Norton.

Schore, A. (1994) *Affect Regulation and the Origin of the Self*. Hove: Lawrence Erlbaum.

Schore, A. (2001) The American Bowlby: an interview with Allan Schore. Telephone interview by Roz Carroll in March 2001. Excerpts published in *The Psychotherapist* Autumn 2001.

Schore, A. (2003) *Affect Regulation and Repair of the Self*. Hove: Lawrence Erlbaum.

Schwartz-Salant, N. (1982) *Narcissism and Character Transformation*. San Francisco: Inner City Books.

Soth, M. (2005) Embodied countertransference. In: Totton, N. (ed.) *New Dimensions in Body Psychotherapy*. Maidenhead: Open University Press, pp. 40–55.

Totton, N. (1998) *The Water in the Glass: Body and Mind in Psychoanalysis*. London: Rebus Press.

Totton, N. (2005) Do bodies tell the truth? *Association of Chiron Psychotherapists' Newsletter* no 30, summer, pp. 8–26.

Trevarthen, C. and Aitken, K. J. (2001) Infant intersubjectivity: research, theory and clinical application. *Journal of Child Psychology and Psychiatry* 42(1): 3–48.

Winnicott, D. W. (1972) *The Maturational Process and the Facilitating Environment*. London: Hogarth Press.

Chapter 6

To touch or not to touch: a relational body psychotherapy perspective

Shoshi Asheri

The aim of this chapter is to open a window to the way in which I, and we at the Chiron Centre, have been grappling with the controversial issue of touch within the psychotherapeutic encounter, both theoretically and clinically.

I will start by looking at some key relational developments in Chiron's philosophy, which have impacted profoundly on our use of touch. I will continue by illustrating my updated understanding of the place of touch in the therapeutic encounter, with two clinical examples: one of a client who is struggling with compulsive overeating and the other, of a client who is questioning her sexuality. I will pay particular attention to my countertransferential process while negotiating the dilemma: to touch or not to touch, and, if to touch, how to touch.

Intersubjectivity and touch

In the spirit of the Chiron tradition I would like to start the theoretical exploration by referring to a lived experience, which illustrates an underpinning issue we have to consider each time we wonder if touch is appropriate as a therapeutic intervention. I used to be married to an artist. I spent many years being an object of his artistic gaze while being a subject in a loving intimate relationship. He was very passionate about his work, so the camera was almost inseparable from his eyes. This, in combination with my passion for psychological enquiries, led us to many wonderful and painful heated arguments. I would say, 'I sometimes want your eyes on me not via the camera' and he'd say, 'The camera is my eyes'. I'd say, 'How can I feel touched if you are hiding behind something?' and he'd say, 'I'm not hiding. I feel like I'm touching you with much more than my eyes when I'm behind the camera'. I'd say, 'How do we know that you are not simply afraid of direct intimacy and you are gaining distance and power by turning me into an art object?' and he'd say, 'How do we know that you are not using your psychological gaze to gain power and avoid the intimacy of my looking at you right now?' . . . and on and on we'd go. Then he'd show me the picture he'd created and my argument would be pulled from under my feet. I felt touched deep into my soul. I felt seen. I felt discovered. I felt loved in a way I couldn't predict. I would look at him, recognising something about him 'the artist' *and* 'my husband' and he would rush to his camera because in that moment he saw something in my look he hadn't seen before. I would say, 'Can I have you right now, not the artist?' and he'd say, 'I am the artist' . . . and off we'd go.

One reading of this encounter is that we were attempting to negotiate what relational psychoanalysts refer to as the paradoxical nature of *intersubjectivity*. As Benjamin (1990: 186) suggests:

> Intersubjective theory postulates that the other must be recognised as another subject in order for the self to fully experience his or her subjectivity in the other's presence. This means, first, that we have a need for recognition and second, a capacity to recognise others in return – mutual recognition.

Intersubjectivity, as Benjamin suggests, is not recognition alone. It entails the ability to sustain an ongoing paradoxical tension between recognising the other as possessing separate subjectivity, existing physically, emotionally and mentally outside one's own omnipotence, and negating their separateness by the pull of our internal fantasy, transference and set of projections, which are created by our intrapsychic dynamics. Stuart Pizer (1992, 1998) talks about the challenge of negotiating mutual recognition as a challenge of bridging our essential separateness and our essential relatedness, our need to deconstruct the 'otherness' to suit ourselves and our need to find the world of otherness in order to locate ourselves in relation to external reality. Our challenge is to develop the ability to sustain the paradoxical tension between the needs, not as either/or but as both/and. Inevitably, we lose touch with our ability to hold the paradox. Either the internal dynamic or the external reality takes over, and a 'breakdown' of the intersubjectivity occurs.

Back to my lived example. There was something compelling, magnetic, or, dare I say, erotic, in these arguments. Probably to do with the 'embodied charge' we experienced when attempting to hold the tension of the paradox as both/and. Him as 'artist' and 'loving partner', and me as 'art object' and 'subject of love'; both distinct yet part of the same system. It became deeply painful each time the holding of the tension of the paradox collapsed into the either/or dynamic. Then we would find ourselves within the limitation of dualism where only one reality can exist. Either I was an object or a subject, either he was an artist or a loving partner, either he was right or I was right. Within this polarised framework, it felt as if only one of us could exist.

When relating to my client through the lens of my position as a therapist, I find myself negotiating a similar tension. When I wonder if it is appropriate to touch my client I cannot help but consider the fact that I'm negotiating the tension between internal and external realities. On the one hand there is an intrapsychic reality of both my client's and my own past relationship with touch (which may be associated with anything on the spectrum from love, care and nurturing to deprivation, exploitation and abuse). On the other hand there is the interpersonal reality of here and now, me and you and the concrete experience of possible physical contact between us.

When I ask myself 'to touch or not to touch' within the therapeutic encounter, I face a paradoxical tension which can easily collapse into a 'yes' or 'no', 'right' or 'wrong' answer, as indeed happened historically, within the field. As we know, within the traditional psychoanalytic framework, following Freud's departure from applying touch to his patient's body in order to encourage emotional expression and regression in favour of the 'talking cure' (Freud and Breuer 1895), touch has been perceived as gratifying the client's infantile needs and making concrete what should remain symbolic. It is seen as interfering with the neutrality of the therapist's position, hence it can derail the transferential dynamic. It potentially encourages aggression but more dangerously, touch can lead to transgression as it stimulates sexual arousal in both client and therapist. In short, within this framework we have to conclude that 'no touch' is the only safe and appropriate answer. Then again, we can take the traditional body psychotherapy stance which, in its rebellion, moved away from its psychoanalytic roots by idealising the body over the mind and by adopting a more humanistic framework, and say that touch is life-giving. It helps to enhance a sense of self and self-boundary by offering an experience of nurturing and containment. It facilitates the mobilisation of frozen energy in the body caused by traumatic or painful past events. Touch can soften body armouring and bypass cognitive resistance, it can elicit memories and unexpressed emotional and physical material that are locked in the body. Hence it is an essential enabler of affect regulation. In other words, through the lens of this framework we are led to conclude that touch is not only appropriate, it is the 'answer'.

I believe that one of the most fundamental developments in Chiron's training in recent years (see Eiden's and Soth's chapters) has been the notion that we cannot deal with the question of touch without taking into account our understanding of the therapeutic encounter as an embodied intersubjective engagement. As such, we have to consider the question of 'touch' as an integral part of negotiating the paradoxical tension between attending to the intrapsychic dynamic within both participants and the interpersonal dynamic between them. In this sense, having an unquestionable rule that touch is always 'right', or appropriate, will contribute to the collapse of the paradoxical tension of the intersubjective engagement as much as will the notion that touch is always 'wrong' or inappropriate. Although in practice the collapse of the tension is inevitable, our updated philosophical premise is that we need to hold the *possibility* of touch, as it can be both an appropriate or inappropriate therapeutic intervention.

It is heartening to notice the evolution of parallel thinking not only within other body psychotherapy training (Totton 2005, 2006) but also outside a body-centred approach. For example, Barbara Pizer (2002: 840) has arrived at a similar conclusion from her perspective as a relational psychoanalyst:

> In my view whether or not we believe in or feel comfortable with any sort of physical contact in the psychoanalytic setting, if we arbitrarily split off on theoretical grounds as a viable possibility in all circumstances, we invite dissociation.

Who is being touched? Who is touching?

The assumption that intrapsychic change is primarily possible through inter-personal means and that immediacy and emotional availability are essential to the therapeutic task has led many relational psychoanalysts to what I regard as an inevitable conclusion: there has to be a reconsideration of the exclusion of the body from the consulting room (Aron (1998), Maroda (2002), Orbach (2004, 2006) and B. Pizer (2000), to name but a few). The question is, what would the inclusion of the *actual* body within the context of a psychoanalytic relationship look like? While relational psychoanalysts deal with this 'hot issue', body psychotherapists deal with a similar dilemma from the opposite direction. We have had no question about the inclusion of the body; the challenge for us has been to negotiate the paradox between having some 'expertise' in our ability to apply touch which can release emotional and/or physical pain, and our understanding of the therapeutic relationship as an engagement between two people's psychology, neither of whose experi-ence is privileged over the other's. In other words, how do we creatively negotiate the paradox between touch as a medicalised intervention and touch as a relational event? This is our 'hot potato', and body psychotherapists at Chiron vary in their styles largely according to how they choose to engage with this paradox. The dilemma we are persistently grappling with is: when is it therapeutically valuable to meet the client's desire to be 'treated' by touch and when is it more valuable to challenge this desire and facilitate a process of necessary disappointment? In this process the client can learn that we don't necessarily have the power to 'fix' them with touch. What we can offer is our availability to engage in a relationship, which can reveal the body/mind patterns that need disruption and reorganisation.

In my own work I find that what guides and monitors my interventions when facing this dilemma is the notion that intersubjectivity is a develop-mental progression. As Benjamin (1990) describes, the developmental pro-cess entails a capacity for mutual recognition that is only gradually and imperfectly acquired. A desire for touch from a client who has very little sense of their own subjectivity, and perceives me as an object of fulfilment of their need or drive, is completely different from a desire for touch by a client who has a sense of their own subjectivity and perceives me as a subject with a separate set of desires. My therapeutic considerations about the appropriateness of touch and/or the nature of it will be fundamentally different in these two cases. For example, I may consider physical holding, which could be soothing and comforting for a client in a regressed, preverbal state, who is experiencing little or no sense of where they begin and where they end. The intention of the touch will be to promote a sense of vertical connection and skin boundary, where separateness and connection can become a 'felt experience'. But the same touch which embodies an experience of the therapist as a 'gratifying object' whose subjectivity is not yet relevant, is completely inappropriate with a client who is presenting an oedipal or interpersonal conflict, where the most relevant issue is their struggle to recognise my subjectivity and the pull to hold on to me as an object of fantasy. In this case the touch, if applied, or the decision not to touch needs to facilitate the client's ability to explore and bear this *conflict*. This again will be different from a response to a client who presents a post-oedipal request for touch. The therapeutic aim, in this case, is to create a context for the client to engage as one adult with another adult. In this situation, the challenge for the therapist is to dare to go beyond the safety of a parental position. Responding to a post-oedipal request for touch will carry all the considerations involved when mutual recognition between two adults is negotiated. However, as it is a therapeutic framework, the therapist holds the delicate and complex responsibility of taking into account not only the mutuality of the relationship but also the asymmetry of it. In my experience as a therapist and as a supervisor, the controversial issue of touch is particularly heightened in the face of a post-oedipal request for touch because the therapist is invited to walk to the edge of their subjectivity, where the line between their response as a person and their responsibility to hold a therapeutic reflection can become extremely fine.

Taking the developmental dynamic into account when considering touch is a fascinating and many-layered subject, which deserves a chapter in its own right. I am aware that by presenting such a generalised and simplified overview I run the risk of creating an impression that the process is linear or that there is a prescribed schema of when and how to use touch according to the developmental stages presented. However, our updated understanding of the psychotherapeutic process, where self and mutual regulation take place, is influenced by contemporary neuroscientific thinking (see Carroll's and Stauffer's chapters) and by post-classical analytic thinkers like Fairbairn (1952), Sullivan (1953), Winnicott (1960, 1971), Searles (1977) and more recently, Bromberg (1993, 1996). Hence, we see the self as de-centred and fluid and perceive developmental progression and growth as a non-linear, ongoing dialectic process. Thus, during the process and at any session, we will be presented with shifting 'states of selves' organised in a fluid, ongoing dialectic. Therefore, when we wonder whether or not to touch, we need to ask ourselves which 'state of self' are we touching at each particular moment, and which state of self is evoked in us in response. We may wonder if a particular touch or a decision not to touch can facilitate a reconnection with dissociated parts in the client and/or ourselves. Back to our example; if we decide to respond to a regressed client by applying a soothing, maternal touch we need to hold in mind that in the same moment another self state exists, which may or may not come to the foreground. This 'other part' of the client, for example, can experience this very touch that was soothing 'the baby' a minute ago, as invasive or manipulative a minute or a session later, because a dissociated memory of inappropriate touch at a later stage in the client's life has been evoked. A touch can be containing for a client, so that a trauma can be explored. Yet the same touch can lead to a re-enactment of a trauma and turn the wounded healer to a wounding healer in that moment (see Clark's and Heitzler's chapters). This isn't necessarily a reason to avoid touch altogether, but rather another reason to perceive the dilemma and the application of touch as a living, creative, dialectic process of constant negotiation.

I find Bromberg's (1996) metaphor of 'a twilight space' very helpful in describing the process of intersubjective engagement. Although he doesn't refer to touch as part of this process, in my experience, holding the possibility of touch as an intervention intensifies the embodiment of the intersubjective space. In those moments when the symbolic material is leading me as therapist to engage with the possibility of a concrete touch with my client, I find myself entering into what he describes as a 'trance'-like state of consciousness, like the moment before entering sleep, when both wakefulness and dreaming co-exist. It is a twilight space 'in which incompatible selves, each awake to it own "truth", can "dream" the reality of the other without the risk to its own integrity' (Bromberg 1996: 519). In this space it is clear that this touch is happening here and now between me and you, yet it is also holding a symbolic meaning of past experiences and/or future possibilities. It is about you and me and it is beyond us. We can both potentially be changed by this engagement if we can keep negotiating the multiplicity of our reality, moment to moment.

In short, taking into account the multiplicity of self and the non-linear and dialectic nature of growth has challenged us, Chiron psychotherapists, to be much more subtle and creative with our notion of touch. We have had to change the traditional body psychotherapy emphasis on catharsis or gratification, which aims at undercutting or melting defences, to a touch that is multi-faceted, with a capacity to discriminate between and hold multiple realities and meanings. In each session, within each interaction, we are challenged to be attuned to the unique experience of both the client and our own shifting subjectivity. We have had to learn a new dance which includes moving flexibly and fluidly from one form of touch to another or to a decision not to touch at all, according to the shifting sand of the intersubjective meeting. This understanding also requires from us a willingness to engage responsibly, moment to moment, internally and at times externally (in an explicit dialogue with our client), with the question: to touch or not to touch, and if to touch, whom are we touching at any moment, and what is being touched in us? Whom are we choosing not to touch? Is there a part of us that is remaining therefore untouched?

I believe that this high degree of self-monitoring and accountability that we apply moment to moment before touching is partly inherent in the contemporary thinking that now guides our work, but paradoxically it is also a positive outcome of having to grapple with the controversy and the shadow aspects of traditional body psychotherapy. The challenge and the art of the work for us lies in the ability to translate the analysis of the relational dynamic into therapeutic interventions which may or may not include a concrete touch.

Clinical examples

Sarah, a teacher in her mid-fifties, came to me after being in Jungian analysis for seven years. She felt great appreciation for her previous therapist, felt that she had done a lot of important work but felt that her therapy 'got stuck' because it didn't 'touch' her body and 'my body is the biggest problem as you can see'. She was severely overweight and this self-deprecating humour was also a big feature of hers. She was depressed, worried about her health, and although functioning well professionally and engaging with family and friends, she felt inwardly extremely isolated, disconnected and unable to create real intimacy with either friends or sexual partners. She hadn't been in an intimate relationship for the last 20 years. She tried massage for a while but ultimately, she found it 'unbearable'. 'What I really want is to be held so I can at last let go and be little. I feel like I've been holding myself all my life. My mother couldn't hold me emotionally or physically and the only way I can be with others is to hold them. My therapist used to encourage me to imagine being held by her, it was great for a while then it became futile because I knew it could never really happen . . . physical holding was not an option within her framework.' Sarah's hope was that I, as a body psychotherapist, would do it for her.

There was something in Sarah's wit, intelligence and psychological literacy that I found very engaging and attractive. Her pain induced deep compassion in me. My arms wanted to go towards her. I felt a strong pull to gratify her desire to be held. At the same time, I was aware that her longing to be held as she has never been held before, was a regressive fantasy that, if mindlessly fulfilled, could obscure the psychic reality of grief and frustration about what didn't happen. For my part, I came to understand her desire as regressive because of the nature of what was happening within me . . . a kind of 'draining', an inner sense of loss of agency. It seemed as if my own separate desires (I might want or might not want to hold her) were irrelevant to her.

Also, I became aware of my own wound of maternal deprivation, which I too compensated for by taking care of others; a signal for me to pause and wonder about my pull to gratify her. Finally, included in the experience of my somatic countertransference was that the felt idea of actually holding her physically close to me filled me with uncomfortable sensations of contraction or even repulsion. Clearly, grappling with these two contradictory realities put me in conflict. I felt torn between my wish to hold her on the one side, and a strong reluctance to do so on the other. In the familiar terms of projective identification I was experiencing, at least in part, Sarah's dissociated conflict even though she was expressing this unambivalent deep longing to be held by me. The outer shape of her body and her current life situation spoke to me of her many layers of defence against such contact. But the vital question of the moment was, what should I do with this uncomfortable conflict that now resided inside me? And anyway, was Sarah the only one dissociating? I found myself entering with her into a theoretical discussion about body psycho-therapy and touch and how touch isn't assumed in the way I work. I could sense that as we were reflecting on it, a skill she was so capable of, she became more and more 'reasonable' and less and less emotionally connected while I sank more and more into the comfort and the safety of my reflective pos-ition, losing touch with both her conflict and my own. Ultimately, I could experience a 'felt sense' of an opportunity gone dead.

Thinking about it after the session I was reminded of Bromberg's (1996) notion that the analyst's involuntary response to the patient's dissociated self-experience is to dissociate herself, and of Schore's (2003) study of self-regulation and mutual regulation in the therapeutic dyad. Schore suggests that the dissociation, i.e. the movement from right brain to left brain of one of the couple, is perceived and immediately reacted to by the other. In this case, as I moved away from emotional engagement into the use of dissociative observation in order to calm down my discomfort, I could sense that Sarah felt it. What I mean to convey here is that although my formulations and reflections in dialogue with Sarah were theoretically 'true', our conversation was 'inauthentic' and I believe that she sensed it. We were both retreating from the emotional charge of her request.

Fortunately for us both, Sarah's desire for actual physical holding would not be driven underground by such disembodied exchanges. When she asked once again to be held I felt more prepared to step into the risky zone of both our uncomfortable truths. I agreed to hold her. My hope was that the physical holding, if carefully engaged, would provide a concrete 'third', where the symbolic conflicts in both of us could be explored; she would be able to experience a 'felt sense' of the discrepancy between her longing to be held and her fear of it, and I would be able to unfold my corresponding experience of my wish to hold her and my reluctance to do so. I invited her to come and sit closer to me and organise us physically according to her image of being held.

Sarah said that her fantasy was to put her head on my lap, and for my hand to stroke her forehead. But she decided that felt 'too greedy'. She put my arm around her and leaned her head down over my shoulder. With that gesture, I sensed my body partly contracting. I figured that this embodied ambivalence was not only mine; I figured that Sarah was most probably bypassing her dissociated resistance. So I asked her to slow everything down and pay close attention to what was happening in her body. Sarah had shifted from feeling an initial triumph of 'getting what she thought she wanted' to the realization that her body 'left the room' and it happened just as soon as she came close to me. Sarah couldn't take in the physical contact she so longed for and now was available to her. Her disappointment was immense.

Gently, I suggested that she could move away and sit at a distance that would reflect where she really was in relation to me. She slowly moved to the far corner of the room, facing away from me, crying. We spent many sessions sitting at this distance as her life story unravelled before us. I could experience her relationship with her extremely controlling mother who fed her when she, the mother, was hungry and removed the plate when she, the mother, had had enough. In the space that Sarah created between us we could experience directly Sarah's loneliness, her self-hate and her rage. We could see that I inevitably had become the controlling mother, withholding my touch but now, I had also become a new figure of possible contact. For Sarah, food had seemed to be the only conceivable comfort within this battlefield. Yet we had now arrived at a place where her pain and rage was more contained in our verbal work, as her reluctance and fear of physical contact was more conscious to her. At this juncture, we altered the parameters of touch. Primarily, I would guide her to touch her own body as a way of illuminating the vertical connection or disconnection between her body and mind. For example: 'when you talk about your mother what is happening in your body? . . . Put your hand where you feel emptiness and stay with it . . .'.

Sarah came to realise that as our working alliance became more solid and the emotional intimacy intensified, she would have different ways of using her body and her mind to 'vacate' the room, and later at home, eat as she felt the emptiness in her belly so acutely. We worked on her increasing her ability to tolerate the discomfort that our growing emotional contact presented her with. There was a point where she wanted to dare to come physically closer in a way that was more in tune with how she felt in relation to me. I remember us exploring in minute details a position which would accurately illustrate our current connection. We worked very slowly and delicately until we ended up sitting extremely close to each other, yet not quite touching. The body heat of our closeness was felt between us yet we were both facing away from each other. A fascinating parallel process started taking place. As I was feeling this position reflecting so well my internal conflict between my love and connection to her and the reality of my physical contraction when I came close to her, Sarah was experiencing in her body the split of her conflict. The right side of her body, which was the furthest from me, was pulling towards me, wanting to bridge the physical gap between us. Her left side, which was nearly touching me, was contracting away from me until a severe pain was running from her neck down her arm. In a sense, this was the ultimate embodiment of the conflict that held the paradoxical tension between her intrapsychic relationship with her internalised mother and her new inter-personal relationship with me. When I invited her to put words into her sensations, she said, 'I feel in a conflict between my desire to feel our bodies touch and my fear that my body will repulse you as it repulsed my mother and now it repulses me'. Having shared this with me made her feel very exposed, yet her shame was held now by both of us and between us. I could feel a wave of great affection for her uncompromising honesty. I could also feel my con-traction dissipating. She was now holding this contraction/repulsion more consciously in herself and within her body. We then spontaneously found ourselves moving very minutely nearer, still holding the little gap where the battle needed to continue for a while longer. The knowledge that she felt repulsed by her body and that she is in an ongoing battle was not new to her, but instead of dissociating from it by vacating her body or numbing it with food, she was gradually learning to contain it within her body with another body in the room. In other words, she became more embodied and so could stay longer within our relationship. Her fantasy of putting her head on my lap hadn't disappeared but it shifted from a regressive desire to an adult desire to be casually lying with her head resting on another person's lap, completely relaxed in her body and able to share her feelings and thoughts shamelessly.

Now, three years into our work together, Sarah is in a loving sexual rela-tionship where she can actually make her fantasy real. As to her overeating, although she feels relatively more in control of it, it is still a daily struggle. Recently, when I was on holiday we agreed that she could email me rather than fall into her pattern of dissociating from our connection. With her permission I'm quoting her words:

> I'm in a process of dumping food as a friend and it's so hard because it's always kept me such good company . . . maybe I can get used to the loss and maybe staying in touch with you this holiday is part of a process of finding another company.

As you can hear, in our work the symbolic has become concrete and the concrete has become symbolic. In this particular relationship, touch has been a key to holding the paradoxical tension of our intersubjective engagement. When I work with Sarah, I often think of Little's (1985) claim that therapy may require a representation of the principle of reality by concrete means. A symbolic, deductive, conclusion-reaching process is sometimes not enough. I also think of Orbach's words:

> Symbols are useful for symbolizing but the body, struggling to come alive, struggling to be held, may well need more than symbols. It needs

to be engaged with, struggled with, to feel welcomed, put upon, invaded, affronted, moved, turned on and turned off by a body in the room.

(Orbach 2004: 41)

It would feel incomplete to consider the possibility of touch in psychotherapy without engaging with the most controversial aspect of it: the risk of sexual transgression. This is a subject that deserves much more attention than this chapter allows. However, I want to bring a clinical example that supports the argument that the risk of sexual transgression doesn't have to lead to the elimination of the *possibility* of touch from the therapy room.

In 2004, at a UKCP conference, I gave a talk called 'Erotic desire in the therapy room: dare we embody it? Can we afford not to?' I want to develop one of the clinical examples I brought in that paper for our purposes. It's about a client in her forties, married with three young daughters, a nurse who was extremely disciplined, conscientious and hard-working. Her beautiful red hair was arranged in a tight bun on top of her head. She felt in midlife crisis, restless and dissatisfied about her current life but at a loss as to what she actually wanted to change. All she said about sexuality was, that 'it's not much fun', and another side comment about not letting her girls keep their hands under the duvet before they go to sleep because 'you never know what they might get up to'. A while into our work together she walked into the session with her lovely red hair all loose. I heard myself spontaneously complimenting her looks. Immediately she apologised for coming in before arranging her hair. I managed to hold the moment and help her identify the pleasure she felt before the apology, which she didn't let herself stay with. She blushed, managed to stay with it for a few seconds while starting to tell me an erotic dream she had had. Very quickly then she stopped and put her hair up again. I became aware of my unruly hairstyle and the danger of being seen to have pleasure in the freedom it represents for me. For a split second I had an image of her letting herself have 'a moment under the cover' but it was soon gone. I said: 'I feel as if you let something happen under the cover but decided to put your hands out again because you never know what you might get up to'. This became part of our symbolic language in the sessions and slowly she tolerated longer moments of 'exploring herself' under the cover, so to speak. This moved to a crucial point when she realised she was getting pleasure out of me witnessing her. Eventually, after many layered explorations, she recognised her 'new feeling' as wanting me to 'join her' under the cover. This very delicate budding of daring to have sexual pleasure and exploring the possibility of having it with another person is so precious and can so easily feel crushed. How can I, as a body psychotherapist, welcome it without either crossing necessary boundaries or implicitly sending a message that this is not allowed?

This is a point where the symbolic has to remain symbolic, not only for ethical reasons but also because making it concrete may foreclose possibilities rather than open them. Moreover, taking the developmental progression into account, I was searching for an intervention which would enable her to experience the legitimacy of having her erotic feelings in relation to me and at the same time support her having to tolerate the disappointment in me being a mere object of fantasy. The hidden nature of her longing to 'let down her hair' gradually became apparent. I understood her request as a desire for me to mirror the possibility of being in possession of female sexuality. I took into consideration the fact that we had talked in the past about the boundaries of our contract. She knew that touch was a possibility which might or might not happen. She also knew that sexual touch was an absolute taboo. However, should the ethical boundary of sexual abstinence prevent the exploration of the erotic charge which was clearly entering the therapy room? I invited her to sit in front of me on the floor. We sat cross-legged, our knees close to each other but there was no physical contact. I asked her to close her eyes and go vertically into her body and very slowly, bit-by-bit, feel the sensations. I asked her then to open her eyes and look at me and try to feel what happened in her body while she looked at me. I invited her to allow her eyes slowly and freely to look at my body while my eyes were rested on hers. As the erotic charge was growing her body started shaking. This was the moment I asked her to verbalise what was happening (often I use verbal reflection as a way of containing what can develop into over-stimulation): 'I feel so excited and so scared. I assume nothing can happen here so I know my fear is not about actually touching each other . . . my fear is about feeling so much pleasure in my body by the thought of it . . .' You can hear how the symbolic can be embodied simply by having the *possibility* of touch translated to a living experience within us and between us. While this was happening I checked my somatic countertransference very intently.

I felt myself responding to the erotic desire, I felt deep excitement as we were entering into unknown possibilities but I was interested to realise that I didn't experience it as sexual desire. I noted that it was not located in my genital area. In my assessment it was not that I was resisting sexual desire between us but that the dominant desire in the room was *her* desire to flirt with unthinkable possibilities, and I was a vehicle for it. For her, allowing so much erotic pleasure in her body was unfamiliar, but to feel it with and maybe towards another woman, was unthinkable. Over time, we went through a period where she needed delicate holding of the thoughts and fantasies in relation to her attraction to me, which inevitably led her to question her sexual orientation. Neither she nor I knew if her sexual orientation was at the root of her restlessness. After a few years of working together holding all unthinkable possibilities open, she concluded that this was not the issue. She gradually managed to have her hair down and be in possession of her own attractiveness. She also realised she had a secret passion for horses which she really wanted to have in her life. Eventually, she moved to the country with her husband, daughters and a horse. How much of it had to do with us managing to embody unthinkable possibilities? I haven't yet found a way to measure it. But I believe that there is a profound connection between the embodied process we had and the translation of its meaning to her life outside therapy.

Presenting these clinical examples is like plucking two or three chords when in fact a whole orchestra is playing a complex piece of music at each session, during each intervention. Nevertheless, I hope it gives a flavour of the many dilemmas and considerations that go into any therapeutic relating which may include touch or may include a decision not to touch.

Conclusion

I believe that in the light of contemporary thinking about the relationship between body and mind, all therapeutic approaches need to reconsider the place of the body and the possibility of touch within their distinct therapeutic framework. However, I also believe that working with touch, as a relational psychotherapeutic event, requires an appropriate training. What the Chiron training has taught me is the importance of embodying our understanding of the relational dynamic *experientially* in our teaching and the need to be trained to pay very detailed attention to the subliminal, non-verbal and right-brain to right-brain interaction.

I think of touch as having an innate therapeutic impact that cannot be replaced by words, and I perceive spontaneous, social touch as humanising the process as a whole. However, it is also clear that the therapeutic frame gives 'touch' a multiplicity of meanings that must be taken into account. In my practice I use touch very selectively. Some of my clients I don't touch at all, because other ways of engaging therapeutically seem more appropriate. Yet, in my experience, knowing that touch is a *possibility* significantly deepens the scope of the relational work.

Based on my clinical practice, these are some of the conditions which I have found need to be present in order for touch to be effective:

1   When the clients know that touch is a possibility but not an inevitability (it may or may not happen).
2   When the touch is guided by the client's material and not by my own need or agenda.
3   When the nature of the touch is varied and unpredictable as it is not dictated by a technique (although technique may be involved) but by the unique meeting that the client and I co-create.
4   When the nature of the touch corresponds to the client's presented 'self state' and can move fluidly with the shifting sand of the intersubjective engagement.
5   When the touch is intended to deepen the engagement with unconscious material and not when the touch is a way out of an uncomfortable issue or an uncomfortable dynamic.

6   When there is an indication that the symbolic needs a concrete manifest-
     ation but not when the concrete manifestation limits the possibilities
     which the symbolic could open.
7   When there is an alignment and congruence between the dynamic of the
     therapeutic relationship and the nature of the touch.
8   When the ethical boundary of sexual abstinence is held as an essential
     foundation of the structure.

Finally, I believe that when people come to us they usually come with a
recognition that their habitual patterns of being and relating have become a
source of suffering. We are faced with an implicit or explicit task to unsettle
their habitual patterns. I see it as an expression of longing to meet life and
aliveness differently from before. As a therapist I want to require from myself,
and the medium I use, what I invite my client to do: to walk to the edge of my
safety zone and flirt with possibilities which are less familiar and less settled
within habitual patterns of predictable therapeutic interventions.

Bromberg (1998: 237) acknowledges the contemporary quip that 'psychotherapy is a good profession for someone who wants to do something dangerous without leaving the office'. The 'danger zone', as I see it, is the zone
where therapeutic change can happen. It's where both my client and I dare to
flirt with a sense of aliveness that starts where habitual ways of relating end.
We do it by daring to walk to the edge of our subjectivity and step into an
intersubjective engagement. Including the body and the possibility of touch
in the work facilitates the embodiment which is an essential guide to and
monitor of the process as a whole. The issue is that this very embodied
process escalates the intensity of the intersubjective engagement. When the
intensity escalates, the fear of the symbolic flirtation with aliveness becoming
a literal flirtation also escalates. As we know, this has been a major reason for
the touch taboo. What has been lost along the way is the idea that this
dangerous line, if walked consciously, skilfully and ethically, can be highly
fertile and potentially transformative. I believe that in the light of contemporary thinking our therapeutic task within the Chiron approach, and
outside of it, is to develop subtle and creative ways to walk this line in a way
that is resolutely safe and ethical yet it is not confined by safety and ethics.

References

Aron, L. (1998) The clinical body and the reflexive mind. In: Aron, L. and Anderson,
    F. S. (eds) *Relational Perspectives of the Body*. Hillsdale, NJ: Analytic Press.
Benjamin, J. (1990) Recognition and destruction: an outline of intersubjectivity. In:
    Mitchell, S. A. and Aron, L. (eds) *Relational Psychoanalysis: The Emergence of a
    Tradition*. Hillsdale, NJ: Analytic Press, 1999.
Bromberg, P. M. (1993) Shadow and substance: a relational perspective on clinical
    process. *Psychoanalytic Psychology* 10: 147–168.

Bromberg, P. M. (1996) Standing in spaces: the multiplicity of self and the psycho-analytic relationship. *Contemporary Psychoanalysis* 32(4): 500–535.

Bromberg, P. M. (1998) *Standing in the Spaces*. Hillsdale, NJ: Analytic Press.

Fairbairn, W. R. D. (1952) *An Object Relation Theory of the Personality*. New York: Basic Books.

Freud, S. and Bruer, J. (1895) *Studies On Hysteria*. Penguin Freud library, Vol. 3. London: Penguin.

Little, M. (1985) *Transference Neurosis, Transference Psychosis*. London: Jason & Aronson Press.

Maroda, K. J. (2002) *Seduction, Surrender and Transformation*. Hillsdale, NJ: Analytic Press.

Orbach, S. (2004) The John Bowlby Memorial Lecture – The Body in Clinical Practice, Part Two: When Touch Comes to Therapy. In: White, K. (ed.) *Touch, Attachment and the Body*. London: Karnac.

Orbach, S. (2006) Foreword. In: Galton, G. (ed.) *Touch Papers: Dialogues on Touch in the Psychoanalytic Space*. London: Karnac.

Pizer, B. (2000) Negotiating analytic holding. *Psychoanalytic Inquiry* 20(1): 82–107.

Pizer, B. (2002) Blowin' in the wind – considering the impact of 'inadvertent touch'. *Psychoanalytic Dialogues* 12(5): 837–846.

Pizer, S. (1992) The negotiation of paradox in the analytic process. *Psychoanalytic Dialogues* 2: 215–240.

Pizer, S. (1998) *Building Bridges: The Negotiation of Paradox in Psychoanalysis*. Hillsdale, NJ: Analytic Press.

Schore, A. N. (2003) *Affect Regulation and the Repair of the Self*. New York: Norton.

Searles, H. F. (1977) Dual and multiple identity processes in borderline ego functioning. In: Hartocollis, P. (ed) *Borderline Personality Disorders*. New York: International University Press, pp. 441–445.

Sullivan, H. S. (1953) *The Interpersonal Theory of Psychiatry*. New York: Norton.

Totton, N. (ed.) (2005) *New Dimensions in Body Psychotherapy*. Maidenhead: Open University Press.

Totton, N. (2006) A body psychotherapist's approach to touch. In: Galton, G. (ed.) *Touch Papers: Dialogues on Touch in the Psychoanalytic Space*. London: Karnac.

Winnicott, D. W. (1960) Ego distortion in terms of true and false self. In: *The Maturational Processes and the Facilitating Environment*. New York: International Universities Press, 1965.

Winnicott, D. W. (1971) Dreaming, fantasying and living: a case history describing a primary dissociation. In: *Playing and Reality*. New York: Basic Books, pp. 26–37.

Chapter 7

The body–mind dynamics of working with diversity

Carmen Joanne Ablack

Introduction

If you have played in a children's carnival band from the age of four until you are nine, you never forget how to 'wine ya' waist' and you just know it is one of the ways you express joy and a sense of freedom. Then when you dance as a black teenager amongst white peers you tone it down, you do not express in quite the same way because you are conscious of feeling and being different, even if this difference remains unnamed between you and your friends.

As soon as one of those friends asks about your experience of dancing when a child and shares their experience of doing tap and soft shoe shuffle, something new is experienced by both of you at an embodied level, there occurs what Gendlin (1996) describes as a felt sense. He goes on to write that having a felt sense leads you to become more deeply yourself. This is the dynamic of diversity for me. A shared experience of difference that is newly sensed and that deepens the inter- and intra-psychic experience for each person involved.

I believe there is a need for a process of culturally competent work, in psychotherapy and other client-based psychological disciplines, that attempts to embrace all the conflicted thoughts and feelings that will arise. In the psychotherapeutic relationship, I think we have a responsibility to sit with and engage in the dynamics of diversity. Our job is a tricky one of making the space safe enough for such exploration, and not making it so safe that we allow the energetic charge and passion of the diversity to dissipate from the relationship. It is with this endeavour in mind that I embarked on running Working with Diversity in Psychotherapy courses at Chiron. I did this initially with my dear lately departed colleague Joachim Boening, and then after a couple of years I led the workshops with some delightful and engaged assistant trainers who were Chiron graduates.

In this chapter I will use the term culture not just in reference to race, but to all aspects of identity be they sexual orientation, gender, race, heritage, class, disability, role expectation, family tradition, etc. In other words, I am talking of identities of function and form as well as those more frequently addressed by societal definition (this theme is further explored in Keary's and Waterston's chapters). For an exploration of the emergent figure in group therapy, which is a background to my thinking on this aspect of the work, see Carl Hodges (2003).

Physicists have a term 'phase shift'. Simply put, and with apologies to any physicists reading this, it means the point at which something profound happens. For me most of the debate spoken and written on difference, transcultural, multicultural, intercultural and diversity issues needs to undergo a phase shift. The debate is not about right and wrong or good and bad, however therapeutically expressed. Paradoxically, that would be the wrong debate. The phase shifts I am looking for will only come from a mutually shared sense of diversity. One that is embodied, articulated and integrated into the daily practice of psychotherapists inside and outside the therapy room.

The framework

Working with diversity is, in my framework, a dynamic of conscious relationship. As conscious as you and I are able to make it, at any given moment. Even when we sit in a so-called stuck place, if we are both aware and acknowledging of the 'stuckness' around our difference then we are working with diversity and sharing an experience of synthesis in the stuckness. I intend to build upon this from casework and by drawing upon my experiences of working with these issues as a trainer and supervisor of psychotherapists.

A new client arrives at my doorstep and rings the bell; a colleague has referred her, and this is our first meeting. I walk down my staircase doing my semi-conscious rituals of straightening the mat, checking the toilet door on the first landing is closed and generally settling myself with familiar actions before meeting a new, unfamiliar person.

I open the door, she looks at me, her eyes widen and she half-screams 'Fucking hell, no one told me you were Black!!!!' She appears to be White.

I respond, with a lot of calmness in my voice, 'Well . . . you'd better come in and we'll go upstairs and talk about it . . .'

As we make our way up the stairs a small part of me wants to giggle. I realise I am a little taken aback, but do not think I am really shocked by our initial face-to-face encounter. I find myself not speaking as we go up until we get in the room. Most of me is intrigued by this unusual and dramatic introduction to the relationship.

I do the usual of pointing out the coat hook and inviting her to sit. Under this, I am aware of my sensing of the client, her breath, the colour in her face; in particular I note that her lips have got colour in them now. I realise she went quite pale at the doorway when she saw me. We both sit; she chooses the seat nearest the door and facing to look out the window.

'So,' I say softly, with a question in my voice that I hope is invitational, 'I'm Black and you didn't know?'

The client looks at me a moment and then giggles, and then she stops smiling, saying quietly and seriously 'I wasn't expecting you to be Black, and now I look at you more, are you Black? Or are you mixed or what . . . What are you?'

There is a catch in her voice and I recognise a sensation in my belly that tells me this is really vital for this client. All the while I am noting her question is not, who are you or what is your cultural mix; the catch in her voice comes with the words 'What are you?'

At the time I do not think about all the possible meanings her question could have; that comes later when I reflect on the session and look back on what happened. But here, with the client, I stay in touch with my body and note that my breath and muscles are at ease. I briefly get an image of a baby bird just emerging from the shell, squeaking for its mother – I also put conscious pondering of this away for later. Instead I lean a little bit forward and say, 'What am I? It looks like it is hard for you not to know?'

A part of me is frankly amazed and a little thrown at the immediacy of all this, but my breath and my muscles are still relaxed and I can sense my own awareness of a real fragility in this client. I attend to her whilst trying to stay aware enough of myself, trying to be attuned enough to my countertransference.

'I . . . I . . . I'm not sure why it is so important; I just wasn't expecting you to be so different to me . . . You're really tall as well . . .'

'Huh . . . so I look different, . . . I'm a different height and . . . maybe . . . there are other ways I might be different to you and this might be important too?'

She smiles briefly leans back and says, sounding a bit amazed, 'You don't mind . . . I mean, you don't mind that I asked or that I have a problem or anything . . . you're just asking me about it and . . . you're okay? . . . I mean with me . . . um . . . with me asking you?' She looks me in the eyes as she says all this, and then lets out quite an audible breath.

I also breathe out so the client can hear my breath; this is a conscious non-verbal communication choice. I want to convey that I am taking her seriously and that it is okay for us to be looking at this.

'I don't mind . . .' I consciously speak on my out-breath, quietly, so that the words carry the weight of the breath, re-emphasising that I am present, aware and really attending to her.

She rejoins 'I guess it is important but . . . I still don't know why?' her breath tails off as she looks at me and relaxes back further into the chair.

I feel my shoulders drop in response and become aware that there are tears somewhere at the back of my eyes, as I breathe out quietly. I have no idea, at first, why I am on the edge of tears and then I wonder briefly if it has after all been a shocking experience of 'greeting' at my door.

I respond, 'That's okay, maybe we don't need to know right now, maybe it will emerge if we work together . . . my guess is it may mean a lot of different things . . . it may take time for us to find out . . .'

She sits upright, 'Yes. I think it will take time and I don't want to go to someone else . . . I think I need to take the time to find out . . .' She looks at me questioningly 'Don't you? I mean do you think it would be good for me to find out?' Her voice becomes a little louder and more demanding.

I can metaphorically hear the creak of a potential trap door in the background. I decide to be cautious rather than direct with my response: 'Well, . . . a part of therapy is that you find out things about yourself, your um . . . behaviour, feelings, motivations and . . . only you can decide if and when you do that . . . I . . .'

She jumps in, but quietly, 'I think I had better do this, I don't want to feel so . . . I don't know . . . I think I don't feel all that safe in the world . . .'

'Is that what you would like to happen, that you feel safer in the world?' I ask this in a slightly more matter of fact tone, consciously grounding myself (and hoping it will do the same for the client).

'Yes, more than anything else . . .' She cries a little. It is like watching a young toddler cry; the tears roll down her face as she continues looking at me. I can feel the tug on my heart; I already know she has moved me deeply.

'I don't think I have ever really felt safe,' she smiles shyly at me, 'I guess you are it, I guess this is where I am going to do my therapy . . . I'm still scared . . . um maybe more apprehensive.'

'Sure,' I say 'That's okay. Hopefully in this space, with me, you can explore the scary, the apprehensive and the differences too . . . in your time, when you are ready . . .'

Whenever I worked with, thought about, wrote notes about this client, I would touch such a place of heartbreak. It is a particularly exquisite pain, full of awareness, love and the sensing of the paradox of the fragile robustness of the therapeutic relationship. It is experienced with the body—mind.

I have used this case example many times on training courses at Chiron and elsewhere; it is often straight White trainees who are the most surprised and outraged by the vignette. This has to be seen in the context of it not being that shocking to a Black (Asian, gay, disabled etc.) person to have someone from the majority group comment on their colour or appearance or way of being in an apparently 'rude' manner.

I believe this seeming difference in response needs to be addressed and understood in the context of survival. I am clear I did not feel fearful of the client's negativity or outraged by her reaction at the door. I understood that she was expressing something more than a surface reaction to my Blackness.

Yet I know I feel anger, hurt and outrage at being treated badly. However, I would go literally mad if I allowed myself to feel it every time an incident, slight, comment or racist interpretation happened with a client, a supervisee or a colleague. All these have happened many times over the years, to say nothing of experiencing the wider world of the communities we live in. I believe there is a place in us all where numbness in the face of offence can become a habitual survival technique. This raises an important ethical paradox in any invitation to let go of an armouring that keeps me sane yet numb. There is a reality to 'it is not safe' and yet it is not safe, for any of us, in so many ways.

So we come back to body—mind awareness and exploration of paradox. It is an exploration with no definitive answers but rather with real awareness of the living diversity dynamic contained in the meeting of the wounds – wounds that both therapist and client have each uniquely endured and from which we are all attempting to recover.

The work of the therapist is to come to understand that their reactions are both reflective and not reflective of difference as the particular group and/or individual experience it. My sense of diversity and my unique relationship to my difference is a constant thread that my therapist must pay regard to even in the face of 'not getting it'.

Experiencing through the body–mind

My body–mind awareness is partly formed as a reflection of my own experiences as a client, practitioner and trainer and also as a human being. I identified with her words 'I don't feel all that safe in the world'. Yet my identification and her experience have different internal images and different narratives. In the exploration of both, something of the essence of what is in the relationship, at that point, can be elucidated. They remain (at least) two narratives; two sets of imagery and also potentially, a shared or felt sense in the room. (See Carroll's and Reynolds' chapters for more aspects of narrative and imagery in body psychotherapy.)

Many writers before have explored in different ways the experience that I use the song line 'stepping out with my baby' to describe. I step out the front door into the world and something just shifts into place; these days I wear it lightly, it is a type of armouring. It is an awareness of the neighbourhood, the current political climate, the country and the energetic charge of being a Black woman on the street; and 'the baby'?

That is the real me, the me that is only partly on show and that I am careful to expose only when I feel safe enough. It is not a thinking process but rather one of sensing and being. I step out with that aspect of self below the surface, with a sense of protecting myself learnt from the first wounding received and added to by subsequent experiences.

Do I think this is different to everyone else? Probably not. What I would highlight is that, dependent on identity and context, each person's 'stepping out' is influenced by their specific cultural context and experiences (remembering that culture refers to all aspects of identity). It is our job as therapist to understand, appreciate and explore this with the client from the truth and reality of our own experiences, if we are attempting a truly integral-relational way of working.

The interplay, between the socio-cultural and historical-political background and framework of the therapist and those of the client, is always present and has an impact whether worked with consciously or not. It is, in my experience, a dynamic of the body–mind, beyond just thought, beyond our beliefs or rules given.

The very way in which you breathe in my presence – as you allow yourself to be impacted by my Blackness, height, weight, accent, posture etc.; how I breathe back in your presence – all this is a dynamic of our relationship. It forms an unspoken dialogic reality that we can only hope to partially comprehend or be aware of at the best of times. It is that Gendlinian felt sense (Gendlin 1996) and leads each person to becoming more deeply themself.

As I explore over time with clients, trainees or supervisees, the meaning of our differences and our similarities, the work always seems to take us to a depthful exploration of an existential–transpersonal axis that is, at once, unique to the particular relationship and universal to the work. This inevitably involves the developing and refining of attunement in both the client and in me to the subtleties of impact on body–mind, heart and spirit. The exploration seems to take a life of its own, demanding we pay attention to our capacity to be with what is emerging and our resistance to looking. It has the delicacy of following the light catching and disappearing in a prism.

In the language of Chiron, the client and I engage in following a holistic phenomenology of relating to the best of our/my ability to allow this to happen. It is intra- and inter-subjective and intra- and inter-psychic and thus relational.

Such relationality requires me to stay connected to the interlinking of feelings, images, sensations and thoughts in myself and supports a similar connectedness in the client. As I and/or the client notices how these different aspects reflect each other, I strive to understand the parallels between them and to use such understanding to deepen the client's awareness and thus my own. Oftentimes, it is the understanding of the client that deepens our work and educates me.

My ability to foster the relational in the therapy comes from an attendance to the somatic countertransference as an ongoing process. I have to attend to my body, my tone of thinking, my breath, the state of my voice, the quality of arousal or deadness that I feel moment by moment in the client's presence; all this, and more, moves in and out of my field of awareness. It is my responsibility to reflect the transferential pressures back into the relationship and to be willing to transparently explore them with the client.

In a conversation with my colleague Michael Soth, he referred to a process of extending Freud's (1912) concept of 'evenly hovering attention' to our energetic perception, attunement and somatic resonance in the relationship with the client. In attempting to work within an integral-relational body psychotherapy framework these become basic fundamentals to the process.

When working with diversity as part of trying to foster the development of an integral-relational exploration, I must be able to hover, to land, to crash even, and then to dare to hover again, whilst staying as conscious as I can of the process. It seems to me that a truly valid position emerges from such a dynamic apprehending, a holding of not just the tension, but also of the elements provoking and providing the tension.

The work of diversity, in my experience, will always lead to moments of unresolved paradox. Can I stay with the client in their painful exploration of their identity? How is my sense of identity affected and challenged by their exploration? Can I understand my awareness and tensions as intrinsic to the process? The task then is not for the paradox to be resolved, but rather to be apprehended, understood and ultimately not grasped, as the awareness both informs and eludes me simultaneously. (See Soth's chapter for the Chiron journey with paradoxical understanding.)

This then is the real 'phase shift' – can I bring myself to stay with the notion of the unresolved paradox whilst simultaneously unravelling its unending layers?

This is the true dynamic in the work of the body psychotherapist. It requires an embodied intersubjective engagement that is a fundamental part of the work of body psychotherapy (see chapters by Asheri, Eiden and Soth in this book).

As I traverse the topography of life history and developmental injury in the client and in myself, the challenge is to stay connected to the intertwining of sensation, feelings, images and thoughts in myself and in the other. I need to remain aware of how these different levels reflect each other, compete with each other and yet require me to attempt to understand their parallels and paradoxes.

When working with issues of identity and identification the therapist has to be aware of what is 'frozen' in the landscape and what is running underground, as well as attending to what is shown. It requires a development of the ability to perceive through the body and through the felt sense as well as an ability to stay with the ever-fluctuating experience of embodiment and disembodiment of relating. The therapist needs to develop the ability to identify and work with their own counter-resistance by paying attention to pressures, and energetic and emotional 'charge' in the therapist's body–mind.

This counter-resistance can form part of what Isha Mackenzie-Mavinga (2005) has beautifully captured with the term 'recognition trauma'. In the context of this chapter, the recognition of the resistance can be a traumatising experience for the therapist, as they have to face the reality of their own cultural awareness limitations. I have to be willing and eventually able to continually revisit the question of 'Who am I really?' when it comes to my limitations of awareness and tolerance for my own and others' identities.

If the exploration with the client takes me into the unknown waters of my own history, can I swim? Do I struggle to breathe? Am I able to tread there long enough and with enough awareness to notice that I am in the unknown and I am frightened? Each time in the therapy relationship that the shared experience of difference is ignored, the diversity is occluded and can become an undermining influence on any other areas being addressed. Both people are wounded by this avoidance.

At the excellent Queer Analysis Conference presented by Pink Therapy in October 2004, I shared an idea that had been bubbling for a while. In response to Dr Jack Drescher talking about the 'seen as normal' of any majority group's position, I responded that not only are the majority normalised, they are in fact neutralised in defence against owning their identity. I would further characterise this as a numbness, as in trauma where differentiation can be experienced as an anxiety.

I believe all therapists have a responsibility to work with the numb and the over-sensitised aspects of themselves and their clients in relation to the dynamic of diversity, in order for the therapy to truly work towards some sense of healing.

I sit in a workshop at an internationally attended psychotherapy conference. We are there to look at, learn about and explore mindfulness in a cognitive-behavioural framework. The participants include three obviously Black people, at least a couple of people with disabilities that can be seen, there are a myriad of cultural groups represented, a mixture of ages, sexual orientations, heights, weights, knowledge, experience, beliefs etc. The workshop leader, without irony, says something along the lines of being 'uninterested in differences' and implying they have little import in the greater scheme of things. The clear implication from her perspective is confirmed when she adds that the attention given to differences 'gets in the way of our humanity'.

As you have read, I hold a somewhat different perspective. I understand the thinking behind the teaching that ultimately our differences are not important; of course we are more than the sum of our identities. However, my perspective would be that, without attention to difference and more importantly, without actively engaging with the dynamics of diversity, we could not truly be with our humanity. It is through the shared experiences of diversity and synthesis that we help to elucidate our humanity.

Cultural competence

Let us go back to my earlier definition of culture as all aspects of identity; at this stage I would add known and unknown. Now we have the fuller definition of culture as all aspects of identity, known and unknown. This leads us to the fostering of a sense of culturally safe enough, in order to truly explore what is not safe, what is known, what is not known and what may lie beyond. Each relationship is understood as unique, containing a power-dynamic, and is culturally dyadic both inter-psychically and intra-psychically.

The appropriate use of cultural awareness and safety, and attention to their absence, empowers the client and the therapist to express degrees of experienced/felt risk and safety as part of the relational dialogue.

Alongside cultural safety, as therapists we need to attend to cultural proficiency (Coye and Alvarez 1999). It is not enough that we are aware; the work requires that we are willing to be constantly wrong footed and yet continue learning how to dance. Coye and Alvarez are asking that organisations and health care practitioners develop frameworks and practices in which there is cultural competence at every point of contact and intervention.

I am suggesting something more – cultural safety and proficiency in the therapeutic relationship require that the psychotherapist remains engaged with the dynamic of diversity as an identifiable relational interaction. Practitioners need to inhabit the dynamics of the therapeutic relationship with an understanding and an ability to work with the paradoxical and elusive nature of the relational. As therapists we need to learn to recognise and welcome every point of contact and intervention being informed by culturally competent, proficient and safe practice whilst understanding that we will always meet paradox at this place. We need to understand that if we approach the work without our holistic, somatic attunement to the relational dynamics of diversity, we will be truly lost. The paradox being that this sense of loss is inevitable. It will be revisited consciously and unconsciously by the therapist, the client and by both. In her chapter, Carroll refers to the co-construction of the relationship. In his chapter Soth can be understood as bringing more into focus the de-construction/re-construction necessary for all that we attempt to co-construct. It is an endless surrendering, to receptivity, to acceptance of our defence against being 'constructed' by the client and to the repetition and need for surrender to the enactments necessary for a truthful relational interaction. (See Soth's chapter for further exploration of these themes.)

These concepts of cultural safety, competence and proficiency came into my teaching in the last few years of working at the Chiron Centre on the initial training in Body Psychotherapy. The paradox of all teaching, I have discovered over my 25 years or more of doing it, is that we are often teaching the what of the how we would like things to be.

My course, Working with Diversity, was a struggle to establish; there was resistance from some other members of staff. This is of course understandable; diversity and synthesis can be very challenging and scary territory. There were concerns expressed along the lines of 'I don't want trainees coming from the workshop and challenging me about my culture and what it might mean to me'. Or 'telling me what they think of me because of who I am or who they perceive I am (and I am left with my wondering about what was meant)'. My only response to this is, 'Why not? Do you imagine it is not already in the field?' Of course it is; consciously or unconsciously, it is present, waiting to be tapped into, to enhance the work. The question this begs is can we allow ourselves to surrender to the constructive de-construction of such questions and comments from our clients, trainees, supervisees and colleagues?

The other initial response was no matter how often I talked about Diversity and multiple identities, what people heard was Race. I still have this experience at meetings and conferences today; over the years I have recognised this will happen, but at times I feel less inclined to 'wait' for many of my profession to understand it is about all senses of identity and the meanings we make of them.

It reflects for me a deep wound of numbness, where many of us are still not in a meaningful relationship with the complexity and richness of our own multiple heritage and identity states. If we are working towards real relationality, this richness cannot be ignored or sidelined; it has to come to the centre of our thinking, being and doing. It will bring a depth of paradoxical experiences that ultimately cannot be resolved, and yet that is the challenge of a true embracing of relational being.

Below I have set out some questions I first heard many decades ago in my days of attending co-counselling workshops. I have worked with these for over twenty years and still make discoveries each time I facilitate or answer them myself. They are deceptively simple questions until you sit and allow them to resonate through your body–mind awareness.

My suggestion is that you try these questions maybe within a staff, supervision or peer group and then use different configurations, of race, class, ability and disability, family position, familiar roles etc. I have learnt that it is important for each person to be given uninterrupted time to ponder and answer the questions.

When did you FIRST KNOW that you are a man/a woman?
What do you like about being a woman/a man?
What do you find difficult about being a woman/a man?
What would you like to be different about being a man/a woman?
     My additional question:
How do you sense, feel, breathe, and experience your body, mind, heart and
     spirit as you talk (think) about this?

It can be illuminating when you put the word psychotherapist as the identity at the end of each question. These questions (whatever the 'identity' explored) seem to bring to the fore an exploration of existence and meaning that transcends, yet holds awareness of, the initial identity that engendered such exploration in the first place. The explorer is integrating with, relating to and transcending their felt sense of self identification, whilst trying to come to terms with the paradoxical nature of understanding and not understanding at the same time. (See Soth's chapter for a further exploration of this.)

Conclusion

In this chapter I have chosen to concentrate on working with diversity mostly from the perspective of 'across differences', because that is the main journey of the work I did at Chiron in this field; for example, I was often the only

Black person in the training room and the only Black person in a quite multi-heritage staff group.

Another landscape I work with addresses the paradoxes of 'within identities'. Or to be accurate, I explore what could be called 'apparently within the identity' – because once we drop below the surface, we are swimming with the cross-currents and under-tows of sameness and differentiation as experienced from the perspective of 'but aren't you supposed to get it? You are like me'. Thus we are with paradox again, what seems like sameness rarely is and yet we must not ignore the surface similarities or the underlying differences.

In conclusion, I see the work of dynamic diversity and synthesis leading to an enriched humanity that has an elusive and almost unknowable beingness. The true competence in this work, for me, comes with being able to more than tolerate the paradox; it is about actively embracing it and learning to stay with the irresolvable whilst simultaneously attuning to its teachings, to the best of my ability. This is a competence I am still trying to attain.

References

Coye, M. and Alvarez, D. (1999) *Medicaid Managed Care and Cultural Diversity in California*. CA: The Lewin Group.

Freud, S. (1912) *Recommendations to Physicians Practising Psycho-analysis*. The Standard Edition of the Complete Psychological Works of Sigmund Freud. Trans. J. Strachey. London: The Hogarth Press, 1960.

Gendlin, E. T. (1996) *Focusing-Oriented Psychotherapy*. New York: Guilford Press.

Hodges, C. (2003) Creative processes in gestalt group therapy, In: Lobb, M. S. and Amendt-Lyon, N. (eds) *Creative License: The Art of Gestalt Therapy*. New York: Springer, pp. 249–259.

McKenzie-Mavinga, I. (2005) *A Space to Contemplate Understanding Black Issues in Counsellor Training and the Therapeutic Process*. Copyright: Isha McKenzie-Mavinga 2005; copies available from attherapy@aol.com.

Part II

New directions and applications

AN INTIMATE PERSPECTIVE

Linda Hartley

Chiron training encourages individuation, and this is borne out by a rich diversity of specialisations, theoretical and clinical orientations, and styles of working amongst its therapists. This section focuses on applications, demonstrating some of the approaches to clinical practice and theory that have evolved with specific client groups and therapeutic issues. In these chapters there is a weaving together of the threads of theory and practice, outlined in Part I, into individual expressions of body psychotherapy. There is a strong focus on working with both developmental and acute incident trauma, and the integration of neurophysiology within various relational models. Case material, enriched by descriptions of the therapist's personal process within the relationship, offers an intimate view of the practice of individual body psychotherapy.

In Chapter 8, Kathrin Stauffer brings into focus the application of neuroscience to psychotherapy. As the psychotherapeutic community has embraced neuroscientific theory, finding validation within it, little critique of its usefulness to psychotherapy practice has been made, Stauffer argues. She invites us to question this liaison and to allow the two fields to have validity from their own different perspectives, rather than going along with an assumption that neuroscience is of more value, which is implied when it is used to underpin and validate psychotherapy; she continues by giving examples of ways in which she has found neuroscientific findings to be helpful in clinical practice. Stauffer's argument echoes Schaible's earlier plea for the psychodynamic and biodynamic models to be evaluated within their own frames of reference, as she explores one of the current integrative challenges facing the body psychotherapist.

Following on from Stauffer's description of how neuroscience may inform clinical work, Margaret Landale elaborates on the way she uses it to help clients develop practical skills and resources. She explores the core issue of autonomic regulation, introduced by Schaible and Carroll, as she addresses psychosomatic distress arising from developmental injury; unresolved emotions impact on the physical body, creating a range of painful and debilitating physical symptoms and disorders. Her work demonstrates a holistic and integrative approach that embraces body process, emotions, mind and the practice of mindfulness meditation, and also addresses transference issues as they arise within the case study presented. The practice of mindfulness of the breath as a tool to help the client deal with both physical and emotional pain, and the process of innate imagery arising from within the body, are explored.

Addressing another kind of bodily wounding, Anne Marie Keary then offers a moving account of her work with disability. It is a subject not often addressed in the body psychotherapy literature, yet one that is crucially relevant as it explicitly addresses the wounded body. Keary challenges us to open to the emotional impact of living with a physical disability, and the effects it has upon attachment and relating. Her writing is at times shocking, ruthlessly honest and penetrating, as she dares to look at the unbearable and explore how, through an embodied relational approach, it may become possible to tentatively bear it within a shared experience of suffering. The immediacy of her writing draws us into the dynamics of re-enactment and the process of the Wounded Healer; through allowing her own vulnerability to emerge into the intersubjective space, the healing power within it is revealed.

In Chapter 11, Morit Heitzler gives a detailed description of an integrative approach to trauma therapy. Basing her chapter around a therapeutic process with a client who had suffered an acute traumatic incident, she skilfully weaves together the methods of somatic trauma therapy, relational body psychotherapy, and EMDR (eye movement desensitisation and reprocessing). The case study reveals how underlying developmental trauma can surface during the working through of an acute incident, and how an integrative approach can enable both levels to be successfully addressed. She shows how a transferential dynamic facilitated the process, whilst acknowledging that in this instance a more thorough working through of the relational dynamics and underlying developmental trauma was prohibited by the time limitations of the therapy.

Following on from this, Tom Warnecke develops a theoretical approach to developmental trauma in Chapter 12, as he explores the complex phenomenon of borderline personality disorder (BPD). It is fundamentally a relational disorder, he argues, with disturbances experienced both somatically and psychically by client and therapist alike. By integrating relational theory with an embodied approach, he develops a way of working which addresses some of the core issues of a client with BPD. Similar in many ways to the symptoms of post-traumatic stress disorder, the 'embodied disorganisation' of BPD is evoked by the therapeutic relationship itself, and can be addressed through an embodied and relational approach.

In Chapter 13, Jane Clark turns her attention to the trauma of childhood sexual abuse, demonstrating a way of working with polarised aspects of an abused client's inner world. She gives a dramatic account of therapy with two clients, which took her beyond the boundaries of her own knowing, through the mire of re-enactment and parallel process within the therapeutic relationship. She courageously enters into the drama of facing the abused and the abuser within her client, and within herself, acknowledging how her own wounds are evoked and how they participate in the healing process. Her writing vividly portrays the theory of inevitable re-enactment and parallel process described by Soth.

Chapter 8

The use of neuroscience in body psychotherapy: theoretical and clinically relevant aspects

Kathrin Stauffer

Background

In recent years, neuroscience has paid increasing attention to mechanisms of what is called affective self-regulation, which have come to be seen as important for how we experience ourselves and the world around us. These are the processes by which we are able to cope with everyday events and also with stressful experiences. On the whole, they are habits; and as the habits of processing and digesting what happens, they form the foundations of what we call our coping style. What is newly percolating into the collective awareness of the professions is twofold: that these mechanisms are not innate but acquired in infancy and early childhood; and that the learning of affective self-regulation is critically dependent on attachment to, and intensive interactions with, a primary carer. In other words, we 'learn' to emotionally self-regulate in the way – and to the extent – that we see it mirrored in our earliest caregivers.

A number of books in recent years have drawn attention to the parallels between these findings and psychotherapeutic attachment theories (see e.g. Schore 1994; Gerhardt 2004). As Chiron psychotherapists, whose training includes a module on human anatomy and physiology, we are assumed to find these books especially significant, as colleagues and members of the general public credit us with a knowledge of neuroscience and an ability to use it in our clinical practice. In this chapter I would like to start with a brief summary of the neuroscience of early attachment, focussing on what might be relevant to psychotherapists. My main interest, however, is in the relationship of these biological findings to the practice of psychotherapy. As a former life scientist, I regard this relationship as my own version of a wound that can never quite heal, in the tradition of Chiron. The bulk of the chapter will address this topic, first in an examination of what the motivation is for psychotherapists to underpin their clinical experience with scientific data and explanations. Following this I will attempt to take the notion of holism seriously and show some of the adjustments in our thinking that are necessitated by a holistic point of view. I will then go on to illustrate, using case material from my own practice, how I can see neuroscience fitting into the practice of body psychotherapy.

My thinking has been greatly helped by many lively discussions with my colleagues John Waterston and Jane Frances.

Traditional body psychotherapeutic thinking about emotional self-regulation

As it happens, body psychotherapy, and in particular biodynamic psychotherapy, has had the knowledge for a long time that the self-regulation of feelings is critical for the healthy functioning of human beings. Moreover, body psychotherapy has always thought of these processes as embodied, as involving the whole body and mind, and as accessible to everyday experience. For a fuller discussion of this extremely important topic, see also the chapter by Roz Carroll in this book.

Biodynamic psychotherapy emphasizes the importance of the autonomic nervous system in mediating these emotional processes. The autonomic nervous system has two branches that operate roughly like a seesaw. The sympathetic nervous system generally mediates processes of arousal and shifts the awareness of a person upwards and outwards in what has become known as the 'fight-or-flight' response; whilst the parasympathetic nervous system generally mediates processes of calming down and shifts the awareness downwards and inwards. In healthy self-regulation, these two operate alternately and together mediate the vasomotoric cycle, or emotional cycle (Boyesen 1980). Every person tends to have habitual 'shapes' of vasomotoric cycles that form the basic patterns of emotional self-regulation.

Emotional self-regulation and the ego

What is new is that neuroscience is slowly elucidating the processes that determine how these patterns are generated in the brain before being transmitted to the periphery via the autonomic nervous system. What is new in the domain of neuroscience, but not perhaps in the domain of psychotherapy, is an appreciation of the importance of these processes for the formation of our sense of self (Damasio 1994, 2003).

It can be argued that emotional self-regulation is one of the primary tasks of a healthy ego. The development of the capacity for self-soothing and a knowledge of, and trust in, one's own ability to make things better form one of the foundations of a stable sense of self. Biologically, these abilities are dependent on an ability of the whole organism to be displaced away from a state of equilibrium and subsequently to return to equilibrium.

As it turns out, and as particularly exponents of attachment theory have argued for a long time, the capacity for emotional self-regulation is dependent on good-enough early parenting (Bowlby 1969; Winnicott 1971). Deficits in this function, whether never acquired or lost through some traumatic event, will have adverse effects. These effects could in their mildest form be so-called stress-related ailments like insomnia or tension headaches, but could also present disabilities for a person in coping with difficult life events on a spectrum from mild neurosis to serious mental illness. It is a long-standing contention of psychotherapy that they could also lead to acute or chronic physical illness. The severity of the effects would depend on the severity of the deficit and also, critically, the age at which the development went awry, as well as the degree of incidental trauma a person has experienced.

The neurobiology of affective self-regulation in the context of early attachment

The current literature seems to describe two components in the processes of emotional self-regulation, a 'cellular' one and a 'humoral' one. The 'cellular' one, or the neuroanatomy and neurophysiology of self-regulation, comprises all the processes to do with connections between neurones and between different parts of the brain. It has been described in great detail by Schore (1994) and, in simplified form, by Wilkinson (2006). The 'humoral' component, or the biochemistry of self-regulation, refers to the habitual levels of certain chemicals and their connections with life events. This aspect has been covered by Martin (1998) and more recently in greater detail by Gerhardt (2004) as well as several others. The two are intimately interdependent, and in functional terms the division is not meaningful. Nevertheless I am choosing to follow it, mostly because it is clearly present in the literature, which suggests that it facilitates thinking about these very complex processes. In biology it is also often feasible to study either of the two, but not both, components, which may have given rise to the division in the first place.

Neuroanatomy of self-regulation

In the brain, neuronal processes and connections grow rapidly during the first few years of life and are also rapidly pruned, depending on their repeated use. Gerald Edelmann describes the establishment of functional neural pathways and circuits as dependent on a phenomenon that he calls re-entry, which appears to be very similar to resonance (Tononi and Edelman 1998).

It is trite to say that we learn by imitation, by mirroring what we see. What is only just being appreciated (Schore 1994; Gallese *et al.* 1996) is the extent to which our brains physically develop by imitation. Mirroring, or resonating with another's neural activity, seems to be the major mechanism by which the infant's brain acquires its habitual pathways for doing most life tasks. So there is a process of resonance going on within an infant's brain which establishes stable pathways for information exchange; but this process appears to be itself stimulated by the resonance with another (the caregiver's) brain.

Among the habits that we acquire in this manner early in life, there are the ones concerned with affect regulation, or emotional self-regulation. These are the very basic patterns of being able to experience, express, contain, and soothe strong feelings. Since life will persist in throwing things at us that stimulate strong feelings, it is important to be able to regulate them. How well we are able to do this will determine some very basic aspects of how full a life we are able to live. This includes our resilience to life's stresses; our ability to relate to others by containing their feelings and allowing them to contain our feelings; and our potential to take risks and thus be successful in life. It is almost impossible to think of an area of life where our ability to regulate affect does not have a major impact.

The picture is emerging (Schore 1994) of how, during early development, various areas of the brain gradually mature and become active. Whilst it is not strictly true to say that various areas of the brain are the seat of cognitive and psychological functions, it nevertheless appears that brain areas are something like foci, or specialized centres, for particular functions (Damasio 1994). Thus we develop by gradually adding more and more functions to the ones we already have. It is particularly interesting to look at the brain regions that are able to integrate information from different brain parts or somatic nerves, and that are able to regulate the functioning of other regions. These brain regions, notably the orbitofrontal cortex, can be thought to constitute something like a sense of an ego, a sense of being able to think and to influence the world around us.

One of the themes that seem to emerge from neuroscience research, which confirms something psychotherapy has always known intuitively, is that healthy psychological functioning involves the participation of the whole person, and that the various forms of pathology can basically be seen as forms of fragmentation. The same seems to be true for the functioning of the brain. In the case of trauma it has been so well documented that we now find people referring to 'hippocampal' and 'amygdaloidal' thinking and feeling (Wilkinson 2006). But it is also increasingly clear that any kind of response to challenge that involves even a temporary loss of ego resources represents a loss of connectivity between different parts of the nervous system. As a body psychotherapist, I would include here the loss of sensory input from tissues other than the brain (including the peripheral senses, visceral sensations and input from the enteric nervous system), or the loss of its integration with the processes that happen within the brain itself.

It is to be hoped that future research will address in particular the question of how, and to what extent, deficits in early development can be compensated for in adulthood. At present, researchers appear to simply extrapolate from early attachment as, for example, Allan Schore does in a recent paper (Schore 2007). However, this does not quite seem to do justice to the complexity of the processes involved. The surge of neuronal sprouting and connecting slows down to a trickle by the time we reach adulthood, and we therefore cannot assume that psychotherapy will just foster the growth and establishment of connections in a client's brain that did not get established in the person's childhood. Rather, we have to look for some sort of redistribution of function (Stauffer 2003). It might conceivably be of clinical use to psychotherapists to learn more about these mechanisms.

Biochemistry of self-regulation

Research here has focussed on cortisol and its function in how we tolerate stressful times in life. Cortisol is useful because it is easy to measure, and because it forms such a plausible and clear interface between the nervous system, the endocrine system and the immune system. In fact it is hard to think of a part of the body that might not be affected by cortisol. From these studies we have a sense of chemical habits which will determine our emotional habits. Gerhardt describes in her book at great length how particular patterns of early attachment are correlated with particular patterns of cortisol secretion (Gerhardt 2004). Although not stated in her text, it is easy to link these patterns with Frank Lake's concept of transmarginal stress that switches a particular ego defence into its opposite (Lake 1986).

It appears to be as yet unclear what the roles of other chemicals might be in establishing emotional self-regulation patterns. We can, however, speculate about some candidates for more soothing functions. One would be oxytocin. Its role in social attunement has been elucidated in recent years, and has given increasing weight to oxytocin as a hormone involved in bonding, affection, nurturing and wellbeing (Uvnäs-Moberg et al. 2005; Lim and Young 2006). Another interesting and suggestive recent observation is that brain-derived neurotrophic factor (BDNF) is negatively correlated with depression (Shimizu et al. 2003). BDNF is one of a group of so-called neurotrophic factors, the substances that rescue neurones from being pruned and thus preserve a more complex connectivity in the brain. So there is a suggestion that depression goes along with the loss of connectivity in the brain. We don't know if the availability and distribution of BDNF is susceptible to the quality of early attachment, but future research is likely to elucidate this.

All of these scientific findings have generated a lot of enthusiasm among colleagues, confirming as they do that psychological suffering is not 'all in the mind' but has a tangible, structural, biological basis. It is hoped that this scientific 'proof' will herald in a new age where the powers that be will make more efforts to ensure that all infants receive mothering that is as good as possible.

Personally I feel that these hopes speak of a relationship that we psychotherapists have with biological science that I am not altogether comfortable with. It seems to me that this relationship between neuroscience and psychotherapy merits a bit more thinking about, and I propose to do this in the following.

The relationship between psychotherapy and neurobiology explored

Ken Wilber makes the point that biology and psychotherapy look at the human organism from two fundamentally different perspectives (see e.g. Wilber 1996). Biology looks at humans from an external, objective, generalized, and prospective point of view. Psychotherapy looks at humans (or rather, us) from an internal, subjective, particular and retrospective point of view. Both perspectives are complementary to each other, but neither can be expressed in terms of the other. Another way of phrasing much the same insight is Reich's elegant principle of functional identity which he proposed as existing between physical patterns of muscle tension and emotional coping mechanisms but which can easily be generalized to any life process (Reich [1933] 1972). From this kind of consideration, it is clear that neuroscience and psychotherapy should, if anything, confirm each other's findings.

On the one hand, the recent books present us with neuroscience confirming psychotherapy. It was described by the attachment theorists in the 1960s that a deficit in early attachment leads to disabling sequelae throughout life (Bowlby 1969). It is questionable whether the additional knowledge (for instance, that a particularly disabling response to stressful events might be mediated by the systems that regulate the levels of cortisol in the brain) will contribute anything to the therapeutic work that we do in the consulting room.

On the other hand, biology has always relied on intuitive, experienced reality as the ultimate test of the validity of its findings – in other words, biology has always required confirmation by psychotherapy. One consequence of this is that neuroscience is forever laboriously establishing phenomena that psychotherapy already takes into account. The question then is, what has neurobiology to contribute to the practice of psychotherapy? Can neurobiology come up with any facts that are genuinely new to body psychotherapy, facts that we can learn something from for our clinical practice? Does neuroscience actually change the interventions that we might use with particular clients? Or does it change the way we might think about our clients? And can we therefore say that neuroscience makes a valuable contribution to our work – because by affecting our thinking it will affect the therapy our clients get? If our thinking changes, do our clients benefit, or is that just a wishful fantasy?

These are questions that psychotherapists need to think about. One big difference between science and psychotherapy is that science defines itself as operating in a value-free space. This is not the case for psychotherapy: psychotherapists are tightly bound to a code of ethics and practice and, at the very least, expected to act at all times in the best interests of their clients. So we have to examine every new piece of theory in this light, and study it for its potential usefulness for our clients.

I suspect that for some practitioners there is a hope that by phrasing what they do in a scientific terminology, they might become more 'acceptable'. This sort of project has quite a long history: for instance, both Wilhelm Reich and Gerda Boyesen liked to give their work a cloak of respectability by couching it in scientific terms (Reich 1969; Boyesen 1980). It seems that these two pioneers felt a strong need to relate their quite revolutionary findings back to an established conceptual framework. I wonder how much of their motivation was the hope to influence and change the profession and perhaps even the whole world in a profound and comprehensive way. In hindsight we can say that this type of scientism has not contributed to the acceptability of either Reich's or Boyesen's work by conventional medical science or by psychoanalysis.

One of the problems with Reich's and Boyesen's sort of undertaking is that neuroscience is mostly prospective, which means that it is mostly concerned with making predictions. Supplying information on the cellular or molecular processes that might be responsible for particular macroscopically observed phenomena is not strictly speaking within its remit, and such 'explanations' can rarely be incontrovertibly established. And so psychotherapists who have in the past tried to claim a medical or scientific basis for their work have used science in order to build an ego for themselves (and for the wider profession); but an ego cannot be built on the basis of scientistic arguments. The result will inevitably be a rather grandiose and narcissistic ego without a true foundation in realistic and integrated self-confidence. In both Reich's and Boyesen's case this seems particularly tragic, as they have both made enormous contributions to the field, and their work requires no proof other than people's experience.

I have written elsewhere about my experience of the desire to be accepted by an 'establishment', and about my conclusion that membership of that (fantasized) establishment is not dependent on scientific orthodoxy but on my experiencing myself as acceptable (Stauffer 2004). I would therefore question whether phrasing body psychotherapy in biological terms in order to gain acceptance as competent professionals is a particularly meaningful project. I would further argue that we are in real danger of losing something of the essence of our work if we limit ourselves to scientifically 'acceptable' language, tempting though this may be especially for body psychotherapists who can easily acquire a 'medical' image. I believe that the goal of acceptance is best served by stating just exactly what clients can expect to gain from body psychotherapy, and by doing this truthfully, in clear language, and with a regard to representing the full richness of the work. Furthermore, I think that hopes of changing the whole field of mental healthcare are not realistic, and we need to come to terms with our limits in this respect.

Holistic thinking

I want to challenge the belief that the life sciences establish some sort of absolute truth, as opposed to the subjective, and therefore less valid, psychotherapeutic teachings. As outlined above, the fact is that psychotherapy makes its statements from a different perspective from biology, but in its own frame of reference, the truth of those statements is the same as that of biology in its particular frame of reference, in that both describe the same phenomenological reality. The belief that one frame of reference is more valid than the other reflects the power structure of our society and in particular a widespread habitual defence against feelings. If we take the notion of holism seriously, we are basically forced to embrace cultural relativism and accord equal 'truth' to different perspectives on the same phenomenon – as long as the descriptions of the phenomenon are accurate.

There is another, related, widespread assumption that needs challenging. It is that, if you observe a structural alteration in the brain of a person who is suffering from psychological symptoms, this observation implies that the structural alteration is the cause of the symptoms. This stands in contradiction to the concept of functional identity which I hold as central to any form of holistic therapy. If we take holism seriously, we have to assume that any symptom is the result of multiple events on all levels of the personality acting synchronically. The concept of linear cause and effect does not work in holistic thinking. That of synchronicity is more useful, and sometimes more poetic and symbolic ways of thinking are most useful. Equally, we cannot assume that if there is a physical 'root cause' to a symptom, then the therapy must also happen on this level.

Using neuroscience in psychotherapy

I want to finally describe how I think scientific information can be used in psychotherapy. My thesis is fairly simple: as a psychotherapist, I regard neuroscientific information as an interpretation, and I would attempt to make use of it in the same way, and according to the same considerations, as any other interpretation. I propose that knowledge of neuroscience has two main applications. One is for me as the therapist and provides me with a map that helps me orient myself in the process, and that facilitates my appreciation for points of similarity and points of difference between me and my clients. Thus it serves much the same purpose as, for instance, knowledge of character structures (Totton and Jacobs 2001). The other is for the client and might help a client to gain more compassion for themselves and more facility in talking about their experience, in symbolizing their experience and thus being more able to contain it.

I would like to propose that using neuroscientific information in psychotherapy is an ego-building intervention. In the context of psychotherapy the main use of a strong ego is to help us contain our distress when being with a client who is more or less overwhelmed by their distress. I would very much see this in the context of the topic of emotional self-regulation that I have discussed above, and think of science at its best as a tool that can help us to acquire more functional habits of self-regulation and self-soothing. These habits may both serve us in the practice of our work, and also our clients who may learn them from us, explicitly or implicitly.

Clinical examples

I want to add two examples from my clinical work to illustrate aspects of how I could see science fit into the consulting room. The first is a case vignette that illustrates how I was able to make use of a piece of 'medical' knowledge with a client who came for therapy with chronic pain. It was useful both in providing me with a focus and a line of inquiry, and also as a way to conceptualize something to the client that helped her communicate and contain great distress and gradually improve her symptoms. In my second example, I will present a case in which the terms 'knowledge' and 'understanding' themselves became part of the therapeutic relationship. The case illustrates how these words have their own meaning for different people and in different therapeutic relationships and therefore have to be set against the background of each client's needs and their individual personality.

Anne

Anne, a woman in her mid-forties, presented with severe chronic low back pain and was mainly eager to receive biodynamic massage for pain relief and pain management. She was not keen on psychological interpretations, and it was clear that she experienced such interpretations as attacks, as being criticized and blamed for her illness. There was a longish history to her back pain with a recent marked exacerbation following treatment for bowel cancer. She had received surgery and chemotherapy for this, and at one point was given a 50% survival chance after five years. Treatment appeared successful, but Anne found herself unable to return to a normal life and became progressively disabled with the back pain.

Anne had a background in life sciences and found scientific explanations helpful. I initially emphasized the connection between post-traumatic stress and chronic pain, and encouraged her to talk about her bowel cancer. She did this readily albeit with some scepticism, not expecting anyone to understand 'what it is like to have to say to myself if I'm still alive on my fiftieth birthday, I will be lucky'. Mostly this part of our work served to establish some trust and ease of conversation between us.

However, I only felt that I had gained an access to her deeper experience of back pain when I remembered that chronic pain goes with a chronic up-regulation of the sympathetic nervous system (Munglani and Hunt 1995). I shared this information with Anne. Her response was to describe to me how the onset of pain always came with the thought 'Oh my God, oh my God, it's all going wrong, what am I going to do?' – and a panicky and hopeless feeling she had always been ashamed of. In the context of a link between chronic pain, anxiety and depression, this feeling became much more containable, and much easier to talk about. It also made a good deal of sense of my observation that she had a strong tendency to freeze when she was anxious or in pain. It appeared that she remained in this frozen position for long periods of time if she did not actively mobilize her musculature in order to undo the startle. Together, we developed over time a picture of her nervous system that would reset to a default state of pain in the absence of sufficient here-and-now input. Anne learned to develop more resources that would override this default state, such as talking to a friend on the telephone, or doing something pleasant.

Anne has meanwhile returned to her country of origin, and on reaching the age of fifty appears to have regained her sense of being able to live again.

Sarah

Sarah has been in therapy with me for several years. She finds life very hard, a great struggle. She feels that she isn't really a member of the human race, and a recurring image is of herself outside, peering in through a window at life that's happening inside. She doesn't experience herself as able to do things or affect the course of her life, and is forever plagued by fears of loss. She manages just barely to hang on to what she has: a poorly paid job, a flat, two or three friends. A sexual relationship has never been possible for her, nor any kind of professional training.

She appears to live in a state of frozen terror, and her ability to exist with these high levels of anxiety seems to form a large part of her identity. She has slowly learned to express some of her feelings in therapy, and typically she feels a lot better at the end of a session. Thus, over time, our sessions have acquired the shape of a vasomotoric cycle, an energetic movement that represents a life process: charge – expression – discharge – relief. Through this type of emotional self-regulation, Sarah has become able to tolerate more feeling, to distinguish different feelings from each other, to put words and feelings together, to develop resources for managing her feelings. We have done a lot of good work and she has gained a great deal from the therapy.

But right from the beginning, she would periodically say: 'If only I could understand!' She explained to me that she felt a need to know why she was the way she was, what had happened to disable her so much. So I did my best to help her 'understand' by relating here-and-now feelings to her childhood experiences. This did not have much of an effect and didn't stop her from exclaiming, every so often, 'if only I could understand!' I felt rather irritated at first: here I was, feeding my client all these helpful explanations, and she just ignored them. Gradually I got interested in what was happening. I did not have a sense that Sarah was rejecting my 'understanding', rather she just wasn't taking it in, as though it all went over her head. At the same time, it seemed important to her that I should understand. For a while, I thought in terms of how regressed she was, how she needed to be babied and pampered until she would be willing to start growing up.

But in the end I found it more fruitful to relate this observation to the observation of how she was slowly learning to self-regulate, and how this had at first only ever happened in therapy, sometimes only in physical contact with me. What if understanding was another self-regulating mechanism? So I began to conceptualize 'understanding' as a part of the mothering that she needed from me, and related it to the ability to self-regulate that she had never been able to acquire and was now slowly gaining. I could see that she had to receive it from me to start with, and would have to be allowed to internalize it in her own time. More and more I saw a containing ego that was quite frail and would crumple at the slightest challenge, leaving her regressed, with the feelings of a very small child lost in an incomprehensible world of terrors, and deeply ashamed of her own stupidity.

There were several pieces of information about Sarah's childhood that I thought relevant to her adult experience. Her start in life was a difficult one: she was the first child of a mother who had never wanted children in the first place, and would have much preferred to have a son. Moreover she was born prematurely and had to spend the first weeks of her life in an incubator. I could see that this early deprivation would have left her with a severe deficit in self-regulation. Specifically I thought it must have left her very impaired in her capacity to tolerate close contact without feeling invaded. But it seemed quite difficult to convey my sense of this to her, as this time in the incubator did not appear to interest Sarah very much.

So therapy continued, and I hoped that she would start to 'understand' when she was ready to acquire this piece of independence from me. Indeed it happened in the course of a phase when she was growing more able to take the initiative and control her own life. One day she went back to her image of standing outside a window and watching a life that just wasn't for her. I said, quite gently, I wonder if this should be the other way around – if you were inside looking out it could be a memory of being in the incubator . . . And suddenly, Sarah was thunderstruck. How could she possibly have missed this for so long? It made things so very clear, and the sense of suddenly understanding something about herself was quite exhilarating.

A couple of sessions later, Sarah told me that for the first time in her life, she could hold her head high and didn't have to feel ashamed of herself – because now she understood that she was as she was for a reason, and it made all the difference. Over the next weeks and months, Sarah's growth started to accelerate substantially, and is still much faster than it was before this.

Clearly, understanding the connection between starting life in an incubator and adult difficulties in forming relationships must have produced a tremendous sense of relief, of containment, that facilitated this formidable growth spurt. But in addition, I also see the understanding as part of a process that was accelerating because the foundations for growth were finally sufficient. It was another piece of the process that Sarah could internalize, and gain her own control over: an ability to contain her feelings by conceptualizing the link to her history.

Conclusion

In conclusion, I propose that in clinical practice, background information from neuroscience primarily serves to contain distress, both the client's and the therapist's. This is useful to the extent that it allows the process to happen at a higher level of energy and therefore, hopefully, at greater depth. As the containment of distress is a central ego function, the integration of neuroscientific information into psychotherapy may be ego-building for individual clients, and the judgement of whether to use it in some way may be helped by this consideration. Whether ego-building for the therapist is necessary or desirable must rest with individual practitioners and perhaps their supervisors and therapists. Most certainly, neuroscience should never be exploited to help psychotherapists defend against their (and their clients') feelings. It would therefore seem of great importance that psychotherapists make a clear distinction between defensive uses of information in order to escape from feelings (which will lead to internal fragmentation of both therapist and client) and more constructive uses of information in order to contain feelings (which can help us become more whole).

But the exercise might also be ego-building for the profession. It is thus useful to the extent that the profession needs ego-building. The caveat here would also be that care has to be taken lest the ego be a precocious ego resting on narcissistic superiority (Philips 1995). By itself, neuroscience cannot serve to give the profession of psychotherapy a sense of self-worth and confidence to engage with other health professionals. This needs to come from a deeper level of internal nurturing. But once the foundations are soundly established, this particular ego function can perhaps come into its own and help to stabilize a more adult functioning of our profession.

References

Bowlby, J. (1969) *Attachment and Loss. Vol. 1: Attachment*. New York: Basic Books.
Boyesen, G. (ed.) (1980) *Collected Papers on Biodynamic Psychology*. London: Biodynamic Psychology Publications.
Damasio, A. (1994) *Descartes' Error*. London: Putnam.
Damasio, A. (2003) *Looking for Spinoza*. London: Random House.

Gallese, V., Fadiga, L., Fogassi, L. and Rizzolatti, G. (1996) Action recognition in the premotor cortex. *Brain* 119(2): 593–609.

Gerhardt, S. (2004) *Why Love Matters*. Hove: Routledge.

Lake, F. (1986) *Clinical Theology*. London: Darton, Longman and Todd.

Lim, M. M. and Young, L. J. (2006) Neuropeptidergic regulation of affiliative behaviour and social bonding in animals. *Hormones and Behavior* 50: 506–517.

Martin, P. (1998) *The Sickening Mind*. London: Flamingo.

Munglani, R. and Hunt, S. P. (1995) Molecular biology of pain. *British Journal of Anaesthesia* 75(2): 186–192.

Philips, A. (1995) *Terrors and Experts*. London: Faber and Faber.

Reich, W. (1969) *Die Funktion des Orgasmus*. Cologne: Kiepenheuer & Witsch.

Reich, W. (1972) *Character Analysis*. New York: Noonday Press. (First published 1933.)

Schore, A. N. (1994) *Affect Regulation and the Origin of the Self*. Hillsdale, NJ: Lawrence Erlbaum Associates.

Schore, A. N. (2007) A neuropsychoanalytic perspective of development and psychotherapy. *Energy and Character* 35: 18–30.

Shimizu, E., Hashimoto, K., Okamura, N., Koike, K., Komatsu, N., Kumakiri, C., Makazato, M., Watanabe, H., Shinoda, N., Okada, S. and Iyo, M. (2003) Alterations of serum levels of brain-derived neurotrophic factor (BDNF) in depressed patients with or without antidepressants. *Biological Psychiatry* 54(1): 70–75.

Stauffer, K. A. (2003) Thoughts on psychotherapy with trauma survivors: 'repair' and 'healing'. *Energy and Character* 32: 60–62.

Stauffer, K. A. (2004) Cinderella goes to the Ball. *AChP Newsletter* No. 28, p. 24. Available online at http://www.stauffer.co.uk/Publications/Cinderella.

Tononi, G. and Edelman, G. M. (1998) Consciousness and complexity. *Science* 282: 1846–1857.

Totton, N. and Jacobs, M. (2001) *Character and Personality Types*. Buckingham: Open University Press.

Uvnäs-Moberg, K., Arn, I. and Magnusson, D. (2005) The psychobiology of emotion: the role of the oxytocinergic system. *International Journal of Behavioural Medicine* 12(2): 59–65.

Wilber, K. (1996) *A Brief History of Everything*. Boston: Shambala.

Wilkinson, M. (2006) *Coming into Mind*. Hove: Routledge.

Winnicott, D. W. (1971) *Playing and Reality*. London: Tavistock.

Chapter 9

Working with psychosomatic distress and developmental trauma: a clinical illustration

Margaret Landale

> It's true, we do store some memory in the brain, but by far, the deeper, older messages are stored in the body and must be accessed through the body. Your body is your subconscious mind, and you can't heal it by talk alone.
>
> (Pert 1999: 306)

Introduction

In this chapter I will be talking about psychosomatic distress and how the body can provide a vital resource for the therapy. At base psychosomatic distress refers to unresolved or poorly regulated emotional arousal levels which have a detrimental influence on the main systems of the body such as the immune, hormonal and respiratory systems and of course the ANS (autonomic nervous system). This can lead to a whole range of psychosomatic conditions or medically unexplained symptoms (somatoform disorders), ranging from severe headaches, fatigue, backaches and gastric problems to chest or abdominal pains and respiratory problems. And we can include anxiety disorders and depression here too.

Severe forms of psychosomatic distress are often rooted in early childhood trauma and can also manifest as self-harming, addictions, eating disorders and borderline personality disorder (BPD). Clients who suffer from psychosomatic conditions are typically further distressed by both the often chronic and debilitating pain with which they live on a daily basis and by the lack of medical explanation or treatment available. This leads to a vicious circle in which these increased emotional arousal levels further decrease the client's capacity for emotional self-regulation and potentially aggravate the symptoms further.

I have chosen a clinical illustration to discuss some of the typical dilemmas which both clients and therapists encounter in this work. Anne's[1] case also demonstrates how by engaging flexibly with embodied, emotional and cognitive processes, significant shifts can occur.

In the context of this chapter I am going to talk about two distinct phases of this work. The first considers how to lower arousal levels by building a practical alliance with the client. This involves providing a rationale based on stress and trauma principles and enrolling the client in developing the necessary practical skills.

The second phase, which builds on the client's ability to monitor and manage their arousal levels, involves a mindful enquiry directly into the symptoms through imaging processes.

Anne's story

Anne was in her early thirties when two of her brothers died in quick succession. A few months later she began to experience severe and debilitating pains and spasms in her lower back and thighs. On several occasions she became completely paralysed and was unable to move for days or even weeks. Thorough medical checks failed to provide a physiological explanation and over a period of three years she tried a range of treatments to little effect. Anne was truly distressed when she came into therapy. The ongoing pain coupled with increased fear of loss of movement was taking its toll. She had, however, begun to seriously consider the possibility that her symptoms were emotionally driven and when she heard that I was specializing in psychosomatic disorders, she contacted me.

My first impression of Anne was of a confident and lively woman. She came across as open and engaging and very articulate in presenting her problems. However, her confident and extrovert manner contrasted sharply with aspects of her body language and indeed her symptoms. Given that Anne had suffered persistent pain over a long period of time, it was understandable that her movements were deliberate and cautious. Yet there was more to it than this. All her movements seemed carefully planned and carried out in a cautious and highly deliberate manner. The contrast was stark. Here was a bubbly, lively woman – but this aliveness was conveyed almost entirely by facial expression, voice and verbal content. There was some gesturing with her arms as she spoke, but I was struck by how lifeless her hands appeared.

The body can reveal a great deal more about a person's emotional identity than the spoken word. In fact all aspects of body language are a powerful resource for the therapist to glean insights into the client's unconscious. I was curious how these first impressions might relate to Anne's history.

Anne was the third child of four, and the only girl. Her mother was a strong and dominant woman, who brought her children up with firm rules. In Anne's words: 'We were all burdens to my mother, to be controlled, washed and dressed'. I believe that Anne's mother wanted to do the best for her children, but she was tense and frustrated dealing with the nitty gritty reality of a young family. She was especially intolerant of emotional outbursts or neediness and would not allow tears. Anne also recalls how her mother intervened and stopped her father from cuddling her when she was four, arguing that it was inappropriate to spoil and indulge children like this.

Anne, being a determined spirit, did not give this comfort up readily and was consequently nicknamed 'super glue'. Anne loved her father, who was affectionate and seems to have favoured her. But he worked away from home for most of Anne's childhood and was therefore unavailable most of the time. Anne's parents argued and fought increasingly until they got divorced when she was in her teens. Her brothers moved out of the family home at this point but Anne decided to stay with her mother.

Following the divorce Anne's mother became depressed and turned to alcohol. Then, just a year later she was diagnosed with breast cancer which ultimately spread into her bones. Anne operated as her mother's sole carer for the next three years until her death. During this time she received very little support from the rest of her family. For example, Anne's maternal grandmother, who lived nearby and was still very active, told Anne that she could not possibly be involved in the care of her daughter because she didn't feel she 'could cope with the horror of it all'.

Anne's mother was also in desperate denial about the recurrence of her cancer and her doctors colluded in this by telling her that she was suffering from bone calcification. Anne was given firm instructions not to tell her mother about the cancer or indeed that she was dying. Anne was left on her own, watching the slow decay of her mother's body, watching her mother struggle to keep hope alive whilst battling against death. She was seventeen. These were difficult and emotionally overwhelming circumstances for Anne. True to her upbringing she soldiered on through her mother's illness and received praise for her resolve and strength. However, we can guess at the cost. Neither she nor any of her family or friends really understood how traumatic this experience was for her.

Insecure attachment

It seemed clear from this history that Anne did not have the appropriate emotional resources to take care of her own needs during and after her mother's illness. We develop patterns of emotional self-regulation[2] in our early childhood in response to our environment and the primary relationships on whom we depend. The quality or security of attachment we experience in our early years is pivotal to our development. Insecure attachment translates into insufficient emotional self-regulation (Bowlby 1997; Schore 2003; Gerhardt 2004; Le Doux 1996; Ogden *et al.* 2006; Siegel 1999).

Anne did not have much access to early memories, but we were able to ascertain some aspects of her early experience. For example, she knew she had learned early to control her bodily functions – she walked early, was potty trained early and learned to read at the age of two. In order to achieve these levels of behaviour and control, she learned to control her impulses and ignore her feelings long before she was developmentally ready to do so. I hypothesized to myself that her embodied mind would have had to organize itself around a fearful denial of her own impulses and needs and her thinking mind would have developed prematurely, set defensively and punitively against her own embodied and emotional reality. Sue Gerhardt captures this when she writes:

> Children who have developed insecure strategies for dealing with their emotions cannot tolerate feelings and so cannot reflect on them. Their emotional habits for managing feelings kick in too quickly. Avoidantly attached children are likely to automatically slam on their emotional brakes when strong feelings start to arise, so that they don't have to be aware of feelings they don't know what to do with.
>
> (Gerhardt 2004: 28–29)

The important point here is that Anne had become so efficient at 'slamming on her emotional brakes' that she no longer knew how to *feel* her distress. I had noticed, for example, that during the early stages of her therapy, whenever I made comments relating empathetically to her early childhood experiences, I met either incomprehension, criticism or was fended off with a humorous or sometimes cynical response. At best we might have a theoretical discussion about the conditions of her upbringing.

Stress

All of this indicated that Anne was not yet able to engage with her underlying issues and that we would need to deal with her current dilemmas first. Anne was able to recognize that she was under enormous stress. Stress is a very helpful and accurate concept to introduce when working with psychosomatic conditions. The usual labels attached to psychosomatic complaints are that the cause is psychological or emotional. Clients understandably find this difficult to accept. The view that the symptoms are expressions of unresolved emotional arousal and refer to unconscious emotional material may leave the client feeling criticized and undermined. It is indeed common for clients to feel that this implies failure on their part, that they are making this all up or are causing it (Broom 1997; Sanders 1996).

The term stress, however, provides a more specific and far less stigmatizing explanation and tends to be more acceptable to the client. It also implies for most people that something can be done about it. Anne understood that she was under a great deal of stress dealing with her symptoms. She fought a desperate battle against her own body and could not find relief. The problem was that her body had become an enemy which she felt attacked by on a daily level. Anne was able to recognize that her coping strategies were not working; in fact she realized that the harder she tried to get rid of her symptoms the worse they became. She also understood rationally that the fear of her own body was likely to exacerbate her symptoms further.

I described the mechanisms of stress to her in very simple terms – that the stress response is activated when we feel threatened and that under normal circumstances, when the threat is over, the body switches into the relaxation response. However, when the experience of threat does not subside, the relaxation response is not activated and we accumulate stress. We also acknowledged that this natural balance between stress and relaxation response might already have been undermined in her childhood and certainly during her mother's illness and we began to look at how she might be able to address this in her current situation.

I was hoping at this point that we might be able to build on Anne's existing coping strategies and resources. It felt crucial not to undermine Anne further by labelling her existing strategies as defensive and therefore wrong. I believe it is important to remember that defence mechanisms have the benign intent to protect and are deeply rooted within the client. In Anne's case her willpower and intellect were vital resources as they allowed Anne to make a commitment to learning new practical skills to manage her anxiety and distress. Having identified stress as an issue we could then begin to look at helping her develop skills for managing stress more appropriately. Over the following weeks Anne began to practise mindfulness and breathing regularly on a daily basis – but I will come back to this later. I would like first to introduce another concept which provided reassurance and direction for Anne – trauma.

Trauma

Anne was quick to recognize that the circumstances of her mother's death had been traumatic. Identifying trauma as an underlying issue seemed to give Anne some sense of identity and relief. The concept of trauma provided at least a logical hypothesis and more importantly, a hope that we might be able to do something about it. Trauma is a common undercurrent to psychosomatic distress and it is helpful to consider trauma-specific clinical interventions in this work.[3]

In this context the significance of working with the body is increasingly recognized. The necessary lowering of arousal levels can most effectively be achieved through skilful influence of the limbic system, namely the ANS and the limbic brain. Developing the client's capacity to pay attention to body sensations and feelings is also vital before effective trauma processing can occur. Babette Rothschild (2000) talks about helping the client to learn how to stay safe and aware during the processing of traumatic material. Pat Ogden refers to the need to create 'a window of opportunity', providing access to a safe space between hyper- and hypo-arousal levels (Ogden *et al.* 2006). It is within this calmer zone that unresolved emotional distress can be made conscious, felt and then integrated (Rothschild 2000; Ogden *et al.* 2006; Levine 1997; van der Kolk 1996).

Working with breath

In order to prepare the ground for processing the deeper distress underlying Anne's symptoms, it was my first priority to help her develop her capacity to pay attention to her embodied experience without fear or judgment. As is the case with many clients who suffer from psychosomatic conditions Anne's mechanisms for dissociation were very strong. I therefore decided to help Anne focus on her breath as a way to help her develop awareness of embodied experience.

I have found both breath awareness and conscious breathing techniques invaluable when working with psychosomatic conditions and indeed developmental trauma. Breath awareness refers to a simple monitoring of the breath without trying to influence it. This can help therapists and clients to become aware of habitual breathing patterns – and functions as a prerequisite for establishing mindful awareness.

Conscious breathing techniques refer to simple practical exercises where the client learns to expand their breathing capacity. A simple yet very effective technique, for example, is the 'calming breath'. Here we would extend the length of the exhalation, pause, and then let the body take the next in-breath. The active lengthening of the out-breath encourages a deeper and unforced in-breath which automatically sends messages to the limbic brain that all is safe. This evokes a parasympathetic response from the ANS which tends to manifest directly as a lowering of anxiety. It is important to remember that any breath work undertaken in a psychotherapeutic context needs to build on an active inquiry into the client's direct experience of breathing. This breath awareness informs any development of a regular daily breathing practice so that deeply ingrained breathing patterns can gently be influenced and readjusted. It is essential, however, that psychotherapists who would like to introduce such a direct body approach into their work have experienced and practised breath awareness and breathing techniques for themselves (Harvey 1988; Hendricks 1995; Farhi 1996; Swami Rama *et al.* 1998; Rosenberg 1998).

Anne understood that it would be desirable for her to learn to relax and engaged well with her breathing practice, which we carefully monitored. We realized quickly, for example, that she felt most safe and comfortable when practising lying down and she reported after only a few weeks she was beginning to experience profound moments of calm. She also began to learn to observe not just her breath but also other body sensations and symptoms mindfully. I am using the term mindfulness here in its basic definition, moment-by-moment awareness without judgment. After only a few weeks she was able for short periods of time to observe painful sensations in her body without fear. This was a big moment for both of us.

A mindful approach to pain

The acceptance of pain, both physical and emotional, is one of the most advanced and difficult processes to engage in. It implies learning to distinguish between pain and suffering, to accept that pain may be unavoidable but that suffering is determined by how we relate to it. This is a crucial distinction to make with clients. Darlene Cohen, who suffered from rheumatoid arthritis for many years and used her meditation practice to help her manage her condition, illustrates this mindful attitude to pain when she writes:

> At first my conscious life was all pain. Acknowledging the pain and its power eventually allowed me to explore my body fully and find there actually were experiences in my body besides the pain – here is pain, here is bending, here is breath, here is movement, here is the sun warming, here is unbearable fire, here is tightness – something different wherever I looked.
>
> (Cohen 2000)

Here we see how through the strengthening of the 'observing' function, we can promote an experience of 'being here – now' as well as an acceptance of 'what is' and this makes it highly relevant for psychotherapy. Mindful awareness of embodied and felt experience is a long-established aspect of body-oriented psychotherapy and a natural resource for Chiron psychotherapists. Ron Kurtz's 'Hakomi method' also incorporates mindfulness-based interventions and more recently Jon Kabat-Zin's 'Mindfulness-based Stress Reduction' programme has inspired numerous clinical applications and research trials establishing the effectiveness of mindfulness for a whole range of conditions in both a medical and a psychotherapeutic context (Kurtz 1990; Kabat-Zin 1990, 2005; Germer *et al.* 2005; Baer 2003).

In this context I have found it hugely beneficial to introduce practical elements of mindfulness quite early on in the work and to teach the client that it is possible to pay attention to their direct experience without any judgment and without feeling overwhelmed.

Mindfulness of transference

This mindful approach is also relevant for the inevitable transference issues which arise when working with psychosomatic distress. Anne had no difficulties practising conscious breathing on her own and quickly developed her capacity to pay attention to her direct embodied experience for long stretches at a time. Things were dramatically different, however, when we were together. We discovered that my very presence or attention made her anxious and tense. She felt watched and controlled by me and kept disconnecting from her direct experience after just a few moments. For example, when we began to establish her breathing routine and I asked her to pay attention to her breath – to notice the movements accompanying her breathing, the length of her out-breath and in-breath, which parts of her chest or abdomen were moving – she reported that she found it hard to concentrate on these instructions. I encouraged her to describe what was happening in her mind and she told me that she had gone into thinking about the techniques and what purpose they served. Further explorations showed that she also had anxious thoughts about getting it right and critical thoughts about my instructions, my choice of words and the tone of my voice.

This helped us to engage in the exploration of the negative transference dynamics that were emerging. By acknowledging her direct experience, body, emotions and thinking mind without judging any of these unfolding processes we were able to build trust and safety in the therapeutic relationship. In the context of this chapter I will not be able to go into further depth on this important subject, but Shoshi Asheri's chapter is an excellent exploration of relational issues and illustrates how important a mindful attitude is when working with transference issues.

When we introduce directive interventions such as breath work to help lower arousal levels, we need to be able to shift fluently between guidance and an open exploration of the emerging material, especially the transference. In Anne's case her tolerance to let me gain insights into her innermost, private experience grew and she became increasingly able to focus on and describe her direct experience. This was another crucial building block also for working towards the discovery of the hidden emotional meaning of her symptoms.

Discovering new meaning through innate imaging

Psychosomatic symptoms can also be viewed as metaphors (Landale 2002). This is evidenced by the fact that most people when asked to describe their direct embodied experience will use metaphor to do so. Body sensations and symptoms can function as symbolic representations of unresolved emotional conflicts carried by the body. Of course most of us will be familiar with 'guided' imagery techniques which are used to influence our limbic brain, our emotions and our overall physiology. However, there are limits to the benefits of 'guided' imagery because such images are introduced by the therapist. The point here is that in psychotherapy we are naturally more interested in the client's innate imagination.

The way this relates to Anne is significant. Her thinking mind was acting as if it could come up with a clever solution to her problems, proposing new strategies at every turn – but in fact she was dissociated from her emotional experience. In her innate imagination she was dealing with unresolved feelings of fear, grief and hopelessness and she could not begin to consciously comprehend, let alone influence, her symptoms. Tuning into her innate imagery was a potent way of accessing her embodied emotional experience. For example, by focusing on a body sensation and asking her to describe it by its shape, colour, size or sound we were able to tap directly into her imagination and thus her unconscious.

Of course this way of working is not new. Freud in his early work engaged with innate imaging through free association as did Jung with his 'active imagination'. Indeed before illustrating how innate imaging helped Anne to release some of the distress she was holding, I would like to quote Jung, who refers to these processes when he writes:

> In the intensity of the emotional disturbance itself lies the value, the energy which he should have at his disposal in order to remedy the state of reduced adaptation. Nothing is achieved by repressing this state or devaluing it rationally. In order, therefore, to gain possession of the energy that is in the wrong place, he must make the emotional state the basis or starting point of the procedure. Fantasy must be allowed the freest possible play.
>
> (Jung, quoted by Rossi 1993: 39)

So back to Anne; her decision to engage with a breathing and mindfulness routine had already allowed a less anxious awareness of her own body. She had an open psychological mind and had accepted the idea that psychosomatic symptoms might be an expression of unresolved emotional conflicts that she held in her body. When I further explained to her that by paying attention to her symptoms – without preconception – we might get those symptoms to reveal some of their meaning, she was willing to explore this further.

In my experience it is important to pace this work so that the client can get used to the process and feel comfortable with it. Psychosomatic symptoms tend to come in clusters and the most pronounced symptoms are deeply entangled with anxiety and resistance. To try and engage too early with the underlying distress can be over-challenging or even terrifying for the client. In Anne's case her lower back pain was off limits in this respect – our tentative attempts at engaging with this pain had confirmed that her resistance was too strong – and we had therefore begun to work with secondary symptoms or sensations.

I would like to focus now on a breakthrough session that happened around three months into our work when Anne arrived at her session complaining about a persistent pain in the right side of her chest. She kept rubbing it as she spoke and was clearly agitated by it. I asked her if she felt ready to focus on these sensations and she agreed and decided to lie down. I said: 'Take a moment to let your attention turn inward, notice your body lying down, feel how the weight of your body is being carried by the couch right now – notice also the steady rhythm of your breathing as your are lying here, supported by the couch'. I was intending with these instructions to help Anne make a state shift, to coax her away from her thinking, conceptualizing mind and help her instead to become more inward focused and receptive. I wanted to engage her limbic brain and my suggestions were aimed at making her feel more present and relaxed. By starting from a containing and calm position I was hoping that we were laying down an immediate memory trace to which we might need to resort later if the surfacing emotional conflict that I suspected was held deep within her symptoms became too distressing.

I then encouraged her to focus her attention on the sensations she was feeling in her chest. She said: 'It is like something acidic, like acid burning just underneath my skin – the whole area feels so sensitive to touch – sometimes just having a shower sets it off. I don't feel it when I feel relaxed.' And as she talked her hand was making circular movements, pressing down the right side of her chest. I was immediately struck by the term acidic, an evocative and disconcerting image. I am always on the look-out for charged images like this as they can be entry points to deeper innate work. But this description emerged right at the beginning and I could detect fear in her voice as she talked about it. I was also instinctively guided by my own response to the term acidic, it is not something one would touch directly and without protection so I decided to take a more cautious approach.

I said: 'As you keep focusing on this area could you describe the shape of it?' Anne responded immediately saying: 'it's round'. 'Round' I echoed 'and has it got a colour?'

'Reddish – like when you've scraped off your skin. It's raw, like an inflammation. Acidic – coming up my oesophagus – like a very sharp bruise.' Anne's unconscious had given us three evocative, visceral images – inflammation, acidic and bruise. Again I had to make an instinctive decision about which one to engage with. I decided to go with the last one and repeated: 'Like a very sharp bruise. I wonder if you have a sense of what might have caused that bruise?' Anne: 'It feels like something attached itself to me – like an alien. Mum used to describe her illness like a spider growing a web, invading her. It feels like webs inside my chest just underneath my skin, growing, turning into metastasis. I have an image of this metastasis, disguising itself as part of the bones, like a growth, like an egg/half egg just sitting there.'

Anne became quiet at this point, her attention was drawn inward. She seemed absorbed and I noticed that her breathing had become slow and shallow. I felt that I had to remain quiet in order not to disrupt her inner focus. Silences have different qualities. Silence can feel withdrawn or detached, terrified, overwhelmed or angry. This silence felt potent. When Anne started speaking again, I could see that she was holding back her tears and it seemed to me that she was having to make a real effort to speak again: 'When Mum was dying I wished for a while that I had the disease, so that I could fight it for her.' She was crying now and after a few moments continued: 'Her cancer felt like something intelligent like an alien which attaches itself to human beings.'

I felt that the repeated metaphor of 'alien' needed to be explored more and I asked: 'Could you describe this alien to me, what does it look like?' After a moment Anne replied: 'It's like an octopus, a beast which wakes at times, something uncontrollable. I couldn't control it, could never really talk to Mum about her illness, so I remember visualizing it a lot. I could not talk to Mum so I just kept imagining it, that beastly creature which ate away at her.' Anne was crying freely now and continued: 'It showed itself, broke out of her skin, her skin full of metastasis, horrible smelly, decaying her. I was so frightened of her body – that this beast would animate her – I felt it reaching for my body – trying to attach itself to me also like I was linked to Mum's pain.' We had reached a point where her embodied memories were surfacing spontaneously and I wanted to be sure that the recollection of these memories did not lead to re-traumatization. My sense was that this was not the case. Anne's tears had a quality of grief and release and it appeared to me that she was sharing and shedding feelings which had burdened her for many years. I felt that this process was taking her into a deeper place of understanding.

The innate image of being linked to her mother's pain seemed to provide a poignant link with her own psychosomatic pain. I wanted to keep her focused on this and suggested: 'Stay with this image of being linked to your Mum's pain. How would you describe this link?'

Anne: 'It's like a mirror image – like the pain is in my body also – to a lesser degree but linking us together – her pain binding me to her, like I had to take this disease inside of me. I couldn't bear to just witness, not being able to do anything, so I kept imagining her pain – took her pain inside of me. I can cope with physical pain. I just don't know how to cope with all this emotional pain.'

I felt deeply moved by the poignancy of this description. Her mother had been unable to acknowledge that she was dying and I suspected that this denial had communicated itself powerfully to the people around her, leading the doctors to collude with this denial and leaving Anne to absorb and internalize her mother's fear and pain. But Anne's mother had been dead many years and Anne had a lot of good things happening in her life now. We had to understand what kept the pain link in place, why Anne still felt she had to carry her mother's pain. I asked: 'And you keep on coping with so much physical pain, what purpose might this serve now?' Anne: 'It helps to show how hurt I am. I don't want to get rid of it because I hold my Mum in there. I can then care for that pain.'

Anne cried for a long while after this. I felt that this was a breakthrough point in our work. I had suspected that grief might be at the core of her symptoms because they had developed following her brothers' deaths. We had already recognized that the circumstances in which her mother died had been traumatic for Anne. But by helping her focus her awareness inward and encouraging her to follow the images which arose spontaneously from her deep embodied knowing, she discovered a hidden meaning to her somatic pain. In that moment her body–mind became whole, giving her a new sense of identity. She was able to *feel* the meaning of her symptoms. She realized that they belonged to her – formed part of her and she began to relate to them rather than trying to eradicate them.

> When the attention is trained on the emotion in question – in particular, on the bodily experience of emotion – it gradually ceases to be experienced as a static and threatening entity and becomes, instead, a process that is defined by time as well as space. The technique of concentration permits the difficult emotion to be experienced as coming from one's own being, and it can then be understood and accepted rather than feared for its brute strength.
>
> (Epstein 2001: 207)

Conclusion

After this breakthrough session Anne began to live with her symptoms differently. She seemed more accepting of her pain and discomfort and less anxious to get rid of it. She observed, some weeks later on, that her back pains had been less frequent and that when they came she saw them not with her previous sense of alarm but rather as a signal to slow down, rest and look after herself. A significant shift had occurred in only three months, showing how much can be achieved even with complex attachment trauma issues when we work proactively with the resources of the embodied mind. Through her regular breathing and mindfulness practice, Anne had learned to pay attention to her body with significantly less anxiety and had begun to trust in her ability to manage her pain. Such resourcefulness can be a prerequisite to the safe processing of emotional charge inherent in psychosomatic distress.

However, I think it is also important that as therapists we are able to handle the delicate balance between structure and phenomenological emergence. I have found regular mindfulness meditation practice to be an invaluable resource in my psychotherapeutic practice. It helps me to pay attention simultaneously to the thoughts, feelings and embodied reality of the unfolding process.

Notes

1 The names and other identifying details have been changed to protect confidentiality – the imagery process described is accurate and published with Anne's permission.
2 See also Roz Carroll's and Kathrin Stauffer's chapters on the subject of self-regulation.
3 For a more detailed exploration of the subject see Morit Heitzler's chapter.

References

Baer, R. (2003) Mindfulness training as a clinical intervention: a conceptual and empirical review. *Clinical Psychology: Science and Practice* 10(2): 125–142.

Bowlby, J. (1997) *Attachment and Loss, Vols 1 and 2*. London: Pimlico.

Broom, B. (1997) *Somatic Illness*. London: Free Association Books.

Cohen, D. (2000) *Finding a Joyful Life in the Heart of Pain*. Boston: Shambala.

Epstein, M. (2001) *Thoughts without a Thinker*. London: Gerald Ducksworth.

Farhi, D. (1996) *The Breathing Book*. New York: Henry Holt.

Gerhardt, S. (2004) *Why Love Matters*. Hove: Routledge.

Germer, C. K., Siegel, R. D. and Fulton, P. (2005) *Mindfulness Psychotherapy*. New York: Guilford Press.

Harvey, J. (1988) *The Quiet Mind*. Honesdale, PA: Himalayan International Institute.

Hendricks, G. (1995) *Conscious Breathing*. New York: Bantam.

Kabat-Zin, J. (1990) *Full Catastrophe Living*. New York: Delta.

Kabat-Zin, J. (2005) *Coming to our Senses*. London: Piatkus.

Krystal, H. (1988) *Integration and Self-Healing*. Hillsdale, NJ: Analytic Press.

Kurtz, R. (1990) *Body-Centered Psychotherapy: The Hakomi Method*. Mendicino, CA: LifeRhythm.

Landale, M. (2002) The use of imagery in body-oriented psychotherapy. In: Staunton, T. (ed.) *Body Psychotherapy*. Hove: Routledge.

LeDoux, J. (1996) *The Emotional Brain*. New York: Simon and Schuster.

Levine, P. (1997) *Waking the Tiger – Healing Trauma*. Berkeley, CA: North Atlantic Books.

Ogden, P., Minton, K. and Pain, C. (2006) *Trauma and the Body: A Sensorimotor Approach to Psychotherapy*. New York: Norton.

Pert, C. (1999) *Molecules of Emotion*. London: Pocket Books.

Rosenberg, L. (1998) *Breath by Breath*. Boston: Shambala.

Rossi, E. (1993) *The Psychobiology of Mind-Body Healing*. New York: Norton.

Rothschild B. (2000) *The Body Remembers*. New York: Norton.

Sanders, D. (1996) *Counselling for Psychosomatic Problems*. London: Sage.

Schore, A. (2003) *Affect Regulation and the Repair of Self*. New York: Norton.

Siegel, D. (1999) *The Developing Mind*. New York: Guilford Press.

Swami Rama, Ballentine, R. and Hymes, A. (1998) *Science of Breath*. Honesdale, PA: Himalayan Institute Press.

van der Kolk, B. (1996) *Traumatic Stress: The Effects of Overwhelming Experience on Mind, Body and Society*. New York: Guilford Press.

Chapter 10

Do we? Can we look at the disabled body?

Anne Marie Keary

Premise

In this chapter I wish to explore some of the issues, questions and ethical dilemmas faced when working with clients who are also disabled. I look at how society deals with the disturbance created by disability, how the body of a person with a disability is objectified and the subsequent effects on attachment and relating. I propose that it is in the process of working through the fragmentation, in an embodied relational way, that space is created to allow increased capacity to breathe. Through this exploration I will weave case material from a client who is disabled, as well as my own experience and perspectives around disability. It is a work in progress, not a detailed case analysis, aiming to pose questions more than offer answers, to help us look.

As I start it is like being stunned. I hit a gap in myself, blankness about putting the words on paper, different to my normal experience of writing. There is a difficulty with shape and structure, things are fragmented and formless, a parallel process of being in bits. I feel my inability, my fear of giving birth to a chapter with a disability. I remember the pain of the arrival of my disabled child into the world and the terror when the experience of difference became personal to me. I know all too well how this shock is carried on, colouring all subsequent gestations in whatever forms they appear.

I am aware of pressure to be an expert, to research and become a specialist, before there is any possibility of speaking, writing, coming out. It is a painful remembering, how I became an expert, not by choice, in cerebral palsy. Around the terrain of disability, you have to find out more and be able to explain to all around what it means. You have to translate, often hiding your own wordlessness. You are outside of developmental norms.

There is a forced deconstruction of reality, with the inner question for me *am I now disabled by the bonding of mothering?* It feels the same as a therapist working with clients who are disabled: does that make me separate, special in a way that can feel objectifying, even patronising? It is also a cheek to dare as an able-bodied woman to put myself close, even by association, to the experience of disability. It is like walking a tightrope between universes.

The client I write about in this chapter, whom I call Helen, was referred to me specifically because she is disabled and I knew of this world of a different drumbeat through the disabilities of my daughter. Working with her is a personal decision to hear more about and look at this world of difference in which one's spirit longs but one's body lags behind. I am pushed to the limits of my therapeutic position and beliefs with the issue of personal disclosure being part of my internal pressure.

I hit a similar dilemma now in writing and interweaving my personal experience, and I realise this parallels part of the difference that comes with disability. It is often a public fact; we may struggle to look, yet the disability itself is often starkly visible. This visibility I am describing, which I enter whenever I am in public with my daughter, my client faces *all the time*. In writing personally I am exposing myself professionally, and yet this is the ground I find myself in. It feels like a forced outing of the difference and in this chapter, by being personal, I am choosing to join partly in that – disability is a public experience.

The backdrop to the work

The process of working with and looking at the effect of disability on an individual brings us right to the heart of the wound of the body in an unbearable way; so we inevitably make ourselves blind, stupid or incapable regardless of the functioning or non-functioning of our own bodies. Essentially we enter into the experience where we are robbed of hope and it feels like a brutal annihilation of the concept of perfection. We have to face how reality has no shape that can be contained or understood in 'normal' terms.

Interestingly, the shape of my work with Helen is unusual for me; I have been working with her for over four years with a gap of ten months when she left the country. Our modes of working have included gaps when she was not able to come, longer session times, telephone sessions, email communication, an ending and then a restart. She is now in twice weekly therapy, with regular text contact. Variations are a feature which both stabilise and destabilise the therapy frame, providing adaptations that sometimes feel essential and at other times indicate the inherent fragmentation.

Helen came to therapy because she felt overwhelmed and frightened by her self-harming destructive tendencies. In our initial session she spoke of feeling her spirit was going before her body and it believed she could do things she could not physically manage. She wondered if a body approach might help her cope better with the despair she feels about her body – a good question!

The sight of damage, of something gone wrong, induces an excited disturbance in the observer, like the voyeuristic response to a disaster (Sinason 1992: 27). We don't know how to handle our desire to stare, or our fear of catching it by association. So we avert our eyes, train ourselves not to look, and tell our children *don't stare, let us all stay blind and not see*! Mainly we do this because we do not know how to look in a way that is not invasive; this fear keeps distance and separateness. We may crave this as we want to stay safely away, so we make the one who is disabled an object; we remove relational possibilities.

There is a massive desire for it all to be okay so we collude by making the disabled cheerful, hiding our knowledge of the opposite. There is a denial that there is another part, maybe underneath the helpless part, that is furious about their lack of control or not knowing. Valerie Sinason writes of the push to be stupid, which means to be 'numbed with grief', so that we dissociate from our intelligence. I catch this when people confronted with my daughter's lack of communication respond 'but she is happy', not able to bear that sometimes we just don't know or can't make sense of different fates. This is important to unpick in our response to disability, as we fall into the areas of not applying our normal thinking and don't use our own sense in the interpretations of behaviour. Consequently we can be fooled by the false smile that can hide scars of self-injury (Sinason 1992: 30).

The first step towards dehumanizing people is to strip them of dignity and privacy (Wilson 2003: 2). Many disabled writers explain it is not really their impairment that causes emotional distress but the impact on their relationships and their ability to manage their environment. There can be a loss of dignity and the disabled person is removed from being able to take control and responsibility for their body. There is confusion when an adult person requires infant care. This disrupts the natural order and creates a constant dyad of client/carer, in which the disabled person is habitually in a client role in many different contexts, leading to infantilisation (Davis 2004: 303).

This set-up has implications for the psychotherapy relationship and the two bodies in the therapy room. The loss model that arises in therapy with disabled clients posits that the disability has to be mourned and it is that in itself which is psychologically devastating. In the early history of psychoanalysis, those with impairments were considered 'unanalysable' due to having 'weak egos' (Asch and Rousso 1985). This contradicts what disabled people say about their problem being the environmental response to impairment (Lenny 1993). It creates a climate of miscommunication, and hurt, which can reduce access to already inadequate provision. Helen is often disillusioned and cynical about the benefit of psychotherapy and the point of sitting talking when she is in such pain. This may be linked to the fact that disability is associated with what cannot be mended so needing therapy also presents the deficit of it not being enough.

People with disabilities as 'the other' – the rejected body

To the non-disabled, people with disabilities symbolise, among other things, imperfection, failure to control the body and everyone's vulnerability to weakness and pain. This projection is given more weight by the actual difference that is seen. With hierarchies of power even within the disabled community, those who have least control of their bodies needing the most care are at the bottom, thus making the body's incapacity one of the most powerful symbolic meanings of disability. Somehow this being 'the other' opens the door for higher rates of verbal, physical and even sexual abuse (Wendell 1996: 64). These events are often unrecognised, like the public stripping at hospitals, damaging self-esteem and sexual identity. What appears missing is the subjectivity of a person; so the observer does not imagine into the experience from the outside, identification gets lost and 'otherness' is maintained. Helen had a lot of exposure to hospital examinations and studies of her unusual body shape, with no benefit from gruelling procedures. This left her strongly opposed to the medical establishment and traditional help models. This experience of 'otherness' has damaged her identity and self.

People who do not conform to physical normality draw attention. Everyday disciplinary body responses like eating, bladder control, dribbling, walking etc. are both instinctive and learnt. When these don't happen in the usual way the disabled non-conforming body becomes the rejected body. Those who appear abnormal are a constant reminder to those struggling to exist in the normal frame that they may slip up and fall outside; as a result it arouses fear and suspicion. Paradoxically it may also reassure us, and make normal feel more normal.

Often people with disabilities cannot make their bodies fit the physical ideals of their culture. They may wish for bodies they cannot have with frustration, shame and self-hatred. Helen's knees barely bend; when she feels hopeless she just wants to curl up in a ball, but she can't have this comfort. She feels her knees are denying her personally in their refusal; she struggles for a realistic and positive self-image.

Fusion and separateness are finely balanced; add a difference like disability and it all gets wobblier. There is a tendency for the therapist to get caught up in the external or concrete issues due to anxiety and our own unconscious response to disability. I have written letters on Helen's behalf to her doctor and social services. I have wanted to assist her in applying for benefits. Yet in this desire I may lose track of her unconscious communication and fail to use the countertransference to her benefit. There can be a pull towards merging to avoid the shock of the difference (Ernst 1997: 30–34).

Assimilating the arrival of a disabled child is of primary importance. How the mother manages this is painfully key, there is a need for her to assume responsibility so that acceptance can emanate in how she is with her child.

Her body response to her child matters, as lack of mirroring affects the body, increasing the non-identification and splitting of the attachment figures. To do that the mother may need to overcome huge feelings of loss and disappointment. It is a brutal reality for the struggling mother that the impact of the terror evoked in the baby by the mother whose face does not light up at the sight of her child is a dreadful and damaging experience (Wilson 2003: 29). It seems an impossible task for the mother and yet it is at the heart of subsequent relating.

Helen's difficulties in relationships manifest in conflicts around attachment and separateness. She is aware of having cut away from her family. She had a prolonged painful separation at the age of eighteen months, with an operation involving a long hospital stay, gruelling procedures involving physical restraints, e.g. being in a body cast for six months. She talks of pulling out her hair when left on her own in hospital, having suppositories forced upon her, refusing to eat, thus initiating her life-long struggle with food.

She lacked the security of attachment so she never managed the separateness that comes from the safety of knowing that outer attachments provide the frame for inner stability. She barely speaks of her relationship with her mother; she rarely visits home and finds it impossible to eat there. Her mother's fussing makes her feel like a difficulty, an object to be taken care of. Her mother's response to her falling was to tell her to get up and ignore the teasing. My sense of Helen's attachment to her mother as it emerges is of a gap, a question mark and a void.

There is an element of terror in her relating as she feels dependency. She recounts the pain she experienced when her father had a brain haemorrhage, and her acute sense of abandonment, deeply unsettling her internal safety. She described the agony of waiting for him to return, fearing he was dead, being inconsolable when her mother went to visit him, sure she too would not return – the details vividly imprinted.

Particular developmental challenges occur around adolescence for disabled people as separation and individuation can be thwarted by the fact of dependency. Helen has managed to separate practically from her family. She has had long-term relationships, with fulfilling sexual experiences, but after a few years they end. It seems to be around the issue of commitment and her last partner did initiate the end because of his difficulty in being alongside Helen. These ruptures have a devastating impact, evoking a massive abandonment crisis. They unsettle her already fragile body image and beg the bitter constant question: 'who would want to be with me and this body when I struggle with being with me and my body?'

Through these attachment dynamics I believe we encounter an externalised and internalised hostility about disability linked to sexuality: the fact that two bodies came together through a sexual act of lovemaking and the resulting child is disabled. This theory holds a relational, internalised point that 'in fantasy and reality parental intercourse has been seen to produce disability' and this is manifest in the body (Sinason 1997: 19).

This reverberates through me, I want to drop it like an unwanted bundle; it evokes a universal fear of procreation going wrong and yet I know it is at the heart of something crucial. This is juxtaposed with societal assumptions that disabled adults are either blindly assumed to have asexual lives, or are seen as symbols of permissive fetish sex – either way often left without resources to develop a healthy adult sexuality (Olkin 1999: 233).

The energy of these complex issues lies between us in the therapy room like an electric current seeking engagement and digestion. The ongoing challenge for Helen and me is to dare to allow space to metabolise the impact of these communications around sexuality and body image.

Looking at the wounded objectified body

Psychotherapy with the disabled body feels like going into the dark places, facing the shadow. As a body psychotherapist my tools feel inept, in need of adaptation. *I feel the limits of my profession, where is the theory about therapy and the disabled body?* Will this questioning be enough to create it?

Facing objectification is inescapable; maybe a particular wound in body psychotherapy where we focus on body sensation, symptoms and posture. Character structure theory, for instance, can be keenly objectifying. Is it adaptable to the disabled world where diagnosis and labelling are internalised so harshly? We use character structure as a map of what happened. What about the body with gaps and disabilities from birth? This questioning goes deeper inside the body: how to talk of grounding when your client's feet don't support her and hurt like hell? How to say: 'feel your body' when her existence feels dependent on overriding it? For me the answer is that with the body focus we are faced with an unavoidable descent into the mess. We are there to pay attention to the body so through the very act of looking the trauma is harder to avoid.

The facts of her body are important to name yet in doing so I join the objectification. This is a constant, the discomfort of which induces an element of dissociation that lies at the core of the experience whether in this writing or in our work. Helen was born with a range of unexplained physical gaps. At the time of her birth there was no one else known in the world to have the same range of multiple congenital disabilities. She has no left arm, no hip joints or sockets, her femurs are not full length, she has scoliosis of the spine, her knees barely bend, and her feet are twisted. She was not expected to walk, but through force of will has achieved this. Her pain is variable, increasing as she gets older. Sometimes she can barely move.

I find Helen fascinatingly beautiful to look at, she has long red brown hair and she dresses in a creative way that both hides and yet does not hide the extent of her physical disabilities. Yet being the object of my gaze is hard for her, as the difficulty around looking is the very thing that embeds the discrimination that follows on the heels of difference.

Mostly I have not got a clue how to do it, how to manage the looking, how to face my inner objectification. I see a lot of disabled adults and children; I push my daughter in a wheelchair and receive the furtive, confused looks. I hear my client speak of her fear and rage at how people look at her, the commonplace taunts that children deliver, 'one armed bandit', 'cripple', whatever.

With disability we can feel the pull to look at distortion, to look outside the norm. As a body psychotherapist I talk about energy, which is also a bodily erotic experience and I believe there is a held back excitement in the unacknowledged inevitable permission to gaze at the difference.

The individual with a disability becomes identified with their body by the nature of their impairment. This may give a link, a commonality, to the trauma of abuse; I say this because disabled people statistically are more likely to be abused as a percentage of the population (Sobsey 1989). I am interested and scared by this. I can feel the appeal of force in the context of such vulnerability; the dynamic of helplessness and surrender is compelling. The feelings are forbidden, dangerous and disallowed, yet that is also the appeal. Therefore the fascination is internalised, hidden to keep it safe; it is even harder to own our erotic looking in this context.

What is in this fascination? Can it be seen as a positive thing, a trying to know, where we imagine ourselves into the body of the other – this time a disabled body? I feel that in my interest in the gnarled contours of Helen's legs, my fantasies about how it (the legs becoming an *it*) challenges my ideas of normal interaction. I see the knee that does not bend, that causes backache, restriction, unbearable pain and I am fascinated, maybe even aroused. I imagine trying to get it to bend to my will, to become normal somehow, not that I really want that, I like the difference – but maybe I like that it makes my own leg feel normal. I move from seeing the whole, to looking at her body in separate bits and part of me finds that satisfying. Energetically, in my body that feels a relief: as if paradoxically I am allowed to enjoy my own fragmentation more.

I have become enthralled with the gaps in my client's body; there are times when all I see is her absent arm. Increasingly I engage with what is missing, I dare to name and feel my objectification of her, becoming the object she most fears. I spent the first two years of our therapy seated in such a way that her less disabled side faced me. I stayed blind. I did not see that our seating positions re-enacted me not seeing the side of her body that held the gap most obviously, her missing left arm. It took a change of rooms for me to catch it and to notice the difference in my body when we sat directly facing each other in a more exposed way. I then chose to stay with the face-on seating arrangement, even though that was harder for Helen; it challenged the silence, a direct bodily confrontation that also contained our shifting dynamic.

The charge of the looking reveals a lot about attachment; at the point where I held my new seating position, it brought up excruciating feelings for Helen. In a move to show her my commitment to witnessing from this new place, I went to hold her right hand; she was sitting upright, I was facing her from her left side, beside her visible gap. It was intimate and personal; she spoke of not being able to hold her own hand. She described the feel of my skin to her touch, how my skin was softer than she expected; I felt uncovered in my flesh. The contact brought up her aloneness, emphasised now that she is single, and the question of whether there would ever be another 'other'. Or do the gaps, as is her fear, keep people away?

I learn that in staying close to the experience of her physical self, I am more available to the unconscious communication, so I can see now the scream that is hidden: 'Is anyone going to engage with what is missing in my body?' The pain is held in the simplest of body experiences, so the internal devils are allowed to be seen through this attention to detail.

These details can hurt. It is not fantasising in Helen's case about not having an arm – this is the real world. She told me about falling and cutting her right arm, her only arm. The terror it invoked of what would happen to her if she lost the crucial use of her arm. Then the helplessness and shame of having to go to a neighbour for help. This is about not being able to put cream on your arm or a plaster when you cut it because you don't have another arm to apply the aid. This is dependency and humiliation, how do we face that in the therapy room? The pain of it forced my dissociation, staying present with it palpable and vibrating in the room had become too much for me at that point. I could not take into vision what needed to be seen, her desperation.

So I fall: 'Have you been putting arnica on it?' I ask. Had I wanted to offer to tend to the wound literally? Probably. My desire to rescue blinds me to the foretasted fact – she can't! In asking this question I become the doer in our internal therapy world. Through my words I taste the shame she has described. But what do I do now as a body psychotherapist? As these seven words land in the room between us, I hit and feel my inability to stay with reality.

Helen is silent. She often questions if I understand and here I show my lack. Now I am the same as everyone else and I get to experience that inescapable fact. I am in the humiliation and feel done to, caught exposed in my blindness. After an agonising silence I say 'I can't believe I just said that!'

Yet for her my response is commonplace, it happens all the time. She shrugs. She senses my disgrace, it calls on her inner grace and she is spacious and allowing. How was it possible for her to do that? Did she need me to have gone through my internal fall, mirroring her real external fall? I believe so. It is a paradox but I get my answer: my job is to pull myself back into the experience from the inevitable dissociation, into my body and to feel the objectification from both sides of doing and being done to.

The unbearable as a way of life

I feel my desire in my writing to make you the reader flinch, to feel in your body a response to the pain I am attempting to unveil. *Why is that?* I long for deep penetration of the other and it is as if then I can feel the real impact in my body. Somehow with that achieved I can allow more softness and finally breathe. My client, who is an artist, reaches similar edges through her work, in her desire to bring the audience into the pain in a searing way; she grapples personally, using her body through performance art to have impact on the other.

This penetrative force is often present in the dynamic of the sessions. When Helen feels her impact on me personally she tends to relax a bit. Sometimes it is harsh and unyielding, other times gentler but insistent. I am thinking of her telling me about her love of hanging baskets and making them as a child with her grandfather; and the fact that she cannot have them in her own garden now. She cannot tend them with one arm, even if she got help with the planting she would not be able to do the ongoing maintenance safely. I started to cry, I just could not bear it and it was as if in that moment the entire world, of not being able to, for her and everyone, was held in that simple desire for hanging baskets. My tears were visible; I was deeply affected, raw and unable to hide. Finally she took a breath and said simply, 'You see it now'.

Weaved through our work is how to look at *the unbearable*. Her attempt to assimilate this leads to a project about how her body works in comparison to others, exploring frustration, pain and self-perception based on being 'looked at'. These (with her permission) are her words:

> This being the daily experience of being overwhelmed by feelings in rela-
> tion to my body and the inadequacy of language in being able to describe
> this experience. By allowing myself to enter into the places that felt
> impossible, has not made the unbearable bearable, but it has shown me
> that it is about finding ways to bear the unbearable.

She constantly questions the cost of her life and the pain she goes through to feel her aliveness. It hurts to walk, to dance, to allow her body to move in line with her spirit. To let out the burning intensity of her rage is deeply threatening. What do you do with all the intensity and objectification? It can feel like a loop of no release that in Helen's case habitually ends in self-destructiveness, so the anger, which needs external recognition, is expressed on the self violently in a hidden way. How then to metabolise, digest this rage and what brings it?

The challenge is to bring it into the relationship, in the hope of breaking the cycle or at least providing an access point to the experience. This is a messy process; Helen's life is complicated by her turning away from need both internally and externally, yet the denial seems to escalate the held back anger of unfulfilled entitlement. She hid her needs to survive; now as she traverses the terrain of her abandonment they cannot be escaped.

A complication of our work has been how I dealt initially with her self-harming. I saw it as a symptom of her response to being disabled, and I underestimated the serious effect of decades of addictive misuse of food. It was a few years into the therapy before I challenged this behaviour. I think here my sensitivity to disability stopped me separating and naming what she was actually doing to herself and her body on a daily basis. So looking through one lens distorted my vision. Another type of blindness, perhaps; I could not bear adding another label to her already over-diagnosed existence. My fear of objectifying meant I failed to be objective.

I constantly feel pulled apart. Should I be treating her differently? As I highlighted earlier, I accommodate Helen in special ways to help contain her self-harming. Her relationship with food and alcohol is conflicted and her self-attacks increase when the work intensifies. To hold the more dangerous affects, she sends me a phone text and I respond. This can happen daily during the week if she manages not to act out; it is a motivation. She also texts at night on occasions if she is about to be sick. The contact seems to help her manage the attack better. It means I think of her daily and she knows that. It also highlights the relational context of her destructiveness. It has helped her see that she might also be sick if I let her down. It gives us access to her earlier feelings of rage with her mother. She started to use food in an effort to control her world from the age of eighteen months when she was in hospital and her mother was not there. She was bulimic all through her late teens, always hiding this from those around her. In their weekly phone calls her mother often asks her if she is eating properly, to which she responds 'yes'.

Yet am I participating in a potentially explosive arrangement in offering her increased access to me outside of the therapy frame, through texts or email contact during my longer breaks? Because it pushes me to my limits, I have to manage my response when I experience how constant demand kills desire. I can feel resentful about the personal cost to me of the work and the access which I give her. The texts disturb my personal space; I struggle to separate my own therapeutic exhaustion from the demands and restrictions on myself as a mother with a child who is disabled. When I hold boundaries with her I feel mean in the face of her serious social and emotional isolation. I can feel unseen by her and caught in the countertransference of the inadequate lame mother, but worrying at the same time about my personal identification and lack of detachment.

Through all of this I am aware how the work is steeped in parallel process. My supervisor and I go to the edge of the relationship to the border with psychotherapy, walking a tightrope between personal process and professional support. It is a living force between us, fuelling the co-creation that Helen and

I have established. It can feel perilous yet my supervisor's presence offers a bridge, mapping this step-by-step journey to mutuality.

When I, in parallel with my client, feel that I simply can't manage, I require tighter holding and more time in supervision. My longing to be held, to hold my daughter and my client exist like a physical yearning in the room. At other times I experience the penetrative desire for impact on my supervisor, mirroring the dynamic between me and Helen. Using the information from these re-enacted feelings provides relief and clears my vision. It helps navigate these personal, practical and psychological borderlands and supports my position that this deeply paralleled way of working is therapeutically key. The disability context adds to the emotional potency of this parallel process.

As I look at the title of the chapter I feel again the deep conflict of the question: can we look? And if we look can we see? I am not sure. Helen speaks frequently of feeling unseen and criticised by me, that I would understand and empathise more if I saw just how much energy it takes for her to survive. The cost of walking up the hill on her way home exhausted; how labour intensive it is to prepare food or clean her flat; how unsettling a fall of snow is when she can't walk her dog as her already precarious balance is disrupted and it becomes dangerous.

I believe I do see her. But I can be tough in response to her daily problems as I assert my professional opinion that she has to defend against her self-harming attacks. At times I feel the awful one who is resolutely uncaring, forcing her to look, to defend; I become like her father whose determination forced her to walk. I stop seeing her pain in order to look at the overall picture.

This is edgy work. Often we are both there in the therapy room feeling as unseen as each other, both hurting, attempting to scramble for meaning. The dynamic of doer and done to is constant, but by working through the dynamics of this barren objectivity there can be hope of a third place, where we find each other again. This is reached through the intersubjectivity of an embodied relational approach.

An example of this is through me acknowledging my harsh response to her. After a weekend where she had been self-harming, I found myself pulling at my hair in the session. It felt impossible. I got her to lie down reluctantly; she spoke of me being far away. I felt far away. I said aloud 'I can't do it'. I felt spent. After a pause she cried deeply: 'This is how I feel all the time and I send myself and other people away'. The harsh force in her was tangible in the room, instead of hidden in the vomiting. I was able to move towards her then and hold her hand from my heart. She was with her deep aloneness and I felt some softness again, more space created to bear more looking.

Ending thoughts

Inevitably, disability is political. I believe that majority culture cannot cope with disability and thus unconsciously splits off from it and unknowingly projects the 'outsider mentality' onto the disabled person. This split creates an internal defensive construction in us all which allows prejudice to form. As therapists this response must be examined.

In my work with Helen I have chosen an engaged human approach where both of us are prepared to be affected and changed, with the assumption that knowing is better than not knowing, seeing is better than not. This means holding the conflict of the relational therapeutic implications and facing the pitfalls of a lack of healthy detachment. It requires surrender to helplessness, yet a commitment to remaining present in the witnessing.

Through all the difficulties of our work, Helen's desire to communicate the impossible – where her hesitation, thoughts and effort show how something overwhelming could be translated into something coherent and understandable – is fundamental to her existence. This quality of looking in spite of it all is inspiring.

I see the work of looking at the disabled body as a voyage into vulnerability, being swept viscerally by deep feelings that are just about held together by cognition, keenly expressed by the writer Mary Jane Owen:

> Those of us with disabilities are precisely the people who prove to society how frail and vulnerable the human creature is. We prove in every way that the 'it' can happen to anyone anywhere anytime, that reality often frightens non disabled people into avoiding us.
>
> It also frightens many of us. We know from the gut out what it feels like to have some system of the body fall apart. The sword has fallen and broken our thin thread of potential perfection. We are already flawed, it happened once and it can happen again and again.
>
> Maybe we have learned to compensate at our present level of functioning. But what about the next assault? How much can we be expected to overcome? We are vulnerable in the worst way to the future.
>
> (Owen 1994: 8)

References

Asch, A. and Rousso, H. (1985) Therapist with disabilities: theoretical and clinical issues. *Psychiatry* 48(1): 1–12.

Davis, K. (2004) The crafting of good clients. In: Swain, J., French, S., Barnes, C. and Thomas, C. (eds) *Disabling Barriers – Enabling Environments*. London: Sage Publications.

Ernst, S. (1997) The therapy relationship. In: Lawrence, M. and Maguire, M. (eds) *Psychotherapy with Women*. Basingstoke: Macmillan.

Lenny, J. (1993) Do disabled people need counseling? In: Swain, J., Finkelstein, V., French, S., Barnes, C. and Oliver, M. (eds) *Disabling Barriers – Enabling Environments*. London: Sage and Open University Press, pp. 233–240.

Olkin, R. (1999) *What Psychotherapists Should Know About Disability*. New York: Guilford Press.

Owen, M. J. (1994) Like squabbling cubs. In: Shaw, B. (ed.) *The Ragged Edge: The Disability Experience from the Pages of the First Fifteen Years of the Disability Rag.* Louisville, KY: Avocado Press, pp. 7–10.

Sinason, V. (1992) *Mental Handicap and the Human Condition, New Approaches from the Tavistock.* London: Free Association Books.

Sinason, V. (1997) W is for woman. In: Lawrence, M. and Maguire, M. (eds) *Psychotherapy with Women.* Basingstoke: Macmillan.

Sobsey, D. (1989) Sexual offences: research and implications. *Transition* (May): 17–18.

Wendell, S. (1996) *The Rejected Body: Feminist Philosophical Reflections on Disability.* New York: Routledge.

Wilson, S. (2003) *Disability, Counselling and Psychotherapy: Challenges and Opportunities.* Basingstoke: Palgrave Macmillan.

Chapter 11

Towards an integrative model of trauma therapy

Morit Heitzler

This chapter describes an integrative model for trauma work, using a case study to illustrate the stages of the unfolding therapeutic process. Each stage is followed by a discussion which explores my thinking and the different therapeutic approaches and techniques I have used. My focus is on the potential – and the difficulties – of integrating the diverse and often contradictory approaches within an overall holistic and relational framework.

The term 'trauma' is often used loosely to describe a wide range of disturbing individual or collective experiences. In contrast to frustration, pain, anger and disappointment which constitute an integral part of human life, this chapter focuses on trauma as a life-threatening experience, with a specific impact on the bodymind system, diagnosable as post-traumatic stress disorder.

Background to case illustration

D. was referred to the Traumatic Stress Service at the Maudsley Hospital following a suicide attempt. A 59-year-old man, his life had taken a dramatic turn two years earlier. When trying to stop a group of young thugs from assaulting someone, D. was badly beaten up. He was treated for multiple injuries, but beyond the necessary medical procedures and investigations was expected to recover fully within a short time. Nothing had prepared D. for what was to follow: he was unable to go back to work, or even leave his house alone. He was constantly haunted by memories of the assault, unable to sleep and plagued by fear and frequent panic attacks. Everything reminded him of the assault and he found no means of escaping from intrusive flashbacks. He could not understand his feelings and was ashamed about being out of control.

An introverted, shy, working-class man, D. belonged to a generation that believed 'if you do not think about it, it will go away'. He spoke to nobody about the inner hell consuming him. But, despite his wife's admonition to 'just forget about it and move on', his insomnia, depression and panic continued to build until eventually D. attempted suicide.

At the Traumatic Stress Service D. was diagnosed with post-traumatic stress disorder following a single traumatic event, and offered 12 sessions with an option to continue for another 12 following a review. This was different from the open-ended contract I was used to, and I therefore approached our first session with a mixture of excitement, anxiety and curiosity.

A person suffering from PTSD is chronically 'stuck' in the experience of the traumatic event and – to various degrees and on various levels – re-lives it over and over again, as if it were happening in the present moment. The activated 'fight–flight' response continues to release the same chemicals and neurotransmitters as if trapped in an ongoing life-threatening situation. The person often experiences 'flashbacks' which 'involve highly disturbing replays of implicit sensory memories of traumatic events, sometimes with explicit recall, sometimes without' (Rothschild 2000: 45). They may also develop avoidance behaviour, trying to anticipate and avoid any trigger that could re-activate the trauma.

As trauma is essentially experienced in the body, PTSD symptoms also manifest through somatic disturbances and dissociation (Herman 1992: 42; de Zulueta 2002: 53; Levine 1997: 136).

PTSD significantly alters brain function. Research shows that not only during the traumatic event itself, but also during any acute re-experiencing of it, it is mainly the brain stem and the limbic system which are activated. The left hemisphere of the cortex is shut down (van der Kolk et al. 1996: 293). Functions such as the ability to talk, to process information on a cognitive level, to differentiate between past and present, to make sense and find meaning, are unavailable during any re-experiencing of the trauma and chronically impaired even between episodes of re-traumatisation. People who are locked in a traumatised state find it exceedingly difficult to talk, understand or make sense of what has happened, and do not benefit from trying to do so. They need to be met on a different level, corresponding to those levels of their brain that are functioning.

The limbic system regulates the autonomic nervous system (ANS) which has two branches: the sympathetic nervous system (SNS) and the parasympathetic nervous system (PrNS). When the limbic system activates first the sympathetic branch of the ANS to meet the danger, and later the parasympathetic to recover from it, these are normal, healthy responses. What turns these responses into PTSD is the chronic simultaneous arousal of the two branches, long after the threat has passed and been survived.

There are different types of trauma:

1   Single event trauma: an incident that occurs once, usually in adult life, typically involving unexpected, sudden shock.
2   Developmental trauma: occurs in childhood and usually carries elements of neglect or abuse. This has a deeper impact on the psychological and physiological structure as it affects the developing child's perception of self and other, and strongly impairs the capacity for self-regulation. This type of prolonged traumatic experience can lead to the development of complex PTSD (Herman 1992) or disorder of extreme stress (van der Kolk *et al.* 1996).

In my practice, I have often encountered clients who sought treatment for a single-event trauma, whilst reporting some symptoms of complex PTSD. They have managed to dissociate memories and feelings of early trauma, to function with some degree of success by numbing, self-medicating, etc. (van der Kolk *et al.* 1996: 282). They have accepted the neurotic equilibrium governing their lives as given, until a recent traumatic event disturbed this shaky foundation. During the process of working with the body and unpacking layers of defences, the connection between the developmental trauma and the recent event can be made.

The human capacity to recover from a single traumatic event is partly influenced by the robustness of a person's emotional resources. People who have experienced a disorganised or insecure attachment (Ogden *et al.* 2006: 48–58) and were not able to internalise a 'good-enough' object, lack the sense of safety and confidence in themselves and the world, and are therefore unable to build a solid foundation of emotional and indeed physiological internal resources. At the root of *any* level of PTSD, then, lies some degree of developmental trauma.

First steps: creating the 'container'

D. arrived for our first session meticulously dressed in a suit and shook my hand nervously. He told me he finds it hard to talk about what happened, and although he desperately wants to get better, he does not want to remember or talk about 'that dreadful night'. He proceeded to tell me about his avoidance tactics: not leaving the house, not talking to people, not watching TV and minimising contact with any stimulus that might trigger a memory or a flashback. This indicated that his trauma was not integrated into a narrative which he could assimilate, contain and share; and that any attempt to demand that he share it could result in re-traumatisation.

My first intention was to establish a working alliance. I gave D. some general information about trauma, PTSD and the typical symptoms of this condition. I explained the physiological mechanisms linked to his flashbacks and panic attacks and acknowledged the psychological purpose of avoidance behaviour as a means of controlling his terror and rage and preserving his sanity.

After using this kind of 'psycho-education' to acknowledge, normalise and make sense of his feelings, we discussed his wish to heal and connect with life again. I suggested a treatment plan which D. expressed enthusiasm to embark on, whilst voicing his anxieties and concerns. At this point, it felt as though we were working as a team, thinking together and sharing our experiences.

In the sessions that followed we worked mostly towards establishing D.'s safe place and looking at his resources. During this time, we hardly talked about the assault and did not specifically focus on PTSD symptoms, staying instead with the first key steps in trauma work – building a safe foundation, and learning the language of the body by tracking the sensations and impulses arising in it (Ogden et al. 2006).

I invited D. to tell me about his family and background. His father was a rigid authoritarian man, a sergeant in the military police, then a prison warden, who also had a successful career as a boxing champion. His mother was a soft, gentle woman, bullied by an aggressive husband who often beat her up. She was unable to protect D. from his father's violence and he was also regularly bullied and beaten. Throughout his childhood D. felt he had to protect his mother, and it was he who, at the age of eight, called the police to rescue his mother from one particularly violent attack. From that day on, the father was explicitly sadistic and cruel towards D., humiliating and assaulting him verbally and physically. D. tried to run away from home a few times but had nowhere to go and felt obliged to return and protect his mother. Prior to this therapy, D. had never talked about his childhood with anybody. Feelings of shame and humiliation – so common in childhood abuse survivors – dominated his perceptions and made him feel guilty and contaminated. He had never made any connection between the first years of his life and the recent assault.

The unpacking of the traumatic event is a painful and demanding process. The client's bodymind system is geared towards avoidance, numbing and suppression of the unbearable memories. These avoidance tactics function with the force of a survival instinct that guides the client toward protecting himself from whatever – in his perception – poses a danger to his psychological integrity. Yet, there is also an impulse in the system towards a true healing that can occur only when the suppressed and denied parts of the experience can be integrated and processed. This conflict, as well as the potentially explosive traumatic material itself, requires a solid, safe and sensitively attuned 'container'.

In working with trauma, the containing function of the therapeutic relationship acquires extra significance, as the trauma has usually been experienced in isolation. Even if other people were involved, as perpetrators, passive witnesses or fellow victims, the subjective reality of the victim is that no-one was there, leaving him to face possible death on his own. Feelings of shame, humiliation and helplessness contribute to this prevailing sense of isolation, and the internalised sense of guilt and badness prevents the victim from reaching out and accepting – let alone initiating – any contact. In situations where the victim is threatened into secrecy, the sense of isolation is more extreme and creates a secondary layer of trauma.

Establishing a relationship in which the traumatised person can share his experience is crucial to trauma work. It is often a slow and tentative journey in which the client needs to test again and again the therapist's capacity to contain the horror of the traumatic experience without being destroyed or overwhelmed by it. In order to pass the client's unconscious tests of her and eventually become the 'containing other', it is crucial that the therapist can demonstrate her capacity to carry both negative and positive transferential feelings. A client who has suffered harm at the hands of others finds it extremely hard to trust that harm is not going to be part of the current relationship and will search the therapist for hidden motivations and investments. He is likely to scan her for non-verbal signals such as tone of voice, directness of eye contact, body movements etc. Like an animal in danger, the traumatised client relies on such flashes of perception and is hypersensitive to the tiniest indication of possible threat or betrayal.

In body psychotherapy this way of perceiving the other through attunement is called 'energetic perception'. The client's experience of the therapist as the safe containing object is measured not by the verbal cognitive exchange between them, but by the client's energetic perception of the therapist's embodied presence and the sense of congruence between the therapist's verbal and energetic messages. This level of relating depends on the therapist's moment-to-moment attunement to her own bodymind responses – to the client, the trauma and the transferential relationship which is constellated in the room. It is only when the therapist can attend to the client and herself as an embodied system that she can provide a container that might feel safe enough for the client.

The next important step is the establishment of a 'safe place': a concrete, observable resource, anchored in the client's life – either now or in the past. It is not an internalised resource like self-confidence. It is a current or remembered site of safety and protection, ideally 'an actual, earthly location that the client has known in life' (Rothschild 2000: 95). When imagining himself in this safe place, the somatic resonance via its smells, colours, sensations and feelings needs to be strong enough to generate an embodied experience of its safety in the present moment.

As the client's bodymind system reconnects with such a sense of safety and pleasure, the triggers activating the arousal of the ANS lose their affective charge and balance is restored. Only when the therapist is confident that the ANS is able to tolerate the level of possible re-traumatisation created by the current processing of trauma can she invite the client to engage further. This limited capacity to bear the internal reactions to traumatising triggers and stimuli is also known as 'window of tolerance' (Ogden *et al.* 2006: 26). Thus, working with the safe place is one of the most effective tools in helping hyper-aroused clients to re-experience the safety of the 'window of tolerance', thus regaining trust in their ability to self-regulate and restore equilibrium.

Other factors crucial to creating a safe container for trauma work include: setting out a clear contract and therapeutic boundaries for the work, re-establishing the client's sense of control of his body and thus safety, and supporting the client in regaining connection with his own power and potential by working with his resources (Rothschild 2000: 88).

The fragmented narrative and the interrupted impulse

Having established the working alliance and some level of understanding of PTSD, identified a safe place and supported the client's resources, as well as gained some insight into D.'s traumatic developmental background, it was time to actively engage with processing the trauma. In our fifth session I invited D. to imagine himself in his garden, the place identified by him as safe. Together we welcomed the sense of calmness and expansion in his body evoked by the familiar images.

I then asked D. to tell me of the events that took place prior to the assault. In describing this, D.'s breath became shallow and he started showing signs of hyperarousal. I asked him to stop and imagine himself back in his safe place, this time actively describing to him some of the images he had shared with me previously. After a few minutes, D.'s breathing stabilised and his body showed signs of relaxation.

Going back to the details of that evening, D. was now able to describe himself feeling scared and intrigued by the sights and noises of the gathering in the shopping mall. Soon his body showed signs of hyper-arousal again, which I pointed out to him, naming the different bodily manifestations, and suggested that he 'go back' again to his safe place. As the level of arousal in his body reduced, I invited D. to tell me about the end of that evening, skipping the actual trauma itself. When his body began to show signs of hyper-stimulation, I invited him to gain control by imagining his place of safety again. D. expressed his appreciation for the rhythm of our work, which had enabled him to feel 'for the first time as if there is hope for me, as if I could do this work and heal'.

We continued working with this method for the next few sessions, narrowing the cycles of the story, until D. was able to tell me the full narrative and describe in detail what had happened before, during and after the traumatic event. His painful story was revealed in increasing detail, with events he had previously 'forgotten' returning to complete the picture. As D. began to integrate the full story, his nightmares became less frequent and less overwhelming.

As we worked on the narrative of the trauma, we paid attention to spontaneous impulses in D.'s body. I encouraged D. to stay in contact with his body sensations and slowly he learned to express them in movements, words and images. A new connection was established between his body, until now largely disconnected and objectified, and his feelings, for which he was acquiring a language of symbols and images. D. was beginning to experience himself as a 'whole' being, and was able to engage more in the relationship with me. He began seeing me less as the 'medical expert' and more as the 'good mother', in whose eyes his emerging sense of self could be positively reflected.

The centrality of narrative to trauma work has been a point of consensus among practitioners of many approaches. It is through the re-telling of the narrative that the split-off fragments of the dissociated experience can be integrated and reclaimed, symbolisation can take place, and a sense of meaning and acceptance be gained. By sharing the details of the story, the client allows the therapist to bear witness to the pain, fear and humiliation which he experienced in isolation, to validate and normalise his feelings and celebrate his survival.

However, most PTSD clients find it impossible to re-tell the story without re-living it, thus causing re-traumatisation. Therefore, one of the aims of trauma therapy is to help the client to 'be able to tell the story of the shocking event without totally reliving it' (van der Kolk *et al.* 1996: 431). That implies closely monitoring hyperarousal and dissociation signals, both of which indicate that the client is no longer able to distinguish between past and present and his sensorimotor system is flooded. The therapist's overall aim is, therefore, to work within the 'window of tolerance'.[1]

There are many useful techniques to monitor and regulate the hyper-arousal during the process of narrative telling (Rothschild 2000; Levine 1997). In my work with D., I used the concept of the 'safe space' and the idea of working with the three stages of the traumatic incident – *before, during* and *after* the trauma (Rothschild 2000: 156); the therapist helps the client focus first on the less triggering parts of the experience, arriving slowly at the heart of the actual traumatic event. Working in this way, the client can reclaim the full experience of the trauma whilst having a sense of control over the process, which is crucial to this stage of the work.

Once D. had begun to tell his story and integrate some of its split-off fragments, he connected with what in body psychotherapy is called the 'interrupted impulse', i.e. the impulse to complete the vaso-motoric cycle towards expression, discharge and relaxation (Boyesen and Boyesen 1981, 1982; see also chapter by Schaible). However, during a traumatic event, powerful enough to threaten survival, the charge accumulating in the system is much higher than in response to day-to-day stimuli. This level of energy cannot be discharged as long as the amygdala (limbic system) perceives the threat as ongoing and therefore continues to stimulate ANS reactions. As the ANS activates more physiological and biochemical mechanisms to deal with the perceived threat, the charge in the body intensifies beyond endurance. At this point, the process of dissociation kicks in, disconnecting the hyperaroused energy from the person's awareness and thus preventing the dangerous 'full-ness' of the experience in the moment. So begins a self-perpetuating cycle in which the ANS is only able to recognise that the threat has passed when the accumulated energy is discharged, but no discharge can happen as long as the ANS is locked in its freezing response. The only way out of the cycle is to activate the SNS impulse (i.e. the fight–flight response) which is blocked under the 'lid' of the PrNS.

If the impulse towards expression and discharge is stopped or interrupted, the vaso-motoric cycle cannot complete itself and reach the relaxation stage. The impulse, however, does not disappear, as the energy inherent in the blocked cycle is constantly motivated towards completion. Rather, the inter-rupted impulse manifests unconsciously and non-verbally (e.g. in small movements or sounds, shifts in the breathing pattern or changes in the direc-tion of the eyes). In D.'s case it took the shape of his right hand forming a fist. If this interrupted impulse is not followed and encouraged towards full expression, the blocked energy usually creates somatic disturbances. For D., this led to constant pain running from his right shoulder down his arm. However, as more split-off fragments of the traumatic event were integrated, the interrupted impulse acquired increasing force and presence, indicating that the blocked energy was more available and ready to be worked with.

Accessing and processing developmental trauma

With intimacy and trust deepening, D. began to share more childhood memories with me. It seemed that the growing connection between his body and its spontaneous impulses unlocked a gateway to more than just factual memories. D. was now experiencing in the sessions some of his early feelings, physical sensations and energetic states. Being in the room with him as he recalled his childhood, I had a clear sense in my own body of the degree of terror, pain, humiliation and helplessness that were his perpetual reality for so many years. Processing some of these early memories in parallel to his recent trauma, D. became aware of the close connection between them.

In our tenth session D. told me – noticeably agitated – of a dream involving an impatient, aggressive man who physically resembled D.'s father: he appeared from nowhere and cut off D.'s toes with a large axe. This dream precipitated a significant memory of an emotionally and physically abusive episode that took place when D. was nine.

Sensing how the relationship with the abusive father presented itself in the room at this highly charged moment, I invited D. to imagine his father sitting in the chair opposite him. D. was distressed, but not over-whelmed. It seemed that he carried in his body a felt sense of his resources, his power and his wholeness, all of which assisted him in addressing his internalised father as an external presence. What followed was a fifteen-minute 'two-chair work' (see chapter by Reynolds) in which D. told his father what he felt towards him as a child and as a growing adult, expressing in a clear and profound way all that had been blocked and suppressed for many years: his rage, shame, fear, humiliation and pain vibrated powerfully in the room, culminating in D.'s demand for meaning: 'Why did you treat me like that? I was your only son, why did you hate me?'

We ended the session with a recall of the safe place and some of D.'s resources. After this session, he had a dream in which his father appeared, not disguised as somebody else, but clear and realistic; now his presence did not evoke fear or distress in D. During the following week, D.'s nightmares stopped, he was able to go out, and felt better than he had for a long time. Something profound had shifted in him. Now it was time to attend to the most persistent aspects of PTSD: flashbacks and psychosomatic symptoms.

The assault had unearthed some early and formative traumatic experiences. As D. regressed back to the frightened, helpless child he had been, memories of his abusive father and of specific traumatic events surfaced. When unprocessed developmental trauma is triggered, it is not possible to work through recent situational trauma without attending to the early layer first. As illustrated through research by van der Kolk *et al.* (1996) and recent neuroscientific studies (Schore 1994; Damasio 1994), the infant's capacity for affect regulation and his ability to make contact are determined by the quality of his primal bond. A disorganised attachment will impair the child's ability to regulate states of hyperarousal and will probably make these already traumatised individuals vulnerable to further traumatisation. When an early trauma is trigged by a recent event, it is therefore impossible for the client to regulate states of arousal during therapy, or use the therapeutic relationship as a potential resource until the early trauma has been addressed and contained.

During and after the assault, D. experienced similar feelings to those that characterised his relationship with his father: fear of annihilation, helplessness and unexpressed rage that turned into self-blame and depression. It is as if the recent event was a condensed snap-shot re-enactment of the violent abuse he had suffered for many years.

D. had remained unconscious of this link because he was attached to the 'bad object' (Fairbairn 1952). In his desperate need to preserve his attachment to his father, D. needed to dissociate from experiences and memories which might threaten that life-giving bond. This is a common defence among children who have suffered abuse at the hand of their primary caregivers (de Zulueta 2002: 56). As I began to provide the 'good mother' figure, including the support and containment that was missing in D's relationship with his frightened, obedient mother, D.'s growing attachment to me enabled him to shift some of the early attachment needs from his abusive father to the transferentially idealised mother-ally I became for him. This, then, enabled him to address his internalised father figure in a way that had not been possible before.

Of course, the dialogue with the internalised father did not constitute a thorough working-through of all the layers and implications of his developmental trauma. In working with D.'s suppressed anger we were addressing the top layer, which had become available to be processed at this stage. Underneath, I could sense a layer of primal longing for parental love and acceptance, which was unconscious in D.'s relationship with his father. This illustrates the splitting that often occurs in people who were abused as children between the 'good' and the 'bad' object (see Warnecke's chapter). In this case, all the 'good' was projected onto me and I became the carrier of the idealised parent. Working through this layer would require a longer process than I was able to offer within the constraints of the setting. However, I do believe that this session, being a fully embodied and expressive experience, was an important stepping-stone towards acknowledging and containing the early dynamics.

The second non-threatening dream of his father indicated that one of the many unfinished cycles in this abusive primary relationship had come to completion. I felt that D. would now be more available to process the recent traumatic event.

EMDR

D. felt more able to engage with his life and family and to distinguish between past and present events. Our work now focussed on his self-persecutory judgment of himself as 'bad, weak and stupid'. D. believed that he had 'caused' the assault by voluntarily stepping in to help the security guard. Feelings of guilt and shame fuelled his self-destructive rage. None of this was affected by verbal discussion as his negative beliefs were anchored in an early stage of development and carried primitive unconscious material, not amenable to rational reflection. I decided to use EMDR to process this part of the trauma.

The part of the event that evoked most distress for him was the moment when he was squashed under a pile of bodies and felt he could not breathe. His negative belief about himself in recalling that moment was: 'I am helpless, I am going to die'. As we talked about it, the level of distress in his body rose. What he would have liked to have thought about himself in the peak of his distress was: 'I will be helped, I will survive'. Although this thought seemed unreal to him, he felt it to be comforting. As we focussed on his body sensations I was aware of the energetic charge escalating in his system. It was time to start our work with the eye movements.

EMDR (eye movement desensitisation and reprocessing) was developed by Francine Shapiro (2001). In using this method, the therapist helps the client recall the memory of the trauma, starting with fragments of the experience which the client can recall readily: images, physical sensations and mental cognition. The therapist then provides some form of bilateral stimulation which can be achieved visually, kinaesthetically or auditorily.

What follows resembles a process of free association, as the client enters a dream-like state, in which images, memories and thoughts arise spontaneously. The therapist does not interpret or invite cognitive discussion of the material that surfaces into consciousness. After a while, clients usually report a noticeable reduction in their physical and emotional distress, recognising the trauma as a past event. This allows a more positive sense of self to replace the former negative cognition.[2]

By introducing EMDR, I was aiming to complete the process of retrieving split-off fragments of the trauma, and felt that we were ready to tackle what seemed to be the main obstacle to his recovery – D.'s sense of guilt and regret. D.'s suicide attempt was an expression of 'survivor guilt' (Garwood 2002). As de Zulueta states: 'By feeling they are to blame, they [the survivors] are at least feeling more in control of what has happened to them. It is a normal response in the face of the terrible sense of helplessness they experienced at the time of the traumatic event' (de Zulueta 2002: 55). She continues: 'This "moral defence" . . . is particularly prevalent in victims of childhood abuse and can best be understood by referring to research in the field of attachment' (ibid.).

D.'s obsessive cycles of shame, guilt and remorse may have served, in a vicarious way, to maintain some sense of control, but they also perpetuated his negative belief about his helplessness and powerlessness, a belief he had carried since early childhood. No cognitive discussion could alter this belief as it was not based on a rational thought process. As long as D.'s sense of self was stuck in that guilt-ridden regressed position, he was unable to follow any of his body-impulses towards the fight–flight reaction, and thus his hyperaroused system could not discharge.

Integrating EMDR and body psychotherapy

As we began processing the charged image with eye movements, D. felt the tension in his body intensifying, and an overwhelming feeling of helplessness. He used the 'stop' signal we had agreed on, which gave him a sense of control and enabled him to choose to continue after a short break. We then did another 'set' of eye movements, and D. again experienced himself suffocating at the bottom of the aggressive heap. This feeling manifested in a rapidly growing charge in his arms and legs. I noticed signs of activation of the SNS (this time without the lid of the PrNS), and encouraged D. to sense the impulse in his arms and legs. He felt a strong spontaneous urge to kick with his legs and push with his arms. I stopped the eye movements and invited him to follow the impulse. D. did not need further prompting; within seconds he was standing in the centre of the room, pushing and kicking, shouting: 'Get off me! Get off!'

His face was red, his hair dishevelled, he had a wild look in his eyes. As he screamed 'I will not let you do this to me! I am going to fight you back!', I realised that I was witnessing a transformative moment. A surge of energy that had been blocked and denied for many years was finding expression, and with it surfaced feelings that had perhaps been too dangerous to feel before: anger, aggression, assertion. D. did not need encouragement or approval; it seemed that he was celebrating his newly found sense of power and freedom. My role was to witness, my presence providing the container and safety for this spontaneous process. Gradually, D.'s breathing calmed, his face acquired its familiar colour, and his body relaxed. He realised that the target-image and negative cognition were far less real and threatening than they had been at the beginning of our session, whilst the positive cognition seemed to be more real.

D. said that when he was pushing and shouting he saw the young assailant's face (which until that moment had been a dissociated fragment) and that this image kept changing into his father's face, and then again into the assailant's face. For the first time D. was able to feel compassion towards the child he had been, unable to protect himself against his father's sadistic assaults, and to see clearly that the violent abuse was not his fault. The session ended after D. again recalled his safe place. His parting remark was: 'I feel as if I have grown taller and wider, I feel so much bigger in my body!'

This session illustrates the power and potential of integrating several therapeutic approaches into the present moment. All the work we had done up to now came together, which enabled D. to break through layers of suppressed emotions and repressed impulses.

I could have continued to work solely with EMDR, rather than inviting D. to move into bodywork, because the way the session had evolved would have been clearly within the understanding and expectations of traditional EMDR practice. Indeed, many EMDR sessions with other clients have demonstrated to me that the level of distress in the system *does* subside, and had I chosen to continue EMDR work with D., the same would have probably happened.

What prompted me to integrate a body psychotherapy approach at that charged moment was my belief that, for profound change to happen, all fragments of the experience as well as all aspects of the person must come together and be felt and expressed (Soth 2005). In D.'s case, 'all fragments of the experience' include his early developmental trauma which resulted in suppression of his healthy aggression and led to a distorted self-image ('It is all my fault'), coupled with and echoed by the recent traumatic event in which he was again as violated and helpless as before. In re-experiencing the most highly charged moment of the latter, the two scenarios came together in the consulting room, manifest in D.'s vision of the faces of the two aggressors morphing into one another. Together, they reflected D.'s internal reality where the two traumas were being implicitly experienced as one.

At that significant moment, it was necessary to encourage what is always absent and fragmented in trauma: the embodied experience of feelings, images and cognitions coming together and being expressed in a relational context. As D. was standing in the centre of the room, shaking his fists against his aggressive father and the young attacker, many cycles came to completion simultaneously. Physically and energetically, the blocked fight-or-flight reflex was released from suppression by the PrNS, and the freezing reaction no longer stopped spontaneous expression. As this cycle of healthy reaction to threat was activated and completed, it appears that the various parts of the brain were able to resume their balanced activity; now D. was able to remember while connected to his feelings, and talk while differentiating between past and present.

At the same time, the stuck emotional cycle of D.'s blocked feelings towards his father found some completion as he was now able to do what had been impossible as a child: to stand up for himself and defend his rights for safety and respect. Transferentially, I think I was experienced then as a mother who did not need him to sacrifice his power in order to protect her, but who could be present and welcoming as he celebrated it.

On a cognitive level, the stuck cyclic activity of the brainstem, which reinforced the neurotic conclusion 'It is all my fault' could now give way to an acknowledgement of the father's cruelty.

The bringing together of *all* levels of the trauma, and the integration of D.'s newly found sense of himself, facilitated the transformation. The result of completing all the blocked cycles, on the physical, emotional and mental levels, was a feeling of expansion.

Ending

Following this, the pain in D.'s shoulder disappeared, as did the numbness in his lower body. He had no further flashbacks or nightmares after that session, and felt able to resume his role as head of the family. He now took steps towards finding voluntary work. He looked alive and happy, and was able to repeat the narrative of the assault without feeling overwhelmed, keeping a clear differentiation between past and present. I knew we were approaching the end of our work together, as D. was no longer a PTSD patient.

With his new-found confidence, D. was able to face one of the last triggers of post-traumatic fear. Together with his son, and later by himself, he went back to the location of the trauma. 'It looked so ordinary', he told me, 'just a normal shopping mall. I looked at it and felt normal myself.'

By now D. was attached to me as the idealised 'good object' he had longed for throughout his childhood. In my countertransference I felt protective and loving towards his budding sense of worth and hope. Although I was aware that we had not processed all layers of transferential feelings, I trusted the good work we had done together.

Conclusion

This chapter introduces an integrative model for trauma work, based on an integration of body psychotherapy principles with EMDR and attachment theory, the latter being one of the key factors in understanding complex trauma. My thinking was informed by neuroscientific research and an understanding of how the brain functions following trauma. I used guided imagery, gestalt dialogue, resource building, tracking and body reading as well as somatic experiencing techniques.

Whilst a relational perspective (Davis and Frawley 1994) is part of my integrative model, in this case several layers of the transference remained implicit and unaddressed.[3] However, by closely monitoring my countertransferential responses, I stayed attuned to such transferential vicissitudes which informed my therapeutic presence throughout all stages of the work.

I have described elsewhere my model of change and integration in therapy (Heitzler 2004). For the purpose of this discussion, I believe that the key principles for integrative trauma work are:

- working with the body
- energetic attunement
- attachment patterns
- resolution of incomplete cycles
- relational perspective.

Many of the approaches discussed in this chapter are taught and practised as comprehensive and complete methods of trauma work. I believe, however, that it was the flexible integration of all these principles into my work, coupled with D.'s courage and determination to heal, that enabled the process to unfold more fully towards change and transformation.

This chapter describes the unfolding of a relatively short and successful process, illustrating one possible way of working integratively with complex trauma. Although this case encapsulates my key beliefs and therapeutic principles, it is by no means typical, as I often experience frustratingly slow, stuck or incomplete processes which challenge me on all levels.

Often, when working with trauma survivors, I feel as if I am called to bear witness to intolerable levels of human suffering. In writing this chapter I wanted to appreciate those privileged moments in which I was called to bear witness to the innate human capacity for healing and growth.

Notes

1 Current research, however, demonstrates the importance of working *at the edges* of the window of affect tolerance. In a talk given recently in London, Schore (2007) argued that only by working in a 'safe but not *too* safe' way, inviting the arousal at the edges of the window of tolerance, necessary transformative enactments can occur in the therapeutic relationship, resulting ultimately in 'expansion of the regulatory boundaries'.
2 Although there is as yet no satisfying detailed explanation for the rapid 'metabolising' of upsetting events prompted by EMDR, research has consistently proven its effectiveness (Mollon 2005). EMDR is now recognised by the National Institute for Health and Clinical Excellence (NICE) as one of the major treatments for PTSD.
3 For example the client's unconscious construction of the therapy and the therapist as the abuser (by which the therapeutic process itself is experienced as a re-enactment of the traumatising relationship).

References

Boyesen, G. and Boyesen, M. L. (1981, 1982) *Collected Papers of Biodynamic Psychology*, Vols 1 and 2. London: Biodynamic Psychology Publications. Reprinted from *Energy and Character*, Abbotsbury Publications, 1969–1979.

Damasio, A. (1994) *Descartes' Error: Emotion, Reason and the Human Brain*. New York: Putnam.

Davies, J. M. and Frawley, M. G. (1994) *Treating the Adult Survivor of Childhood Sexual Abuse*. New York: Basic Books.

de Zulueta, F. (2002) PTSD and dissociation: the Traumatic Stress Service in the Maudsley Hospital. In: Sinason, V. (ed.) *Attachment, Trauma and Multiplicity*. Hove: Brunner-Routledge.

Fairbairn, R. (1952) *Psychoanalytic Study of the Personality*. London: Routledge & Kegan Paul.

Herman, J. L. (1992) *Trauma and Recovery*. London: Basic Books.

Levine, P. A. (1997) *Waking the Tiger: Healing Trauma*. Berkeley; CA: North Atlantic Books.

Garwood, A. (2002) The Holocaust and the power of powerlessness: survivor guilt – an unhealed wound. In: Covington, C. (ed.) *Terrorism and War*. London: Karnac Books.

Heitzler, M. (2004) My personal approach to the theory and practice of integrative psychotherapy. *British Journal of Psychotherapy Integration* 1(2): 63–74.

Mollon, P. (2005) *EMDR and the Energy Therapies: Psychoanalytic Perspectives*. London: Karnac Books.

Ogden, P., Minton, K. and Pain, C. (2006) *Trauma and the Body: A Sensorimotor Approach to Psychotherapy*. New York: Norton & Company.

Rothschild, B. (2000) *The Body Remembers: The Psychophysiology of Trauma and Trauma Treatment*. New York: Norton & Company.

Schore, A. (1994) *Affect Regulation and the Origin of the Self: The Neurobiology of Emotional Development*. Hillsdale, NJ: Erlbaum.

Schore, A. (2007) Presentation at CONFER conference: Psychological Trauma and the Body, London 15–17 September.

Shapiro, F. (2001) *Eye Movement Desensitization and Reprocessing*, 2nd edn. New York: Guilford Press.

Soth, M. (2005) Embodied countertransference. In: Totton, N. (ed.) *New Dimensions in Body Psychotherapy*. Maidenhead: Open University Press.

van der Kolk, B. A., McFarlane, A. C. and Weisaeth, L. (1996) *Traumatic Stress: The Effects of Overwhelming Experience on Mind, Body and Society*. New York: Guilford Press.

Chapter 12

The borderline relationship

Tom Warnecke

It is by exacting that distance between self and other that strangely we
know that we are connected.

(Willow Pearson, 2005)

Introduction

Borderline personality disorder (BPD) has always been considered an elusive
and puzzling phenomenon. Concept and theory are indeed anything but
straightforward. The 'personality disorder' construct appears to suggest a
pathological condition located solely in the client. At the same time, the
borderline dynamic is most famously associated with difficult or unstable
relationships and evokes images of harassed and tormented therapists. But
borderline relationships are challenging for clients and therapists alike. Both
may feel attacked, invaded, helpless, misunderstood or unappreciated by the
other. Borderline patterns of organisation are evidently active across the continuum of intrapsychic and interpersonal fields. The word borderline – 'a line
that indicates a boundary' – incidentally names what is most lacking in the
borderline dynamic.

But the borderline dynamic is also particularly apparent as a bodily experience for both client and therapist. Hyperarousal and catastrophic anxieties,
both cardinal features of BPD, suggest disturbances of very basic functions
and indicate that the organism is in a state of somatic disorganisation.
Diagnostic considerations of BPD are often initiated by the therapist's senses
and bodily experiences. The presence of a borderline dynamic can make
others feel tense and self-conscious or may be experienced as electrifying the
air. Body and psyche of the therapist are impacted by and respond to disorganised or dissociated psyche and body states of borderline individuals.
In this chapter, I propose clinical perspectives to psychological and somatic
phenomena and disturbances commonly experienced by borderline individuals and their therapists.

BPD – a disorder of self

Borderline theory developed initially from an emphasis on intrapsychic organisation into a descriptive 'syndrome' and has since evolved towards the current disorder of self construct with its associated specific aetiology. Like any psychopathology, the borderline dynamic may be compensated to various degrees by the individual. While the actual presenting individual symptoms and abilities to function may differ substantially, there are a number of diagnostic considerations which indicate a borderline dynamic:

- inability to regulate the intensity and duration of affects
- catastrophic anxieties and hyperarousal
- confused or distorted sense of self
- blurred boundaries
- difficulty distinguishing between self and other, and between internal and external space
- lack of psyche–soma differentiation
- disorganised and inadequate muscular armouring
- indications for 'cephalic shock'.

Every dysfunction indicates a relational problem that has not been compensated and the borderline dynamic carries a history of abuse, deprivation and neglect associated with blurred boundaries, dissonance and intermittent contactlessness in unpredictable early relationships. Golomb and colleagues (1994) predict the emergence of BPD from primary environments characterised by high parental over-involvement on the one hand combined with parental inconsistency on the other. Parental focus is towards the adult's needs rather than the child's and children are typically treated inconsistently and as need-gratifying objects. Greenberg (1989) suggests that BPD begins as a healthy adaptation to an unhealthy environment. Becoming borderline, she argues, is the lesser of two evils.

Whilst there is general agreement about the environmental causes associated with BPD, borderline theorists appear to differ in their clinical definitions of core psychopathology. Masterson (2000) emphasises 'abandonment anxieties' which he links to rapprochement failures and faulty separation–individuation. Others see attachment failures and intolerance of aloneness at the core of BPD (Gunderson, Adler, Fonagy). Adler (1985) particularly highlights a lack of self-soothing capacity and 'insufficiencies of sustaining introjects'. From a somatic-integrative perspective, however, I suggest that these clinical perspectives and contributions to the borderline construct complement rather than contradict each other.

Somatic perspectives of BPD

In body psychotherapy, somatic manifestations are seen as dynamic correlations of any psychological processes we observe. Following Reich's concept of organismic structure, BPD disorganisation manifests as a disorganised structure or 'embodied dissonance' (Lewis 1976b). The distorted or confused sense of self at the core of the borderline 'disorder of self' conception indicates severe disturbances in the individual's psyche–soma relationship. Psyche and soma lack differentiation and appear either merged or dissociated. Disturbed attachment patterns, lack of boundaries and the complex disruptions of affect regulation we observe in BPD, suggest a lack of psycho-affective maturation and failures to develop differentiated somatic frames of self-references. The development of implicit and explicit self-experience is grounded in somatosensory experience of stimuli and affects but also depends on interactive experiences of being related to by important others (Krueger 2002; House 1996). Abilities to form affect representations and distinguish physiological, affect and emotional states develop initially when such states are attended to by empathic and intersubjectively attuned caregivers.

The developmental arrest associated with BPD is considered to disrupt the emergence of higher-order psychological functions (Golomb *et al.* 1994). I suggest, however, that basic functions such as affect tolerance and the growth and maturation of a self-referencing bodily self constitute the first casualties of developmental arrest. Winnicott's conceptualised 'true self' is a bodily self that preserves a sense of continuity of being. Winnicott (1952) linked the lack of psyche–soma relationship to experiences of disintegration and depersonalisation, which involves a diminished sense of personal reality, or 'self'. Recent advances in neuroscience have contributed substantially to understanding the reciprocal relationship of psychological and physiological processes.

Affective processes lie at the core of the self in Schore's (1994, 2003, 2006) conception as they are bodily-based phenomena of an intrinsic psychobiological nature. Schore proposes a psychoneurobiological model of 'implicit self' development based on a brain/mind/body system which constitutes the dynamic core of the implicit self. The development of implicit self-functions appears to be crucial for the ability to maintain an integrated, coherent, continuous and unified sense of self. The implicit self is disorganised and dysfunctional in BPD (Schore 2006).

Psycho-affective development and somatic self-referencing are derailed during early development in BPD when parents lack empathic attunement to the child's emotional experience and relate to the infant as an extension of their own organism instead. Such parents are unable to provide a balance of soothing and stimulating responses to modulate the child's autonomic and psychological arousal. The development of bodily self-functions is disrupted further by parental failures to engage with the infant's body senses and psychomotor experiences. Psyche and soma remain undifferentiated and disorganised instead of forming a functional unity as a dynamically self-organising implicit self.

Deficits in self-referencing abilities can be expected to mirror the severity of disturbance experienced by the individual. Impaired psyche–soma integration is evident in the capacity to differentiate between affect, emotion and cognitive functions. It also impacts bodily regulation in the areas of sleep and self-care and manifests in chronic feelings of emptiness, another cardinal feature of BPD. When the steady stream of consciousness arising from moment-to-moment somatosensory self-experience is stunted or perhaps even absent, the individual is left with a painful inner void. Proprioceptive experiences of unbalanced and inadequate muscle tone fuel states of unspec-ified anxiety and nameless dread (Boadella 2005). Thoughts and feelings may seem lost and in search of embodiment whilst affect states are experienced through bodily expressions of distress to avoid overwhelming or frightening feelings. Migraines, headaches or gut spasms may present dramatic expres-sions of affect states or serve as coping strategies for hyperarousal and catastrophic anxieties.

Psychosomatic symptoms, Krueger argues, may equally represent restitu-tive attempts rather than defensive regression and splitting. 'When based on developmental arrest rather then regression, the body and psyche have not been initially integrated in order to later be defensively split or foreclosed.' (Krueger 2002: 96). Psychosomatic symptoms or self-inflicted pain may actu-ally serve the individual as validating experiences of personal reality or attempts to develop internal points of self-references. Images, metaphors or semi-psychotic ideas may also substitute particular affects or emotions.

Deficiencies of psyche–soma functional integration are particularly evi-dent in the sensory–emotional continuum of motor activity and experience. Muscular proprioception facilitates abilities to receive oneself, which is cen-tral to self-experience, cohesiveness and continuity of self. The structuring functions of muscular organisation support the integration of sensory and motor activity with emotional experience. Muscles are organs of emotional experience and expression. Motor and sensory functions are split to numb and reduce the emotional intensity of trauma and make conflicts less over-whelming. Unfortunately, such dissociation also obstructs the development of somatic implicit self-functions.

Motoric implicit self-functions determine the individual's primary capaci-ties to respond and relate (Boadella and Specht-Boadella 1994; Warnecke 2003). They affect the capacity to restrain motor discharge and, crucially, determine abilities to compensate and defend. Both muscular structuring and muscular defences (armouring) are inadequately developed and disorganised in BPD. The lack of surface boundaries is another cardinal feature of BPD. Surface boundaries (Boadella and Specht-Boadella 1994) are closely linked to the phenomenon of muscular tonus and shape our experience of a dividing line between internal space and external space. Inadequate surface boundaries affect the ability to separate inner from outer and distinguish between self and other. An enduring sense of wholeness and security can only develop within well-defined outlines of the individual.

BPD is also characterised by dysregulation of the autonomic nervous system. Borderline trauma responses manifest in chronic sympathetic mobilisation. The impulsive intensity of fear, terror, rage and aggression reflect the extent of acute sympathetic hyperarousal. Impulsive behaviours also suggest a lack of inhibitive functions such as the 'social engagement system' (Porges 2004), internalised feedback systems and boundaries. Borderline individuals have insufficient inhibitory capacity to modulate the sympathetic over-charge and the two branches of the ANS fail to regulate each other. Carroll (2001) suggests that the body is experienced as radically unsafe in instability and trauma. Sympathetic mobilisation and lack of safety are also apparent in 'either/or' mental images or cognitive processing and in head or neck tension, spasms and aches, another feature of BPD.

Neck, facial and cranial muscles are typically engaged in holding together, keeping out, holding back or holding in. Head and neck present the earliest available capacity for an infant to brace itself against shock and to bind anxiety in muscular tension (Lewis 1976b). Paraphrasing Lewis, the head is where the infant can best sustain a holding attitude against the dissonance it is experiencing. Cephalic bracing also affects breathing since diaphragmatic and cephalic spasm share a direct physiological connection (Lewis 1976b). The reliance on cephalic bracing to defend against fragility and vulnerability is characteristic for both schizoid and borderline dynamics.

The borderline relationship – engulfment or abandonment

Minor interpersonal disruptions amplify into intense relational ruptures in the borderline relationship. The relational dynamic of the borderline aetiology finds expression in the oscillation between disorganised and anxious attachment patterns. The therapist is frequently experienced as either 'too close' or 'too far away' and borderline individuals alternate unpredictably between the associated polarities of engulfment and abandonment. Both are potentially the source of intense physiological arousal and psychological distress. Hyperarousal and catastrophic anxieties find expression in despair, rage, clinging or self-destructive behaviours.

Table 12.1 illustrates the range of intrapsychic and interpersonal aspects of 'too close/too far away' anxieties in the borderline relationship. Catastrophic 'too close' anxieties may be triggered by a client's wish for connection but also occur in response to empathic or challenging interventions and reflections by the therapist. In body psychotherapy, touch is also likely to set off such anxieties. 'Too close' anxieties express fears of engulfment or fears of 'being controlled' and may, in particularly regressed states, intensify into infantile devour-or-be-devoured fears, panic and rage. 'Too close' anxieties may also activate abandonment acting out.

Catastrophic 'too far away' anxieties generally reflect deficiencies of self-soothing capacity but also a lack of containment in relationships. They manifest as despair or rage when clients feel abandoned, not met or not heard. The borderline individual is devoid of self-soothing images and depends on external sources to fill the inner void. Fears of such dependency on the support and reassurance of others, however, will inevitably evoke 'too close' anxieties sooner or later.

On occasions when the arousal levels soar even further, conditions of extreme stress, terror or helplessness may evoke a dissociative freeze response (see Heitzler's chapter). Unable to escape, the organism responds by dissociating and simultaneously increasing parasympathetic inhibitory activity. Blood pressure drops precipitously, the racing heart slows to a crawl, tense muscles collapse and animation is suspended as sympathetic hyperarousal turns into hyperparasympathetic dissociation.

The embodied disorganisation and affect dysregulation in BPD is reminiscent of PTSD. The lack of continuity and coherence of self, a central feature of BPD, is also found in the fragmentation of self experienced by victims of massive trauma. However, there is a fundamental and crucial difference in clinical implications. In BPD, trauma responses are evoked by the therapeutic relationship itself. With a history of empathic failures and toxic experiences, borderline trauma is conceived as attachment trauma or early relational trauma (Schore 2002b). Attachment relationships are characterised by co-regulation of affect, i.e. the ability to resiliently regulate affect, and emotional states through interactions with others (see Carroll's chapter). Co-regulating relationships such as a therapeutic relationship are not only desperately

Table 12.1 Catastrophic anxiety and hyperarousal in the borderline relationship

'You are too close'	'You are too far away'
• Fear of engulfment • Fear of invasion or being controlled • Blurred boundaries • Lack of distinction between self and other • Infantile devour-or-be-devoured fears • Lack of surface boundaries	• Inner void • Intolerance of aloneness • Fear of abandonment • Separation anxiety • Experiences of despair and deprivation • Ruptures in the therapeutic relationship
(Disorganised/disoriented attachment) *'Faulty separation–individuation'* (Masterson 1981, 2000)	*(Anxious/ambivalent attachment)* *'Insufficiency of sustaining introjects'* (Adler 1985)

sought but also equally feared by borderline individuals. In their experience, such relationships are toxic, dissonant and have few or no boundaries.

Ambient relational trauma of regulatory failures and disrupted or fragmented intersubjectivity and their re-enactments in the therapeutic relationship can be expected to challenge both participants severely. Empathy and attentiveness may not be quite sufficient when such dynamics erupt. Borderline individuals need not only the structure and support they crave from their therapists but also the capacity to weather such storms and to challenge habitual assumptions and behaviours. Gunderson (2001) identified good affect tolerance, empathic ability and self-sufficiency as the main qualities required from therapists in the borderline relationship. Therapists also benefit from a good sense of boundaries and a well-developed body presence.

But the frequent disruptions of mutual regulatory processes also present crucial opportunities to re-experience traumatic material in affectively manageable doses. In the context of a safe environment and secure attachment, overwhelming traumatic feelings can be mastered and adaptively integrated into the client's emotional life.

Intersubjective dynamic

Borderline hyperarousal, psychological distress and intrapsychic disorganisation find expression in famously intense transference relationships. The containment of affect within the transference facilitates crucial insights into a client's experiences. Valent suggests that severely traumatised people may have no alternative but to communicate their stories of distress through transference and countertransference, which he describes as 'central tools for discerning unprocessed or defended events' (1999: 73).

Somatic transference and the transference relationship offer a participative window to guide us into the intersubjective borderline experience. Pathogenic intersubjective transaction patterns are likely to arise in borderline relationships and find expression in re-enactments of dysfunctional relational dynamics. Stolorow and Lachmann view transference and countertransference as jointly formed intersubjective systems of reciprocal mutual influence (Stolorow et al. 1987). In intersubjective theory, the 'self' is thought to be constituted relationally within ever-changing intersubjective fields, rather than existing as a separate, fixed entity solely inside the person. Taking this line of argument further, Brandchaft and Stolorow (1987) associate the psychological essence of the borderline dynamic with phenomena arising in an intersubjective field rather than a pathological condition located solely in the client.

Moskovitz (1996) likened the borderline experience to being lost in a mirror. From a relational perspective, this metaphor is even more potent and apt. As therapists, we may become the proverbial mirror when we enter into the borderline relationship – a mirror in which borderline clients can potentially find themselves but all too easily also a mirror in which both therapist and client may lose themselves and each other. The success of the borderline relationship depends on the therapist's ability to move frequently and sometimes rapidly between two positions shown in Figure 12.1 – relating from an empathically attuned but differentiated position on the one hand and interacting from within the intersubjective experience on the other.

Somatic dimensions of BPD manifest dynamically in the transference relationship. At the same time, somatic dissonance, arousal and affect dysregulation also find expression in relational ruptures and dissonance. Dysregulated states are evoked by both inter- and intra-personal aspects but equally also manifest and find expression in both dimensions. In Vaughan's (1997) evocative metaphor, the therapist becomes a character in the internal drama who collaboratively rearranges the furniture from a position within the client's internal world (see Clark's chapter). Taking Vaughan's image both literally and from a somatic angle, I suggest that the therapist's body and self-experiences may indeed bridge psyche–soma dissociations and provide crucial links as well as differentiations between the minds and bodies of therapist and client. This aspect of the therapist's functions becomes increasingly significant the less developed a client's implicit self-functions are. Lewis's 'symbiotic manifesto' symbolises the precarious nature of regressed borderline experience in language and makes the risks apparent:

> I am completely helpless. I need you to regress and coo and resonate and be *deeply* attuned to me. I depend on you for my rhythms of tension and gratifications. But your identity must be solid: If your eyes are clear (not disturbed), *you will see me*; I will be mirrored in you, and I will begin to be.
>
> (Lewis 1976a: 6)

Mirroring of either a validating affirmation, or an existential denial, crucially involves the organisms of both participants, Lewis asserts:

> But if your own symbiotic experience . . . was inadequate, your identity will be confused and fused with mine: I will look into eyes that see me as an extension of yourself: *By your very existence, you deny my biology*, you give me a profound conviction that I cannot survive as a separate organism.
>
> (Lewis 1976a: 6)

Relationships rely on sensory experience of eye contact and touch but also on proximity, facial expressions and affective content of voice, posture or gestures. Somatic dimensions are equally evident when somatic transference and countertransference affect our visceral sensations, respiration and sensory-motor experience of self and other. The ability of the sensory-motor system

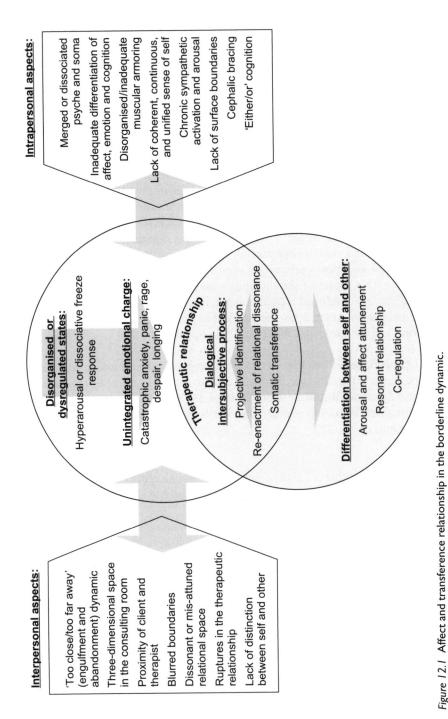

Intrapersonal aspects:

Merged or dissociated psyche and soma

Inadequate differentiation of affect, emotion and cognition

Disorganised/inadequate muscular armoring

Lack of coherent, continuous, and unified sense of self

Chronic sympathetic activation and arousal

Lack of surface boundaries

Cephalic bracing

'Either/or' cognition

Disorganised or dysregulated states:

Hyperarousal or dissociative freeze response

Unintegrated emotional charge:

Catastrophic anxiety, panic, rage, despair, longing

Therapeutic relationship

Dialogical intersubjective process:

Projective identification

Re-enactment of relational dissonance

Somatic transference

Differentiation between self and other:

Arousal and affect attunement

Resonant relationship

Co-regulation

Interpersonal aspects:

'Too close/too far away' (engulfment and abandonment) dynamic

Three-dimensional space in the consulting room

Proximity of client and therapist

Blurred boundaries

Dissonant or mis-attuned relational space

Ruptures in the therapeutic relationship

Lack of distinction between self and other

Figure 12.1 Affect and transference relationship in the borderline dynamic.

to feel movements, postures and emotional states observed in others is also referred to as kinaesthetic empathy. Such involuntary bodily identifications enable not only empathic responses but also transferential experiences of dissociated and unintegrated states. I regularly come to lose some of my somatosensory self-experience in the work with clients fragmented by trauma. Our projective identification with the lack of embodiment and concomitant difficulties to modulate or compensate arousal states may account for much of therapists' infamous experiences in borderline relationships. But the reciprocal nature of somatic transference also indicates the necessity to consider the impact of therapists' responses on clients. How, for example, is my borderline client affected when I feel like I am sitting on eggshells throughout a session? And what would my intrapsychic response to a suicide threat communicate back to the client?

Working with the borderline dynamic

The severity of disturbance in BPD suggests that clinical considerations at the start of the therapeutic relationship should be informed by trauma work perspectives. Directive approaches and crisis intervention techniques are suitable to meet the extent of implicit self-disorganisation and manage hyperarousal and catastrophic anxieties. Clients' needs for containment, structure and support can be expected to dominate the initial phase of therapy. At this stage, therapeutic interventions are primarily aimed towards creating a holding environment and increasing tolerance for positive and negative affect states. Once such basic needs are met in the relationship, the therapeutic process can move towards validation of self-experience, engagement in the relationship and interpersonal learning. The complexities of BPD require a therapeutic approach which meets the deficits of basic implicit self-functions whilst simultaneously engaging with complex levels of self-organisation and relational experience. I propose a clinical combination of intersubjective dialogical engagement in the relationship with resource- and skill-oriented corrective interventions.

Somatic, cognitive or behavioural interventions

The instability of the borderline structure is most obvious in episodes of catastrophic anxiety and hyperarousal. In trauma work, the concept of 'putting the brakes on' whenever arousal becomes too overwhelming for a client is well established and usually achieved with somatic interventions or by utilising a previously established 'safe space' as described in Heitzler's chapter. In BPD, the trauma response is activated by the unfolding interpersonal and intersubjective dynamic in the consulting room. The bodily proximity between therapist and client usually contributes to 'too close/too far away' anxieties and attending to experiences of personal space and proximity may serve to bring arousal and anxiety back to a tolerable level (see Asheri's discussion of this). Borderline clients can utilise the space of the consulting room as a resource and learn to actively manage arousal and stress levels. Attention to self-experience and personal space in the consulting room will also help the borderline client to differentiate between themselves and others and aid the development of self-referencing abilities, as Greenberg describes:

> When she [the client] entered my office, I suggested that she move her chair to wherever she felt most comfortable that day. I also asked her to adjust the lighting to suit herself: brighter or dimmer, ceiling light or standing lamp. Eventually, she began to take the initiative herself.
>
> (Greenberg 1989: 38)

Initial choices of position in the consulting room and subsequent use of space enable clients to acknowledge and articulate their experiences of boundaries, vulnerabilities and relational stress as well as actively regulate them. Since trauma is characterised by an inability to escape, motor activity is crucial in its treatment and prevention. Traumatic memories are somatosensory memories and retrieved as sensory experience. They typically lack both language and narrative. The process of finding words and language creates containment for overwhelming experiences and is inextricably linked to the individual's self-referencing capacities.

> To recognise basic sensations, state of mind, to approximate an experience with words, a patient must have an internal point of reference to recognise basic sensations from an unaltered state of mind; once arrived at this way-station, analyst and patient may identify and differentiate feelings.
>
> (Krueger 2002: 189)

Some clients may find it easier to first articulate their experience of the therapist's micro level behaviour before attending to their self-experience. Differentiation between body sensations, affect and emotional states is essential for emotional integration. Affect de-somatisation is initiated by acknowledging, naming and processing such states in resonant relationships. Crucially, client's disowned experiences need to be first contained by the therapist (Schore 2003). Any intolerable or frightening affect demands active empathic attunement from the therapist to assist in its tolerance, modulation and integration. An absence of such attunement may well be experienced as traumatic by clients. Containment is facilitated by the therapist's ability to empathically register, observe and describe a client's affects, actions and emotional states. Acknowledging rather than interpreting events opens up a shared space for client and therapist to explore and attend to the sensory details of experiences.

Client fears of how their states of turmoil might affect the therapist may also need to be engaged. Frequently, such fears manifest as a need to get away or attempts to hide the catastrophic anxiety when flight is not an option. In the borderline dynamic, action typically aims to create immediate regulation of affects and relational tensions. Likewise, images, symbols and presaging signs may substitute for affect or emotional states. When the context of actions or images suggests that an emotional expression is intended, we can respond as if the anxieties or feelings implied were actually present. As such, validation of self-experience and acceptance of clients' strategies to contain and manage their anxieties initially takes precedence over exploring behaviour and activities in terms of its useful or maladaptive functions. The ability for self-reflection depends first of all on the self-referential capacities of the individual. Borderline clients 'learn to observe themselves by being observed' (Gunderson 2001: 273).

Boundaries shape and define the structures of any relationship. Appropriate boundaries make relational environments predictable and thereby contribute significantly to the safety of any relationship. In the borderline relationship, challenges of formal frame issues such as changes of session times and cancellations need to be negotiated rather then imposed since they constitute integral aspects of the therapeutic relationship and offer crucial opportunities to negotiate the relational environment in detail. Borderline clients may also learn in the process that ambivalence is tolerable and how conflicts can be managed, negotiated and ultimately survived.

In body psychotherapy, the experience of boundaries may also be explored through proximity, movement and touch. Some borderline individuals are virtually unable to distinguish whether a hand is touching their skin surface or penetrating inside. Not surprisingly, touch is likely to trigger hyperarousal and fears of invasion. But touch also provides an interface between self and other which can be actively and explicitly explored in the therapeutic relationship. To validate the integrity of surface boundaries and affirm the internal space within, both therapist and client will need to explicitly attend to their own and each other's experience of self and other. As therapists, we need to rely on our involuntary kinaesthetic empathy to engage resonantly with the continuum of engulfment and abandonment, as the following case vignette shows.

Sara and I had previously explored various aspects of boundaries in depth, from proximity to surface boundaries. She had recently become aware of experiencing considerable habitual anxiety and we intended to focus on physiological aspects of her anxiety on this occasion. We had agreed that I would place my hand on Sara's belly to engage with the movements of her diaphragm. As she lay on the mattress, however, Sara struggled to settle into our contact and seemed to become more anxious. After observing this for a few minutes, I decided to respond by lightening my touch, guided by a felt sense of 'resting my hand on water'. At the same time, I began to imagine myself in a location outside the room whilst maintaining some awareness of Sara and our interaction at the same time. I half expected some furious response to such an act of negligence but none materialised. Instead, Sara visibly calmed down almost immediately and her breathing and diaphragmatic movements deepened notably.

Talking about the experience later, Sara reported that she had initially worried about being invaded. These feelings had then disappeared suddenly and she had begun to enter into an increasingly relaxed and calm state. Eventually, Sara came to feel guarded and protected by my hand. In this instance, a resonant engagement with Sara meant to limit my touch and my presence to a degree of contact she could tolerate rather then confront and perhaps invade her with the kind of contactful touch usually advocated in body psychotherapy. Physical contact generally serves to intensify involvement between two people. Being securely and resonantly held in appropriate circumstances by someone can create a powerful sense of security. Self-referencing requires the capacity to respond to stimuli originating from within the body and necessitates a sense of safety. Interoceptive processes are facilitated by the 'calm and connection reaction' (Uvnäs-Moberg 2003) of parasympathetic 'self-care' activation.

Touch also offers an opportunity to engage with the habitual organisation of motor nervous systems and associated phenomena of relational motor activity and muscular intentionality. Motor activity and sensory experiences predominate in our earliest attachment experiences and become embedded in individual attachment patterns. Muscles are sense organs and the sensory-motor integration of involuntary muscle gives rise to intentions, facilitates the capacity to communicate, and organises expressions of resistance and assertion (Warnecke 2003). Subliminal muscular self-experience plays a central role in the intrapsychic dynamics of self-organisation and is therefore crucial to self-cohesiveness, affect tolerance and integration. Relational motor activity and 'somatic dialogue' (Boadella and Specht-Boadella 1994) rely on the kinaesthetic empathy of the therapist. The affirmative effects and mutual mirroring of somatic dialogue are associated with non-verbal formative processes such as internalisations and assimilations. If I can stay grounded, centred and bounded when hyperarousal and trauma responses impact my bodily presence, my client not only learns that it is possible to cope but may also assimilate the somatic skills.

Relational alliance and transitional phenomena

Kinaesthetic empathy, validation of experience and effective crisis management provide crucial building blocks for the emerging relational alliance. The therapeutic alliance is a subtle, dynamic and interactive collaborative relationship (Safran and Muran 2000). In research cited by Schore (2006), over half of the beneficial effects of psychotherapy have been linked to the quality of the therapeutic relationship. Safran and Muran note that transitional phenomena require an ability 'to experience one's internal world as meaningful, and this in turn requires a fundamental sense of trust in the other's willingness to be interested in one's internal world and responsive to one's emotional needs' (2000: 95). In the interpersonal system of the relational alliance, the therapist may also serve as a self-object function (Adler and Rhine 1992; Schore 1994).

Transitional phenomena flourish in holding environments jointly created by client and therapist. They provide a shared metaphorical space to try out new identifications, to explore different ways of being in the world and relating to others, to test behaviour that promises greater mastery, pleasure and adaptation, and to practise solutions to unresolved primitive conflicts around love, hate, envy, jealousy and aggression. Transitional phenomena are particularly significant to the borderline dynamic as they require a shared simultaneous holding of two paradoxical realities, the pretend and the actual, and increase tolerance for ambivalence. Clients can both own and disown vulnerable aspects such as threatening internal states, feelings, thoughts and intentions while testing out the therapist's responses.

States of uncertainty and suspense may co-exist creatively with omnipotence or feeling unconditionally loved while the inherent anxieties are held jointly in the transitional space, rather than defensively splitting or emotionally flooding either client, therapist or both. New facets of implicit self-functions may arise from previously conflicted intrapsychic material. In the transitional space, both are intermittently held by an intersubjectively available therapist and occasionally transferred to inanimate objects. A small object brought into the consulting room may serve as a self-object placed in the therapist's care for example.

Anna had brought objects to me on various occasions during the first two and a half years of her therapy. I felt touched by her gestures and took them as expressions of her search for connection and yearning for a holding environment. As Anna appeared too anxious to explore any possible meaning, I simply acknowledged and thanked her at each instance. When I eventually inquired about her feelings on yet another occasion, she managed to embrace and acknowledge her emotional investments in the pebble she had brought that day. Anna and I could feel mutually touched and connected by her expression and shared this experience for some time. She then proceeded to tell me about her initial internal response of panic, fury and rage on hearing my invitation to explore. Her impulse had been to smash a water glass which was standing on a side table near her. Her realisation that she had actually been able to contain both her vulnerable feelings and her destructive impulse seemed as significant to her as the subsequent shared experience of mutual connection.

The steady stream of objects and their reception in the relationship not only symbolised the emerging transitional space but also contributed to its construction and led to this instance of psyche–soma integration. The containment Anna experienced in the transitional space enabled her to restrain her impulsive motor discharge. Intense feelings are always accompanied by correlative motor impulses, which include all primitive urges such as hitting, tearing, crying or clinging (Carroll 2001). As Anna was able to differentiate her affective and motor impulses from her emotional experience, she felt safe enough to notice and reflect on her underlying feelings of vulnerability and share her wish for intimacy and connection.

Trauma seems most debilitating when pain and fear are compounded by aloneness and isolation. The subjective sense of isolating estrangement escalates both pain and fear and appears central to the experience of trauma itself. In the experience of traumatised people, their solitary worlds appear fundamentally incommensurable with those of others (Stolorow 1999). A state of resonant attunement with another person, however, seems to send a potent signal to the traumatised organism that the traumatic events are over. Smith (2004) suggests that the prefrontal cortex is 'awakened' by an empathic connection.

In states of resonant and empathic attunement, affect is regulated effectively. Schore (2002a) identified the dual regulatory processes of affect synchrony as the fundamental building blocks of attachment. Such processes create states of positive arousal and interactive repair which are capable of modulating states of negative arousal. Affect regulatory functions are learned when the self-regulating processes of a self-regulating other become 'selfobject regulatory functions'. The affective experience with the externally regulating therapist is internalised in the form of orbitofrontal neuronal representations (Schore 1994). As such, interactive regulation is a core skill of psychotherapy (see Carroll's chapter).

Secure attachment relationships with a balance of soothing and stimulating responses serve as a working model for modes of engagement in therapeutic relationships. Smith (2004) observes that catharsis is fostered by warm, empathic engagement while internalisation is stimulated by separation anxiety in response to a slightly aloof stance of expectancy on the part of the therapist.

> As therapists, we can be empathically attuned to our patients while being fully expectant that they will continue to take risks and grow. The art of being a therapist is to be both highly empathic and highly expectant at the same time.
>
> (Smith 2004: 630)

Resonant attunement and parasympathetic activation support interoceptive and self-referencing capacities, which promote development of basic and higher-order functions in turn. Complex levels of self-organisation such as empathy, ambivalence and ambiguity necessitate awareness and management of paradoxical realities, for example contradictory feelings or some differentiation between one's state and the state of the other. Intuitive psychobiological attunement to self and other requires similar paradoxical awareness from the therapist. In body psychotherapy we can explicitly attend to our own somatosensory self-experience whilst simultaneously resonating with our clients' bodily sense of self through processing subliminal perception, and listening and interacting from an intuitive subjective experience. In the process, we not only contain distress and dissociated experiences by metabolising anxiety and affect states, but also model their integration.

Intersubjective resonance, affect synchrony and interactive repair are subtle and yet complex mechanisms which encourage the borderline individual to connect feelings with situations and behaviours, aid the growth of self-referencing functions, and facilitate psyche–soma functional integration of affect, sensory and emotional experiences, with motor activity. The relational alliance can transform the borderline relationship into a dynamic growth-facilitating environment.

Conclusions

Borderline individuals lack embodiment and have insufficient tools to modulate or compensate hyperarousal and catastrophic anxieties. They experience impairments and intense distress in most significant aspects of mastering their world, from basic self-regulation to the management of relationships.

Such failures of basic and higher-order functions in BPD are conceived as experience-dependent and therefore considered open to change. A clinical approach which combines relational work with interventions aimed to meet the deficits of basic implicit self-functions appears to offer the most hope of beneficial change.

Somatic dimensions are at the core of subjective and intersubjective borderline experience. The borderline relationship is fuelled by the intersubjective experience of borderline disembodiment and deficits of self and regulatory functions. Trauma research and neuroscience can help us as therapists to understand our transferential reactions, our intersubjective somatic experiences, and our struggles to manage our affect states in borderline relationships. Or, in other words, to help us manage our own borderline aspects invoked in the borderline relationship rather then getting lost in them.

The success of the borderline relationship ultimately depends on how well therapist and client succeed in forming a collaborative relationship based on a meaningful emotional connection between two people on the one hand and on our ability to manage the tensions and paradoxes of differentiated and merged states and negotiate the ambivalence and ambiguity of subjective and intersubjective experiences on the other.

References

Adler, G. (1985) *Borderline Psychopathology and its Treatment*. Northvale, NJ: Aronson.

Adler, G. and Rhine, M. W. (1992) The selfobject function of projective identification. In: Hamilton, N. G. (ed.) *From Inner Sources – New Directions in Object Relations Psychotherapy*. Northvale, NJ: Aronson, pp. 139–162.

Boadella, D. and Specht-Boadella, S. (1994) Unpublished biosynthesis training manual. Heiden, Switzerland: International Institute for Biosynthesis IIBS.

Boadella, D. (2005) Affect, attachment and attunement. *Energy and Character* 34: 13–23.

Brandchaft, B. and Stolorow, R. D. (1987) The borderline concept: an intersubjective viewpoint. In: Grotstein, J. S., Solomon, M. F. and Lang J. A. (eds) *The Borderline Patient: Emerging Concepts in Diagnosis, Psychodynamics and Treatment*, Vol. 2. Hillsdale, NJ: Analytic Press.

Carroll, R. (2001) *The Autonomic Nervous System: Barometer of Emotional Intensity and Internal Conflict*. Online: http://www.thinkbody.co.uk/papers/autonomic-nervous-system.htm (accessed 21 January 2007).

Golomb, A., Ludolph, P., Westen, D., Bloch, M., Maurer, P. and Wiss, F. (1994) Maternal empathy, family chaos, and the etiology of borderline personality disorder. *Journal of the American Psychoanalytic Association* 42(2): 525–548.

Greenberg, E. (1989) Healing the borderline. *Gestalt Journal* XII(2): 11–55.

Gunderson, J. G. (2001) *Borderline Personality Disorder: A Clinical Guide*. Arlington, VA: American Psychiatric Publishing.

House, R. (1996) Object relations and the body. *Energy and Character* 27(2): 31–44.

Krueger, D. W. (2002) *Integrating Body Self and Psychological Self.* New York: Routledge.

Lewis, R. (1976a) The psychosomatic development of the self. *Energy and Character* 7(2): 2–14.

Lewis, R. (1976b) Infancy and the head. *Energy and Character* 7(3): 18–26.

Masterson, J. F. (1981) *The Narcissistic and Borderline Disorders.* New York: Brunner/ Mazel.

Masterson, J. F. (2000) *The Personality Disorders.* Phoenix, AZ: Zeig, Tucker & Co.

Moskovitz, R. (1996) *Lost in the Mirror, an Inside Look at Borderline Personality Disorder.* Lanham, MD: Taylor Trade Publishing.

Pearson, W. (2005) From her introduction to the song 'Comfortable Distance' at a performance in November 2005. Online: http://in.integralinstitute.org/avantgarde/ show_willowtrilogy.aspx (accessed 21 January 2007).

Porges, S. W. (2004) Neuroception: a subconscious system for detecting threats and safety. *Zero to Three* 24(5): 19–24.

Safran, J. D. and Muran, J. C. (2000) *Negotiating the Therapeutic Alliance: A Relational Treatment Guide.* New York: Guilford.

Schore, A. N. (1994) *Affect Regulation and the Origin of the Self: The Neurobiology of Emotional Development.* Hillsdale, NJ: Erlbaum.

Schore, A. N. (2002a) Dysregulation of the right brain: a fundamental mechanism of traumatic attachment and the psychopathogenesis of posttraumatic stress disorder. *Australian and New Zealand Journal of Psychiatry* 36(1): 9–30.

Schore, A. N. (2002b) Advances in neuropsychoanalysis, attachment theory, and trauma research: implications for self psychology. *Psychoanalytic Inquiry* 22(3): 433–484.

Schore, A. N. (2003) *Affect Regulation and the Repair of the Self.* New York: W. W. Norton & Company.

Schore, A. N. (2006) *The Science of the Art of Psychotherapy.* Key note presentation at the 4th Biosynthesis Congress, 1–3 June 2006, Lisbon, Portugal.

Smith, J. (2004) Reexamining psychotherapeutic action through the lens of trauma. *Journal of The American Academy of Psychoanalysis and Dynamic Psychiatry* 32(4): 613–631.

Stolorow, R. D. (1999) The phenomenology of trauma and the absolutisms of everyday life: a personal journey. *Psychoanalytic Psychology* 16: 464–468.

Stolorow, R., Brandchaft, B. and Atwood, G. (1987) *Psychoanalytic Treatment: An Intersubjective Approach.* Hillsdale, NJ: Analytic Press.

Uvnäs-Moberg, K. (2003) *The Oxytocin Factor.* Cambridge, MA: Da Capo Press.

Valent, P. (1999) *Trauma and Fulfillment Therapy.* Philadelphia: Brunner/Mazel.

Vaughan, S. C. (1997) *The Talking Cure.* New York: Putnam.

Warnecke, T. (2003) Some thoughts on involuntary muscle. *AChP Newsletter* 25: 20–28.

Winnicott D. W. (1952) Anxiety associated with insecurity. In: *Through Paediatrics to Psychoanalysis: Collected Papers.* New York: Brunner-Routledge, 1992.

Chapter 13

Facing the abuser in the abused in body psychotherapy

Jane Clark

Introduction

Working with a client who has been sexually abused in childhood throws up several dilemmas for body psychotherapists. Body psychotherapy involves touch and abused clients who are drawn to body psychotherapy are aware of this.

At a particular point in the therapy a conflict between a body psychotherapist and client may arise concerning the use of touch. If it does, the conflict can lead to an almighty power struggle in which the internalised abuser in the client rears its head and locks horns with the therapist in a re-enactment of a past abusive relationship.

The conflict calls on the therapist to relate congruently and appropriately with the internalised abuser in the client, hold the client's abused inner child, hold the therapeutic position, hold the therapist's internalised abuser and dare to be real all at the same time.

Background

Before I began the Chiron training programme I worked as a psychodynamic counsellor where to touch or not to touch was not an issue; touch was a taboo. I was taught to understand the value of no touch in terms of appropriateness and good, firm boundaries, particularly with respect to clients who had a history of childhood sexual abuse. It made sense, the client was safe, and I was in no danger of re-abusing, at least not through any physical contact that could be interpreted by the client as abusive.

I experienced sessions where the client wanted to be held, their belief being that experiencing respectful and appropriate physical holding was the only way they could heal the wounds of abuse. I empathised and sympathetically explained that use of touch was considered inappropriate within my codes of ethics and conduct. I struggled with this and tried to compensate by holding them with energy, warmth and understanding. I was keenly aware that the clients experienced rejection, and correspondingly I felt rejecting, in the driving seat and at arm's length.

Theoretically I recognised the wisdom of not rushing to hold the client. To do so would put me in the role of rescuer, both to the client and to myself, and relieve us both of having to bear the weight and relational tension of difficult client/therapist material. 'Rescuing the client' might feel good at the time but it has a shadow side, rescuing implies the client is helpless: 'The more the therapist accepts the idea that the patient is helpless, the more she perpetuates the traumatic transference and disempowers the patient' (Herman 2001: 142). My refusal often enabled the client to get in touch with negative thoughts and feelings about themselves as being unlovable, untouchable and repulsive in some way, material that might not have come to light if blocked by my need to rescue and hold them (see Asheri's chapter).

I struggled most with the taboo when the client's inner child emerged and described how she/he had never been held in a loving way; my refusal to hold felt abusive, the uncompromising rule (code of conduct in practice) felt like a wedge driven unnecessarily and cruelly between therapist/mother and wounded child/client.

I began to question the blanket taboo of touch; this led me to the training programme at Chiron, beginning shyly with one module, Body and Energy.

With the taboo lifted I had to think and feel my way through a client's motives behind their request to be held, and there are many to consider: avoidance; a magical belief that being held will heal all ills; the beginnings of a re-enactment; and a vital clue to the plight of an abused infant, racked with body memories, waiting for a conscious connection to her plight to free her.

The requests of two clients (I will call them Janet and Mary) to be held, and my reluctance to do so, triggered a re-enactment of internalised abusive relationships.

Triggers

In some clients, memories of sexual abuse can lie dormant for decades until a dam suddenly bursts and a wall of remembering pushes through, flooding familiar boundaries and horizons, blurring the client's knowledge of him/herself as a person. Traumatic memories, both mental and emotional, float like debris to the surface of consciousness along with an acute sense of mistrust in self, others and the world. The first step we take in therapy is trust building, which is not an easy task, and all we can hope to achieve is a wary trust. The steps towards trust will collapse and have to be rebuilt and strengthened.

We work towards redefining the blurred edges and boundaries of a therapeutic environment that was once safe, prior to the flood of traumatic memories; as part of that process we need to identify the triggers that burst the dam and disarm them: 'Identifying traumatic triggers is one of the great challenges of trauma therapy' (Rothschild 2000: 116).

Prior to engaging in therapy both clients had coped relatively well in building 'normal' lives. They survived the education system, held down good jobs, married, and had children; both had been highly ambitious and able to achieve their goals.

Janet: memories of abuse flooding the mind

Janet was abused by her father as she reached puberty, aged eleven; until then he had treated her like a princess. She had developed quite a strong ego. The themes within our work included dynamics of dominance and submission, oedipal attachment, the flooding of boundaries, attempts to sabotage the therapeutic framework, and a desire to merge.

Janet occasionally regressed into childlike aspects of her self: a dominant three-year-old, a sweet, engaging, pretty little girl, a seductive princess and an eleven-year-old victim who felt lost and alone, wondering who she really was. Regression in Janet seemed more of a means to demonstrate ages and stages of behaviours than a defence against remembering traumatic experiences. She would keep half an eye on me, scanning for impact. She did not regress to the pre-verbal level.

Janet operated from the mental level and preferred to access her feelings through talking. I worked relationally, referring occasionally to her body sense. She engaged shyly with a little bodywork if it had a psychodrama flavour and there was no physical contact between us.

She came to therapy in her thirties after she discovered her husband had had a string of affairs. She challenged him and he asked her for a divorce. Janet wanted a third child; divorcing him would diminish that opportunity so she pleaded with him to stay with her and have another child. He flatly refused.

Janet was about to lose half of all she possessed, get a job and take on even more responsibility for the children, yet none of this seemed to worry her half as much as being told 'no' by her husband. She felt betrayed, not by her husband's affairs but by his refusal to give her a third child.

Her husband's refusal was so shocking to Janet; it was the trigger that sent her spiralling back into childhood and memories of the abuse. She had coped for many years by clinging to the princess who could and should have anything she liked. She came to therapy because the princess was beginning to break down into its shadow, the lost princess, the victim.

Mary: Memories of abuse flooding the body

Mary was abused by her grandfather; she found it difficult to identify how old she was when it began but her waking conscious memories gave her images of her as a child aged four to six years old.

My work with Mary began with grounding; her body was highly expressive, terrifyingly articulate, twisting and writhing in terror. There was an absence of eye contact and red flushing to her face.

My concern for Mary was a perpetual re-traumatisation through an almost obsessive determination to get to the bottom of 'it' (the abuse) once and for all. I likened it to taking a pneumatic drill down through the shell of her psyche in complete disregard for the soft flesh of her vulnerabilities lining the walls. I would have been lost without all I had learned in experiential group work, including witnessing a Chiron trainer skilfully bringing a trainee/client out of a trance-like, hysterical state.

Mary came to therapy in her forties. She had suffered from a thyroid problem for well over a year and long after the doctor concluded the problem had been successfully treated she was still suffering from the symptoms. She was working as a secretary to a team of child abuse specialists; her job was to type up reports of the content of their meetings, and she felt overloaded. She had taken her memories of abuse to a therapist some years previously and thought she had dealt with them; however, she recognised a re-emergence of them mostly in feeling.

She was insightful enough to recognise the possibility that her body had taken on the expression of the effects of abuse that her mind was unable to articulate.

She came with two major fears: that the expression of the effects of abuse would be misdiagnosed as a mental illness, and that she would lose her husband because she could no longer tolerate sexual intimacy with him without feeling revulsion and rage. For this she felt immeasurably guilty and ashamed. She asked me to trust that she knew what she was doing in wanting to explore and come to terms with sexual abuse, however scary it might get. This was something I noted.

For Mary there were many triggers to remembering sexual abuse: routinely being exposed to cases of child abuse at work; her body lying to her by expressing symptoms of an illness she no longer had; pressure from herself and her husband to engage in sex when every nerve ending in her body screamed out that it was wrong.

She came to therapy to understand the effects of the abuse on her; she needed someone she could trust would not fall at the 'first scary fence', refer her on and leave her in a world of diagnosis and labelling where the madness of abuse might be misinterpreted as Mary's madness ('madness' was Mary's own word.)

Re-enactment of the client's drama

When working relationally, re-enactments of clients' internal conflicts (dramas) happen all the time on many different levels from subtle to blatant (see Soth's chapter). Occasionally a re-enactment can take us right off the map of our theoretical understanding and teach us something new. This was the case with Janet and Mary.

Janet was the first client to draw me into a re-enactment and urge me to let go of my theoretical understanding of what needed to happen and trust in what she believed needed to happen. Mary was the second. Their stories were similar in that they had both been abused and drew me in a very real way into a re-enactment as part of the recovery process. Their individual agendas proved to be very different; nevertheless, the common ground between them was that I had to *'face the abuser in the abused'* and let go of the safe seat, in order to see what they wanted me to see.

There the similarity ends in that Janet was psychologically more robust than Mary; she was sexually abused from the age of eleven. Prior to that she had passed through several stages of childhood development in what she perceived to be a safe environment. Whilst in combat with the abuser within Janet I was aware I needed to take care of the victim within her, but I was also aware that her adult self was hovering in the background, controlling and monitoring the process. Even at the height of the battle she was quite capable of verbalising her feelings and very clear about what she wanted from me.

Mary was abused from infancy up to the age of eleven; her re-enactment was no less forceful and painful than Janet's, but whilst in it she lost the ability to verbalise her feelings and regressed into an infantile state. Initially I misread the regression as a defence mechanism but her body language suggested something else; it was crucial for me to understand her non-verbal communication.

Facing the abuser in the abused – the key to understanding

The drama

As therapist I had been subtly auditioned by my client for the parts I would eventually play in the drama; the therapy room became a stage, and the mattress for body and energy work and the massage table the props and backdrops of scenery for a play. The historical internalised script was for now in the client's hands as each scene was set and choreographed as steps towards the re-enactment of the internalised abusive relationship. The main characters waited in the wings for their cue to take the stage. The cue was a trigger: the client saying 'Hold me' triggering the thought that something wasn't right, coupled with an intuitive feeling to stay well back. Something else needed to happen before I held the client and I didn't know what.

Holding the tension of not knowing can be excruciating but slowly the force behind the request rises up to reveal itself. Within the tension, impulses to act (rescue) have to be sifted through, their therapeutic value and intent questioned. Supervisors past and present, peer group discussions, the latest argument for and against the use of touch, long-term versus short-term therapy ('get them sorted out, back on track'), masochism ('you have to sit here taking this'), my punitive internalised mother ('do you know what you are doing? no of course not') rush in like gremlins, all with clever redundant pearls of wisdom to drop into my ear, as the thunderous silence in the room aches on.

Hold me!

When the request for holding takes on the quality of a demand, it is probably coming from the internalised abuser.

The demand

'I need you to hold me. Why won't you hold me? Refusing to hold me is abusive. You are playing with me.'
　'You can heal me, you know you can. You choose not to.'

Therapist's traps

I have to admit that the first time I heard the words 'you can heal me' my narcissistic wound sucked them in as a soothing anaesthetic that could have seduced me into the arms of inappropriateness. Janet's therapy spanned the early years of my training at Chiron, a time when I was embracing the concepts of body psychotherapy, captivated and ignited by discovery and understanding, caught up in the newness to me of a very old wisdom. I was imbued with a childlike awe at the potential for the mysterious and magical in the laying on of hands. Clients can read us so well.

　The following quote I found by psychoanalysts John Maltsberger and Dan Buie should be enough to sober up a therapist intoxicated with the possibility of being a magical healer: 'The three most common narcissistic snares are the Aspirations to heal all, know all and love all' (Herman 2001: 143).

The plea

'Please hold me until I can heal. If you won't who will, you are my only hope. Please, please hold me.' (Saviour Rescuer)

The conflict

With Janet I had the feeling that I was being asked to resist the demands and pleas to be held: 'Hold me' versus 'Hold the boundaries'.

　Beyond theoretical understanding I felt a mothering instinct for the child/victim and yet I knew the request from the client was tainted. 'I want to hold the child but I won't be seduced into crossing a boundary; this feels like a trap.'

In the demand I heard the plea; in the plea I heard the demand. Impasse!

The seeds of a re-enactment were taking root. 'According to Kernberg, the therapist's task is to "identify the actors" in the borderline patient's inner world using countertransference as a guide to understanding the patient's experience' (Herman 2001: 147).

Traumatic countertransference

I was ashamed to feel a revulsion creeping in as a negative, punitive reaction to Janet and Mary, my once treasured clients who now rocked me with demands, alternating between intense neediness and bullying tactics. I felt an irrational irritation when their adults disappeared, leaving me with a demanding and needy child and an abusive parent bullying me into picking her up.

I felt panic rise when I searched for compassion and empathy within myself, to find they had disappeared. I knew my feelings belonged to the countertransference; at the same time I had to consider that countertransference feelings could have been strengthened in intensity by residues of my own story of abuse. I had to run them, one by one, through my internal supervisor before I dared to act.

The conflict boiled away in its alchemical pressure cooker, preparing to blow the lid on the client's Pandora's box of negative thoughts and feelings. I felt it would not be long before the abuser/victim (the directors) would call me, their understudy, from the broom cupboard back stage to take the limelight as they took up their position in the audience.

Much like in the final act of a Shakespearean play, I sensed I could be duped into playing the victim and, in the swirl of a trickster's cloak, if pushed too far the script could expertly unmask me as the evil abuser.

The conflict seeped into supervision sessions in parallel process (see Michael Soth's chapter). We looked at how my feelings (countertransference) mirrored the client's feelings. With Janet, I understood the dynamics of the re-enactment and the parts I was picking up to play. 'And if you agree to hold her? And if you don't?' My reaction to those searching questions was that the abused and abuser were fused; if I moved to hold and comfort the child I would be playing into the hands of the abuser. Whichever way I moved, I was being abusive. I was trapped and so was Janet. The drama was set.

With Mary, countertransference feelings were much more acute. I felt intense guilt about not holding her and revulsion at the thought of holding her. I felt incredibly burdened and useless. I wondered if I had taken on more than I could manage, seduced by my narcissism into being that strong person who would not fall at the 'first scary fence'. I confined discussion of her case in supervision to theory, referring to my feelings but not expressing them fully. In retrospect I can see how much I carried alone. At the very beginning she had asked me to trust that she knew what she needed to do and to stay with her; if I admitted to myself that I was floundering and that perhaps I should refer her on, it would feel like a complete betrayal; her fears would be realised.

Deep down I trusted her and my ability to stay with her process, but was trust enough? I was afraid if I 'told all' my motives in staying with her might be questioned and at worst dammed. My rationale had such a subjective edge I was afraid I might fall at the first theoretical fence. I hadn't realised how guilty I felt about withholding material until I read the following paragraph in Judith Lewis Herman's book *Trauma and Recovery*. My guilt surfaced in partnership with relief in knowing that I was not alone in holding this position.

> Many therapists treating survivors elect to withdraw rather than to engage in what feels like fruitless debate. Their practice goes underground. Torn, like their patients between the official orthodoxy of their profession and the reality of their own personal experience, they choose to honour the reality at the expense of the orthodoxy. They begin like patients to have a secret life. As one therapist puts it, 'we believe our patients we just don't tell our supervisors'.
>
> (Herman 2001: 152)

Janet's re-enactment

Following several weeks of pleas and demands, Janet arrived for her session dressed to kill. I felt instantly shabby by contrast, and recognised in her superior air that her father's little princess, who had never been refused anything, had arrived. Her rage with me and my refusal was awesome as she systematically attacked the therapy, the therapy world and in particular my lack of skills.

The princess Janet had been abused and reduced by her father but she clung on to an aspect of her that could never be refused. My refusal to hold her regressed her to pre-abuse, setting up a re-enactment of the first scene: enter stage right, the abuser.

Her tone was hostile as she opened with a volley of attacks. She screamed that I was not real, she needed me to be real, and therapy did not belong in the real world. It was an expensive farce, she was no better, in fact she was worse. Her parents had shown her an article proving that therapy should last no longer than a year. Considering it was her father who had abused her I felt slapped and recognised I was now the primary abuser.

During her attacks I held my therapeutic position by putting pieces of her jigsaw together, trying to fit her words 'be real' into place. I could feel her dredging her mind for something to say that would make me feel intensely angry.

She concluded I had a problem with touch, treading on a past truth. I caught the full force of her provocation. To explode back at her would feel such a relief (Abuser). As she chipped away at me, I felt a heaviness on my chest, and a deep sense of injustice and helplessness (Victim).

She read my face with a cold eye, witnessing me swing between abuser and victim, silently feeling it all. I was absorbing her internal conflict, providing her with a mirror to observe victim and persecutor outside of her.

I felt angry and defeated, yet still her words 'be real' rang in my ears. Other words tumbled into my mind: 'will you let me do to you what was done to me, take it and do nothing, or will you turn my attack on me and re-abuse me?'

What did she mean by me being real, surely by being real, taking it personally, I would compromise the therapist position. In *The Pain of Helping* (Morrissette 2004) I found a quote from Figley, who coined the term secondary traumatic stress disorder (STSD):

> As Psychotherapists we learn on the one hand to be objective and analytical in our professional role as helper. We must put our personal feelings aside and objectively evaluate our clients and administer the best treatments according to best practice guidelines. But on the other hand we cannot avoid our compassion and empathy – they provide the tools required in the art of human service.
>
> (Morrissette 2004: 54)

My dilemma was that Janet seemed to want my anger, and helplessness, alive and real to match the reality of her internal conflict. (Be real.) A soft approach could court disdain, experienced as diluting the effects of abuse on her. Objective analysis could be interpreted as distancing, an avoidance. Silence could be read as ambivalence or impotence.

Janet read me well over the years, intuiting reactions in me. As intimately as a partner, she knew my facial expressions, body reactions and my feelings flickering behind the therapist's mask of composure.

The only way I could define real was for me to imagine coming across an act of abuse on a child of mine by an adult. Immediately I encountered panic within myself, and the need to rescue, followed by a murderous rage towards the abuser. I imagined rushing to intervene and finding my supervisor's hand on my arm holding me back and saying to me, 'You can observe but you can't react because you're wearing your therapist's badge.'

Being witness to abuse, believing the client, showing empathy and compassion, being able to withstand horrendous attacks from the internalised abuser without collapsing and/or attacking back were all important stages, but Janet pushed on for congruent reactions. This was quite tricky because the abuser and the abused were two sides of the same moon, one side lit, the other dark. In engaging one I would automatically engage the other and they could suddenly change places, wrongfooting me.

Janet's body language gave me further clues. As she accused me of having the problem with touch she flicked the tips of her fingernails one by one on the back of her thumb like a cat extending its claws (Abuser). I noticed her left hand move to smooth over her mouth as if she were wiping away her words (Victim).

Inspired by a skilful exercise from Charge, a Chiron training module (Charge: Soth Chiron Training 2000) in how to address the abuser and the abused separately and together, I turned my body to her left and spoke to the victim, reflecting back to her the stages we had been through to this point, reassuring her that I was still there for her. She listened until I had finished, then she turned her face to the right where the abuser immediately jumped in with 'You don't fool me, you're angry and therapists aren't supposed to get angry.'

I held on to being 'real'. Uncharacteristically I let my eyes wander to the window, allowing an audible sigh of giving up on the out-breath and fighting on with the in-breath. From the pit of my stomach I responded, mirroring the abuser's tone but in a controlled way. 'Yes I am angry because I think you are determined to spoil everything we've worked so hard to achieve.' The response from the abuser was to emulate a tearful child, 'I so wanted you to hold me.'

I used quiet, controlled anger to fuel my reply. 'I'm not responding to that. You've attacked everything we've built together, using the victim in you as a shield, knowing I won't fight back because I don't want to hurt her; she's your hostage and it's time to let her go.' My tone seemed to both shock and please Janet; she remained silent but the energy in the room had lifted. I dropped back to my usual tone and said 'Now I know what you've been up against.'

Janet wanted reactions congruent to the abuser *and* congruent to the victim. This is what she needed to happen to make sense of her internal conflict, which was insightful of her when we consider that both victim and abuser are hostage to each other and therefore glued together in perpetual conflict, one relying on the other to keep the 'safe' defence mechanism in place. For Janet we had to separate to integrate, and I had to see and respond to victim and abuser as distinct from each other before we could view them as aspects of the same whole.

Facing the abuser in the abused proved to be a turning point for Janet and in sessions that followed she slowly allowed herself to come out of her hiding place, bringing with her aspects once trapped in the folds of the internalised abuser. The fairy tale ending for her was meeting and marrying a new partner and giving birth to her third child. The decision to have a third child was carefully considered, involving not just her new partner but also her existing children, although I am sure the much tamed princess had more than her fair say in the matter too.

Mary's re-enactment

Mary's re-enactment took us deeper than Janet's. Whereas Janet moved into recovery as a result of facing the abuser, Mary regressed.

At first I mistook Mary's regression as a massive defence against seeing the drama to a conclusion: terror of abandonment, fear I would abuse her or collapse into victim, mistrust of my ability to hold the therapeutic framework, or a huge manipulation designed to frighten me into feeling her terror – the possibilities were endless.

Regression as a defence had been a huge theme throughout her therapy. We employed every skill in the book to help her spot the triggers of memory that overwhelmed her into regression: we explored how to ground and balance, how to deal with impulses to regress and re-traumatise, and sought to confine exploration of material likely to disturb her to the therapy sessions.

At this advanced stage of the therapy, sudden regression irritated me. It seemed a backward step. My internal supervisor suggested I did not leap to judge, but wait and see. I caught myself in an arm's length approach, shielding myself from something unpleasant. I moved forward energetically, looked deeper; Mary's hands were moving in front of her face, they reminded me of a tiny baby extending her fingers and locking them into focus. Once focussed, she thrust her fingers forward as if groping for contact and just as suddenly retracted them and folded them into fists, reminding me of the grasp reflex.

She sensed my curiosity and pulled her fists back towards her body, unfolded her fingers and closed her eyes. Blindly she found the arms of her chair and scratched at the cloth. It crossed my mind that I was witnessing a response to something extremely unpleasant and I wondered, given Mary's background, whether it might be abuse.

With superb synchronicity a client gave me a set of Russian dolls as a Christmas present. Together we unscrewed each layer to reveal smaller and smaller dolls, and realised the tiniest one that you cannot unscrew was missing. Mary immediately came to mind, the missing doll symbolising the abused infant.

What if I had witnessed in Mary a rapid involuntary descent into infant body memory? It was as if infant memories were powerfully holding back the adult and the child until the infant had been seen, driven up into view by Mary's hands.

In Judith Herman's book *Trauma and Recovery* I came across a chapter in which she discussed trance and dissociative states as defences and she included two clients' descriptions of their dissociative states. One description stayed with me for days:

> I would do it by unfocussing my eyes. I called it unreality. First I lost depth perception; everything looked flat and everything felt cold.

I felt like a tiny infant. Then my body would float into space like a balloon.

(Herman 2001: 102; my italic)

I needed to make sense of what I was seeing beyond my own limited knowledge. I asked myself how an act of sexual abuse on an infant could possibly register enough to be remembered; an infant does not have the mental capacity to remember and yet, if my intuition was correct, Mary was demonstrating an infant's ability to distinguish the difference between different types of touch and intentions. An infant instinctively reaches out and soaks up gentle and loving touch and holding, reacts to extremes of hot and cold, rough touch and rasping textures, and possibly when large fingers periodically and persistently press a little too hard on their tiny fragile bodies with urgency, accompanied by the sound of laboured breathing and the smells of an inappropriate and cruel intent, the act is so demonic it cannot fail to register somewhere.

I looked to Babette Rothschild's book with the inspiring title *The Body Remembers* for greater clarity.

The infant has the instincts and reflexes that are needed for existence (heartbeat, respiration reflex), the ability *to take in* and make use of nourishment (search, suck and swallow reflexes; digestion and elimination) and *to benefit from contact* (sensory pathways, *grasp reflexes*), etc.

(Rothschild 2000: 16; my italic)

As infants do we grasp and *take in* both positive and negative contact through our sensory pathways? If so, might we consider the infant body as a storehouse of unprocessed memory sensations waiting to be processed into intelligible data? Babette Rothschild writes 'At birth the brain is among the most immature of the body's organs' (Rothschild 2000: 16). Therefore an infant is dependent on an adult registering and responding to its basic needs.

Mary needed my eyes and brain to process infant body memories. Her adult and inner child did not consciously remember and therefore could not make sense of her body sensations and movements. 'I believe that, relative to the brain, the body proper provides more than mere support and modulation: it provides a basic topic for brain representations' (Damasio 1994: xix). I picked this line from *Descartes' Error* that may appear out of context with the rest of his text but it spoke to me about the process between Mary and me. In the absence of brain representations of Mary's infant-like body movements (basic topic being abuse) an adult brain had to register and respond to her basic need (to be rescued!).

Babette Rothschild writes: 'The basic brain system though, is not enough to ensure the infant's survival. The baby needs a more mature human (the primary carer – not always its mother) to care for and protect it.' (Rothschild 2000: 16/17).

By its very nature the infant was not developed enough to take its place in the constellation of characters gathered on the stage but the drama could not go on without her.

Beneath the abused child lay the abused infant's story, stored in skin and connective tissue, muscle, bone and bone marrow. Traumatic body memories waited to excrete into consciousness.

Mary's hands scratching at the cloth on the arms of her chair provided a visible sign of her infant's distress. As I understood what I was witnessing I realised I had misread the infant tone of impotent neediness as belonging to the age of consciousness.

Intense feelings of guilt belonged to my abandonment (through ignorance) of the infant in favour of focus on abuser and abused. Free floating revulsion belonged to my response to an act of sexual abuse by an adult on a totally defenceless infant.

Prior to this session Mary often woke in the early hours of the morning in complete terror, and we tried in vain to find the trigger for this in her environment. After discovering the abused infant, Mary experienced waking in terror but something had shifted, she remembered the session and was able to locate the source of her terror as primitive senses belonging to the infant. She realised part of her terror came from not knowing what the feeling was and where it came from; now she knew, she imagined picking up the infant and comforting her and in doing so she was able to go back to sleep. Mary had gained control of the terror.

Conclusion

Facing the abuser in the abused in a re-enactment, in the client's own way, provided the key to a greater understanding of the client's unique path to recovery. Both clients demanded that I look closer and open my mind, challenging my general way of responding to traumatic countertransference. Mary invited me to question what I considered to be regression to infancy as a defence, asking me to look again and dare to recognise infant body memories expressed in an adult's body.

> The soul breathes through the body, and suffering, whether it starts in the skin or in a mental image, happens in the flesh.
>
> (Damasio 1994: xix)

References

Damasio, A. (1994) *Descartes' Error – Emotion, Reason and the Human Brain* (1996 edition). London: Papermac (Macmillan General Books).

Herman, J. (2001) *Trauma and recovery – from domestic abuse to political terror* (first published 1992; Pandora Edition 1994, 1998). London: Basic Books, pp. 102–152.

Morrissette, J. (2004) *The Pain of Helping – Psychological Injury of Helping Professionals.* New York: Brunner-Routledge.

Rothschild, B. (2000) *The Body Remembers – The Psychophysiology of Trauma and Trauma Treatment.* New York: W. W. Norton & Company, pp. 16–116.

CHANGING SOCIO-POLITICAL CONTEXTS

Linda Hartley

In the final brief section, the perspective widens out into a discussion of group body psychotherapy within a different socio-political and cultural context, and the potential of body psychotherapy to effect social change is explored.

John Waterston examines his work over a period of ten years leading a body psychotherapy group in a post-communist, ex-Yugoslav state. Exploring the connection between developmental theory and critical social theory, he shows how history and economic and repressive social structures impact on psychotherapy. He concludes that the psyche of the Balkans is more amenable to a psychotherapeutic endeavour resulting in meaningful social change than that of the UK, and is ideally suited to this, thus affirming this potential of body psychotherapy.

Paradoxically, as Waterston's context widens out into the socio-political arena, and into the practice of group body psychotherapy, he finds that disclosure of personal detail must narrow in order to respect the safety of participants in a political environment where the activity of body psychotherapy is considered genuinely subversive. I therefore invite the reader to imagine some of the rich processes and interactions described in earlier chapters playing out within the context of a group of peers, witnessed, supported and challenged by them, but 'behind closed doors'. We might see this as another dimension of parallel process, the presence of the historical Iron Curtain still exerting influence.

Chapter 14

Body psychotherapy, social theory, Marxism and civil war

John Waterston

My intention in this chapter is to attempt to connect psychotherapeutic theory and practice with a critical theory of social structure. I will also explore the ways in which such a connection might illuminate the possibilities of psychotherapy as an agent of social change. I will not recapitulate the specifics of body psychotherapy, except where I consider it to have a unique contribution, as I expect the interested reader will by this stage of the book have a thorough grounding in such details.

My interest in developing the connection between social theory and psychotherapy and psychotherapeutic theory has developed through my experiences of group work in one of the ex-Yugoslav states over the past ten years. Whilst I appreciate that it would be useful to illustrate the work with particular instances of case histories, I have chosen not to include specific material because of boundaries of confidentiality and dignity. I have, however, included a flavour of one particular group later on in this chapter to illustrate a very specific cross-cultural phenomenon. Otherwise, I have confined myself to clinical generalities but nevertheless hope to communicate how I have developed my methods of thinking, of formulation and of intervention in an environment where the specifics of history and culture have such a profound effect on the individual psyche. I have come to see the importance of this as I have realised that social change is not simply a process of protesting that existing systems of power, dominion and economy are unjust and ought to be challenged and changed – it is also a matter of recognising that individual and group unconscious and irrational desires, attitudes and impulses towards action are to be found at the root of these systems. The fact of repression throws the self forever off-centre to itself. Traditional social theory, which is premised on the rational, knowable and stable self, is utterly undermined by the psychotherapeutic project. Ever since Freud first argued that consciousness is discontinuous, in being over-determined and dislocated by unconscious processes, it has been possible to see the essence of being as centred not in cognition but in the vicissitudes of unconscious desire.

The strongest characteristic of unconscious processes . . . is due to their entire disregard of reality testing; they equate reality of thought with external reality . . . one must never allow oneself to be misled into applying the standards of reality to repressed psychical structures.

(Freud 1911)

Recent developments in social theory have sought to demonstrate further that the essence of social structure is therefore like constructed.

Discovering Chiron

I trained at Chiron through the late 1980s and into the 1990s having been drawn to them by the faintest whiff of the possibility of revolutionary potential in their work (see Eiden's introduction). Whilst this aspect of the work was rather understated I did have the sense that there was an understanding that psychotherapy, if practised in a certain spirit, could have an impact not only on individuals but also on the wider community; that the solipsistic core of the psychotherapeutic experience might be developed outward and extended into the community from which the original repressive force had emanated, thereby transforming the community. I was being offered a model of psychotherapeutic process which appeared to go beyond self-actualisation and into possibilities of social change through personal change. Being a rather naive but enthusiastic unreconstructed socialist at this time, I was well versed in the Marxist critique that is social theory and was further enthused to discover Erich Fromm (1942) prominently on the Chiron reading list. In the early 1980s I had (heroically to my mind at the time) walked out on a highly lucrative career in property development as being, to my mind at the time, implicated in the 'reactionary forces of contemporary capitalist materialism'. I was young and idealistic, with more spit and fervour than any real analysis of contemporary culture. On reading Fromm (1942) and Reich (1980) describe the reactionary forces imposed by neurotic structuring, it appeared to me that the Chiron Centre for Body Psychotherapy was attempting to address this in a way which did not get enmeshed in the endless rounds of envy, ego struggles and power games that appeared to dominate organised, and not so organised, political struggle.

My experience of political process thus far had been one of confusion and disillusionment at the degrees of dishonesty and outright nastiness I had encountered. I had wondered how the world could become a better place if the people trying to make it a better place were so unremittingly mean-spirited. My initial experiences of the people I met at Chiron were that here was a real interest in employing the psychotherapeutic endeavour to assist in constructing non-injurious social structures. I also encountered individuals who appeared to be genuinely kind, thoughtful and compassionate human beings. In retrospect I now know that this aspect of the Chiron experience called to me more strongly than any political agenda, career consideration or intellectual process. Moreover, most significant to me was that these were kind, thoughtful and compassionate men. Strong, powerful, men who appeared authentically to be striving against authoritarian social structures in and amongst themselves and not only in abstract political posturing.

I feel mightily moved as I write, remembering these first meetings, and the beginnings of a grounded exploration into the possibilities for overlaps between psychotherapy and social theory. In other words, deconstructing the connections between the natures of the individual psyche, in particular the unconscious, the formation of selfhood and the structure of the social order. Given the grounding of the Chiron training and the undoubted privileges of personal therapy and analysis my interest has remained substantially focussed on these questions. In particular, given that psychotherapeutic theory has repeatedly demonstrated that submission to an authoritarian social structure results in individual neurotic misery and untold social disease, why might it be that human beings persist in creating and maintaining such structures?

Upheaval in Europe

When I trained at Chiron in the early 1990s it was a time of enormous upheaval throughout Europe. In the Soviet Union, following the ascendancy of Mikhail Gorbachev from 1985 onwards there began a profound loosening of the strictures of communism with the introduction of policies of openness ('glasnost') and restructuring ('perestroika'). Subsequently, the whole edifice of the Soviet and Eastern European Marxist/socialist project began to dissolve. By the end of the 1980s massive popular opposition to the project led to communist governments finding themselves without mandate or legitimacy. Further undermined by the reluctance of the Soviet Union to send troops in support, power was quickly relinquished to popular, democratic movements.

In June 1989 the communist government agreed to free elections in Poland, and demands for reform in East Germany culminated in the drama of the dismantling of the Berlin Wall and the reunification of Germany. The communist government of Czechoslovakia resigned in November 1989 and in December of the same year a violent revolution culminated in the overthrow and execution of Nicolae Ceausescu in Romania. In early 1990, the monopoly of power held by the communist party was revoked by the Bulgarian parliament and in 1991 popular opposition led to the resignation of the communist cabinet in Albania. In August 1991, a communist-led coup d'état against Mikhail Gorbachev collapsed in disarray and brought to an end the party's control of government and the military. By 1991 the Marxist/Leninist endeavour, which had begun some 80 years earlier with the extinction of the Romanov dynasty in Russia, appeared to be over on the European continent. (For a summary of these momentous events see Crawshaw, 1992.)

The ending of World War I and the extinction of the Romanov dynasty were events around which the next eighty years of European history would pivot. The nations which emerged victorious in 1918 created almost a dozen new nations in Eastern Europe in the hope that the emerging democracies would prevent a repeat of recent history. Unfortunately, by the 1930s a combination of insurmountable ethnic differences within the nations, political corruption due to the naivety of the political process and the great depression had undermined the project. World War II finally overwhelmed the endeavour and the new nations found themselves caught between the Soviet Union and Nazi Germany.

The German armies overran most of these nations in the early years of the war and some – Hungary, Romania and Bulgaria – aligned themselves with the Nazis. Resistance groups became operational in all nations, with the strongest forces being the partisan armies of Yugoslavia and Albania. By 1945, the Soviet armies had occupied all the nations of Eastern Europe, with the exception of Yugoslavia and Albania. Between 4 and 11 February, 1945 the Allied leaders conference at Yalta discussed the terms of Germany's surrender and the future of Eastern Europe. With the Soviet armies firmly entrenched in Eastern Europe, Stalin assured the British and American delegation that he would allow the people of Soviet-occupied territories to hold free elections. Exhausted by six years of war, the British and Americans had little choice but to take him at his word. However, within three years, a series of well-organised and highly disciplined national communist parties, supported by Soviet armed force, had taken control of Eastern Europe and established the Marxist, Soviet model of economic government.

By the late 1940s the 'Stalinisation' of Eastern Europe was complete, with the communist party holding a complete monopoly on power in each country. Independent political parties were abolished, along with meaningful elections, and wide-ranging restrictions on freedoms of association and expression were imposed. The Marxist scientific laws of history determined that the world would eventually become socialist, the governments of the new nations owned the means of production, and housing, employment, education, social welfare and medicine was freely available to all.

During this period, Yugoslavia fell under the aegis of the possibilities of Stalinisation but due to the residual military power of the partisans at the end of the war, and the formidable charisma of its leader, it was able to negotiate a more independent relationship with the Soviet Union than was possible for the other nation states of Eastern Europe. However, the fragmentation of the communist project in the 1980s triggered a series of events which culminated in a civil war of staggering brutality and the eventual break-up of Yugoslavia into independent nation states.

Introducing body psychotherapy to ex-Yugoslavia

My first contact with this part of the world was in the years immediately following the end of the war in 1995. I feel it is important to have given this short history as it extends back to the living memory of the people I have worked with in ex-Yugoslavia, or to their parents' experience. Also, for reasons which I hope will become very clear, I have found it impossible to work effectively in the region without an appreciation of these facts. A case history of any one of the individuals I have met and worked with would, of necessity, include socio-political information in a way that would perhaps be viewed as irrelevant when working in the UK. The relevance of such a perspective stems from the fact that this history is relentlessly alive in the current construction of the psyche of those individuals and groups with whom I have worked. I will return to this in more detail later, but here briefly point out that this phenomenen constitutes the most enduring difference between my work in the UK and the work in ex-Yugoslavia: that the construction of the psyche, in particular the ego identifications, are centred less around the family scene than towards the nation state and the specifics of its history. This is not to say that familial dynamics are irrelevant but that the degree to which the psyche, and selfhood, is constellated around impersonal social structures is that much the greater. Consequently, any psychotherapeutic formulation and intervention has to take this fact into consideration. As a psychotherapist I have found it necessary to immerse myself in an understanding of the political and ethnic history of the region in the same way as I would immerse myself in the individual familial dynamics in the UK.

The question of 'differences' in my observations and analyses as a psychotherapist in the UK and the Balkan experience has been of enormous use in helping me to refine an understanding of the connection between psychotherapy and critical social theory. Most specifically, on the one hand I encounter a westernised, post-industrial, democratic, capitalist structure with the core formative experience being of the atomised nuclear family. On the other hand I find a (recently dismantled) Marxist dictatorship with a more distant structure of oligarchic monarchy, the core formative experience being a familial structure firmly embedded within, and subject to, the strictures and requisites of an impersonal nationalism. The question has been whether the psychotherapeutic endeavour which, for all its vicissitudes over the last one hundred years, remains firmly rooted in the 'westernised' social structure, needs to be radically revised to encompass a psyche constructed in a very different society?

Psychotherapy and social structure

Freud viewed repression as necessary for a social life to operate, the inevitable neurosis as the price of civilisation, and stressed the necessity of the authoritarian social structure as a buffer against primitive barbarism. Social theory has been more concerned with the fragmentation of the self as a result of authoritarian structures and the nature of social relationships, particularly prevailing systems of power. In pursuing my theme of difference I have been drawn to the *Institut für Socialforschung*, or the Frankfurt School, which has, to my mind, provided the most comprehensive and compelling critique of the points on interconnection between culture, society and the human psyche.

Following on from Reich and Fromm, Herbert Marcuse (1956) and Theodore Adorno (1951) sought to explore the fragmentation and alienation of the human subject in the modern world. Whilst I would argue that their analysis of fragmentation, relying as it does on a piecemeal and uniform view of psychic internalisation, is founded on a somewhat simplified view of certain tendencies operating in the capitalist world, they nevertheless have offered an original and insightful description of the relationship between subjectivity and the unconscious, the effects of the progress of history and social, political and economic organisation. According to Marcuse, the dominion (of repression as described by Freud) 'initiates the chain reaction of enslavement, rebellion and reinforced domination which marks the history of civilisation', and 'the unfree individual introjects his masters and their commands into his own mental apparatus' (Marcuse 1956).

That the critique is propelled from the (western) Marxist prospective is all the more enlightening to this current investigation. Moreover, Marcuse and Adorno viewed the revisions of the neo-Freudians, for example Hartmann (1966), Horney (1963) and Sullivan (1966) in their insistence on the autonomous ego-function and illusions of atomised selfhood, as liberal humanist attempts to devalue the revolutionary potential of psychotherapy. In the insistence of the liberal humanist viewpoint of inflated selfhood lies a covert reactionary force which ultimately leads to a dissolution of social cohesion and renders the socialist endeavour impotent.

Marcuse and Adorno propose that psychic repression underpins all forms of social organisation and that the 'reality principle', i.e. that which represses, is structured through ideological, political and economic forces. Therefore, they contend that whilst an amount of basic repression is necessary for the functioning of society this repression need not be absolute and will depend upon the organisation and relative dominion of the constituent forces. Further, Marcuse introduces the concept of 'surplus repression' being specific to particular forms of political and economic organisation and that which is over and above the minimum required for society to operate. Surplus repression is required in the service of dominion and political and economic inequality – in effect it deepens the basic, necessary repressions in the interest of domination within certain social structures. According to Marcuse, the chief features of this domination are: restrictions on sexuality as a result of the ascendancy of the patriarchal-monogamic family, a division of labour based on inequalities of individual worth and the atomising influence of a mass-commodified culture. In a direct overlap with pure Reichian (and Chironic) concepts, Marcuse states 'the desexualisation of the organism is required by its social utilisation as an instrument of labour' (Marcuse 1956).

Adorno (1951) develops this critique by seeing that the ego functions through cognitive testing but, as a result of the repressive and pathogenic conditions of late capitalist social process, it must also effect unconscious prohibitions. In a liberal capitalist society this prohibition is effected through the agency of an internalisation of the authority of the Father via the encounter of the Oedipal situation. However, as capitalism advances and requires a reversal of the processes of self-awareness and self-actualisation the opportunities for human beings to experience caring emotional relationships and an authentically nurturing social scene are tragically diminished.

Adorno contends that the narcissistically weakened self is the prevalent character type in late capitalist society and the historical precursor of this development can be seen in the rise of fascism throughout the twentieth century. The present-day weakness of the ego, together with the resultant need to strengthen the ego through identification with impersonal group ideals, makes individuals highly susceptible to structures of domination and manipulation such as mass marketing, fascism and the culture industry. In Adorno's view narcissism comes to replace internalisation – the individual no longer wants to become like the father but rather like the image constructed and projected by the agents of mass commodification or by the agents of fundamentalist dogma. In other words, psychic identification is no longer to the family but to the corporate logo.

Here we can clearly see a much more sophisticated and convincing recapitulation of Reich's original attempts at social criticism. Therefore, according to this view, the enormous social and technological changes which have occurred in the last one hundred years have resulted in a massive escalation in psychological repression, contributing to attendant neurotic misery and injurious acting-out. This 'acting-out' takes many forms, from self-harm and interpersonal violence in relationships and families, to social malaise and fragmentation, to inter-community conflict and violence and all the way to civil and national warmongering.

The origins of the repressive social structure

I have shown that the authoritarian, alienated social structure leading to repression and individual neurotic misery is prevalent in advanced capitalist society and displayed a credible argument as to why this might be the case. I want to move on to address the question of how this structure might be introjected into successive generations in order that orders of domination and repression are maintained despite the deleterious consequences. The traditional view that society forbids the expression of certain desires and impulses in the name of social order, for example in Hobbes' view of the social contract (Sorrell 1986), is inadequate and redundant. Psychotherapeutic theory posits that the psyche, and thereby the manifest social structure, is formed through a splitting and repression which is the result of its own inherent developmental processes.

Traditional Freudian theory states that the separation of the psyche occurs after birth and as part of the socialisation process. The id resides with the unconscious and drives the activities of the entire psyche while the ego and the superego, whilst being significantly more available to consciousness also contain considerable elements of the unconscious. The superego is the depository of guilt feelings, moral prohibitions and sadistic self-punishment – the 'voice of the Father'. Freud shows that the reproduction of culture in the child is not simply a learning experience but occurs through the acquisition of 'ego ideals', which in turn are the product of largely unconscious processes. 'Ego ideals' are thus formed through identification with significant other persons, most notably those persons to whose authority the child must submit in order to avoid violence, abandonment or humiliation. Further, the cruelty, harshness, and inherent violence of the superego become clear when we consider its essential contradiction, which demands both acceptance and rejection of the child's ego choices. The superego says not only 'you ought to be like this' but also 'you must not be like this'.

The superego is thus the embodiment of the Law, but a law which is riddled with contradiction and so full of double-bind messages as to be incomprehensible and incapable of being satisfied no matter how convoluted individual behaviour may become. Thus, repressed desire comes into being with the introjection of the Law and is a product of the differentiation of the id. The Law cannot but contain all the elements of the cruel and sadistic contents of the unconscious, including the survival instinct which expresses itself through a desire for dominion (Freud [1923] 1962).

Thus, the Law is not an external authority which is imprinted upon a passive and frightened subject – it is an internal construct born of the id's earliest object choices and will thereby be alloyed into the structure of the unconscious itself. This process of the forging of the Law into the structure of the unconscious makes for an indelibly tenacious system of social values, norms of behaviour and prohibitions which actually have no rational authority. The rational 'legitimacy' of the Law is wholly dissolved by the Freudian project as Freud presumes that the workings of conscience are invariably irrational. Morality is constituted through libidinal coercion, supported by threats of violence, rather than through a rationally construed 'rightness'. The Law is shown to be constituted by the vicissitudes of unconscious desire and supports Freud's contention that people both identify with and desire the Law, and to be subject to it. The function of the Law here is to stabilise the vicissitudes of the individual psyche – therein lies its tenacity and the absolute desire of the conscious, socialised subject to reproduce the law in his offspring and to use all means available to bring this about.

Further, perceived threats emanating from 'the other', different cultural norms, alternative rules of Law, can be seen here to be threats to the stability of the psyche. The Nazi threat that my parents grew up with, the 'Red terror' that I grew up with, the 'war on terror' that my son is growing up with might be seen in this light as a threat to plunge the individual back into the mael-strom of psychic chaos – the same psychic chaos that led to the formation, sedimentation and stabilisation of the emergence of the tripartite structure of the psyche itself. Maintenance of culture here becomes akin to the main-tenance of sanity. We see now the tragic situation whereby the repressed individual cannot but reproduce repressive social structures.

The social being that emerges from the process of 'civilisation' is formed through both the introjection and repression of the existing social norms. The socialised psyche emerges through the multiple processes of parental-object identification, materialisation of libidinal and aggressive impulses, modifica-tion of those impulses through the agency of the Oedipal situation and internalisation of the prohibition and thereby, the establishment of the Law. However, the essential ambivalence at the core of the human subject remains – the Law locates man within the dominion and repressiveness of an inter-nalised social power but the unconscious remains the source of resistance against this dominion. The identification and wish for dominion by the Law is matched by a 'reaction-formation' against dominance and constitutes the dialectic of dominion and rebellion. Authoritarian social systems, no matter how apparently complete, cannot contain or wholly annihilate individual unconscious libidinal and aggressive representations and their imperative for expression and manifestation within the existing social order. The displace-ment of the primacy of consciousness in the Freudian model liberates a residue of ceaseless streams of creative outpourings from the unconscious. It is this stream which comprises the very makings of alternative consciousness and is a potential source of revolutionary discourse.

Jacques Lacan (2002) points to a revision of the traditional Freudian pos-ition (wherein the self is forever distorted, and distressed, by social pressures) and presents a self which exists only by virtue of the alienation of desire itself. For Lacan, the struggle between self and society is tempered by the fact that the 'self', including the very structure of the ego itself, is a mis-recognised construct, founded on ideology and illusion. This is in direct contradistinc-tion with the Freudian view of the 'natural' self being continually at odds with the 'un-natural' cultural demands. The Lacanian self is at once less consciously distressed and more alienated from the 'real'. For Freud, the con-stitutive imaginary derives from the primary unconscious, whereas Lacan's imaginary exists prior to the unconscious and is a world of distorted illusions upon which the self is built. The illusory is a mirror image of the real, emanat-ing from a pre-Oedipal stage where the division between subject and object does not exist. The individual is thus cast into a hall of mirrors, and threat-ened with a confusion of psychosis-like intensity unless order is restored by the symbolic structure of received social meanings, differentiation and individuation.

The introjection of the individual into the world of language provides the separation of the imaginary and the symbolic and represses the imagined abyss of the specular image. Through the acquisition of language (and repression) the unconscious is structured and the subject can enter the domain of 'I' and 'not I'. For Lacan then, the entry into social relations saves the individual from psychosis, establishes the structure of the unconscious, introduces the 'self' and 'not self' into the psyche and reproduces the existing social order through instilling the symbolisation upon which the social being will establish its existence. Both neurotic misery and revolutionary potential in Freud emanates from the ceaseless irruptions of the un-reconstituted unconscious. For Lacan, this potential arises because the symbolic is destined to be interrupted by the steady outpourings of the imaginary, by the narcissistic illusions of the ego, and thrown off-centre by the disorderly effects of the domain in the self which is beyond representation.

Given that the socialised being is necessarily alienated from organic drives and any sense of primary self, true revolutionary ideation perhaps becomes literally inconceivable. The revolutionary therefore belongs to the domain of the pre-symbolic, the irrational pre-self, pre-language, world – a return to which requires a deconstruction of the self beyond that which is likely, or indeed possible, in anything but the most extraordinary circumstances.

Psychotherapeutic work in ex-Yugoslavia

I first went to the region in January 1996 to teach biodynamic massage to a group of psychologists and psychiatrists. I currently visit up to six times a year, chiefly facilitating a closed psychotherapy group which has been operative for the whole of the ten years. In addition, I run training workshops in body psychotherapy, mostly as summer schools of four or five days' duration. Whilst the work has undoubtedly been challenging and at times traumatising by association, it has also been the most satisfying and meaningful element in my professional life over the years. I am in little doubt that this is due to the opportunities to combine psychotherapeutic practice overtly with social change and in discovering that the expectation of the group participants is that this is how it will be. In my view, the previously identified ego structure which arises from a formative immersion in a strongly socialised culture, such as experienced in Yugoslavia prior to the early 1980s, tempers the tendency towards solipsistic and atomised psychotherapeutic outcomes. In other words, there is a stronger and more ubiquitous gravitation of the psychotherapeutic process towards integration in social change where ego structure is already identified with what I have previously described as 'impersonal nationalism'. There is less overt emphasis on self-actualisation and more on social actualisation and, the 'rewards' of the psychotherapeutic process tend to move more readily towards community action. This to me has been the most deeply satisfying aspect of the work.

I have been curious to ask the implicit question posed by the Marxist critique of the capitalist, mass-commodified and atomised society that is: will the Marxist/socialist structure avoid the stultifying effects of the otherwise necessary repression that is surplus repression and the descent into mass narcissism consequent upon the impoverishment of the ego? The answer is discovered to be 'no', but with some qualifications. In essence, repression results from submission to an authoritarian social structure which does not adequately support organic life-processes and not from any particular socio-economic relationship.

Freud's original conception that unconscious desire is the organising principle of all thought, action and social relationships lies in direct contradiction to the traditional western emphasis on reason, rationality and conscious control of the self. Further, Freud pointed out that the content of the unconscious will be necessarily repressed as a result of submission to an authority upon which the individual depends for survival. Furthermore, submission to an authority which is in contradiction to the wishes of the primary unconscious results in repression of the contents of the unconscious. The degree to which any individual can sustain repression without psychic distress depends on many things – the maturity and flexibility of the adult ego, possibilities for sublimation through creativity, their place in the social and economic order and opportunities for the 'acting out' of the repressed material either inside or outside of cultural behavioural boundaries. However, there is a limit to accommodation and too much repression leads inexorably towards individual and cultural neurotic misery. Stultification emanates through the social structure being constituted of values and imperatives which are inimical to the wishes of the unconscious and yet require submission to those very values as a prerequisite to admission to the society. In other words, that by insisting upon submission to their authority, societal values create formed individuals of singular neurotic misery (see Freud [1930] 2004).

As I have already briefly written, the chief difference between the peoples of the UK and those of the region is not in the degree or nature of repression but in the ego-identifications resulting from the different political systems. Submission to repressive authority, supported by threats of violence, abandonment or humiliation has, in many respects, the same effect on the developing psyche howsoever organised – whether it be through 'the law of the father', the 'glory of the brotherhood', capital-led alienation or a Marxist/socialist economic order. Nuances may differ but I have seen little evidence of significant qualitative variations in the structuring of neurotic patterning in the two systems. The therapeutic task is essentially to address the imprinted patterns of submission which occur through the socialisation process.

Working predominantly using body psychotherapy I have found a powerful method of loosening this imprinting. The emphasis on the 'felt experience' both transcends the submissions which have necessarily occurred as a result of the excessive dependency of the human infant and also facilitates a return to what Lacan called 'the real'. As the acquisition of language is a powerful transmitter of social values, and hence repressions, the 'felt experience' can access pre-verbal states which can effectively translate into liberation. Likewise, the emphasis on the body reminds the individual that the excessive dependency of infanthood is no more and opens possibilities for a loosening of repressions which feed on this illusion of dependency. Philip Rieff (1979) has written that first (infant) love is always authoritarian and that sexuality, like liberty, is a later achievement and always in danger of being overwhelmed by deeper inclinations toward submissiveness and domination. The inclination to construct human relationships on a submission/domination continuum is rooted in the very first hours of life and destined to repeat itself throughout life. The relationship to authority is introjected pre-verbally and unconsciously. The tragedy here is that truly revolutionary ideation is rendered 'unthinkable' and illusions of the revolutionary are relegated to mere rearrangement of the domination/submission dynamic. My experience is that body psychotherapy can transcend both the language and dominion barriers to the appreciation of individual mastery of the self and brings possibilities for a dismantling of the recurring cycles of domination and submission in the socialisation process.

What this has meant in the practice of body psychotherapy is, essentially, to use the felt experience of individual autonomy as a vehicle for building a previously unconstructed kind of group. The challenge is to construct a social structure (within the therapy group) that allows for a satisfying balance between individual autonomy and desire and submission to the authority and needs of the group – in theoretical terms, to avoid the creation of 'surplus repression' (Marcuse 1956). In practice, this has meant having a continual conscious awareness that this is the task – a task, as I have already suggested, to which the 'socialised' psyche of the people of an ex-communist state might be very well adapted. In working with individuals in the group, the felt experience of the personal process brings about an individuation and a 'belief' in self-containment and self-sufficiency.

The adult self is essentially a self-regulating, self-sustaining organism and body psychotherapy is one of the more effective ways of knowing this (see Carroll's chapter). For example, time and again individuals have discovered that their feelings of dependency, and consequent life-crushing fear and massive behavioural restrictions, have been revealed to be illusory in the light of bodily experience. The group has been an environment where such illusions can be approached and challenged. The approach and challenge is always supported by the conscious use of a re-animation of the motoric ego. This has many times been as simple as verbal, or physical calls to attend to the power of the organic self in the face of seemingly overwhelming social-political and familial constructs.

For example, one the characteristics of the group process manifested as a deep-rooted tendency to interfere in one another's process with the stated intention of helping, or correcting the 'mistakes' other group members were making. Subsequent upon my repeated interruption to these interferences (an intervention I could hardly bear not to carry out as the group's inability to leave each other alone was singularly irritating to my 'individualised' structure) there emerged a deeper fear that one group member's 'mistake' would render the whole group liable to condemnation. I came to view this as part of an emotional consequence of the collectivised psyche wherein the sins of one become the sins of all. The challenge provided by my blocking the interferences and the uncovering of the underlying structure of dependency eventually revealed the illusory nature of the collective responsibility and fostered an ability to tolerate the struggles of individuals within the group process without the need to interrupt. More specifically, the process was supported in that the group member with the impulse to interfere (with the collectivised fear reaction) was contained initially by re-animation of the motoric ego, later by introjection of the felt experience of independent (bodily) safety and eventually through a dismantling of the illusion of collective culpability.

The early stages of the group were very much concerned with this kind of process with a preponderance of one-to-one work with the therapist. As individuals discovered the illusory quality of their dependencies more and more, and were increasingly able to transcend these, the quality of the group changed. I would describe this change as a shift from 'I want to be an autonomous individual' to 'We want to be a (deeply interdependent) group of autonomous individuals'. Herein is the revolutionary potential in the psychotherapy group. From the secure base of autonomous selfhood has grown the desire to form a community without surplus repression. We have found that the security of the selfhood can tolerate a degree of repression as required by the group where, in effect, the individuals *choose repression* in order to serve the community. Perhaps 'containment' would be a better term but, semantics aside, the revolutionary event is that the strength of the emergent autonomous selfhood allows for a freely chosen sacrifice of a part of that selfhood in order that the community might flourish. Moreover, we have also discovered that the experience of this new kind of community is so deeply nourishing – paradoxically, because it involves at times the notion of sacrifice of selfhood – that members of the group have sought to recreate such communities outside of the immediate group.

Conclusion

I have shown throughout how the individual is enmeshed in the prevailing authoritarian social structure to the degree that, especially according to Lacan, the very structure of the unconscious is unable to operate in any other way. Rearranging power structures is not, to my mind, revolutionary. In the light of this, I feel that the truly revolutionary act is perhaps beyond the reach of the human subject other than in very limited and circumscribed environments where a commitment to such, and an appreciation of the massive individual and collective forces ranged against an endeavour, exists in a highly extraordinary way. Over a period of ten years it is just such a circumscribed environment that I feel I have contributed to creating in the groups in the region.

I have tried here to give a flavour of the potentials of working psychotherapeutically in an ex-communist state within the boundaries of confidentiality. In this I have also tried to draw together some of the main strands of social theory as they might overlap with a developmental theory of the individual psyche. I have also attempted to show how an understanding of history and economic structure will have a bearing on the psychotherapeutic endeavour, and some way in which this endeavour might contribute to social change. As I write, after a little over ten years' experience of working in the region, the aspect which occupies me most is a growing realisation that the repressed psyche which also contains a substantial subscription to identifications with more impersonal group ideologies, and particularly an ideology founded upon communal interdependence, is that most amenable to a psychotherapeutic endeavour which will readily evolve into meaningful social change. It is my experience, and that of colleagues also working in the region, that such a psychic configuration is ubiquitous in the states of ex-Yugoslavia and thus enables the restoration of the psychotherapeutic endeavour in this region to its full potential as an agent of social change.

References

Adorno, T. (1951) Freudian theory and the pattern of fascist propaganda. In: *The Essential Frankfurt School Reader*. New York: Continuum, 1985.

Crawshaw, S. (1992) *Goodbye to the USSR*. London: Bloomsbury Publishing.

Freud, S. (1911) *Formulations on the Two Principles of Mental Functioning*, Standard Edition, XII: 225.

Freud, S. (1962) *The Ego and the Id*. New York: W. W. Norton. (First published 1923.)

Freud, S. (2004) *Civilisation and its Discontents*. Penguin Books. (First published 1930.)

Fromm, E. (1942) *The Fear of Freedom*. London: Routledge and Kegan Paul.

Hartmann, H. (1966) *Psychoanalysis, a General Psychology*. New York: International Universities Press.

Horney, K. (1963) *Collected Works*. New York: W. W. Norton.

Lacan, J. (2002) *Ecrits, A Selection by Jacques Lacan*. New York: W. W. Norton.

Marcuse, H. (1956) *Eros and Civilisation*. London: Routledge.

Reich, W. (1980) *Character Analysis*, 3rd edn. New York: Farrar, Straus and Giroux.

Rieff, P. (1979) *Freud: The Mind of a Moralist*. Chicago: Chicago University Press

Sorrell, T. (1986) *Hobbes*. London: Routledge & Kegan Paul.

Sullivan, H. S. (1966) *Conceptions of Modern Psychiatry*. New York: W. W. Norton.

Additional reading

Benvenuto, B. and Kennedy, R. (1986) *The Works of Jacques Lacan*. London: Free Association.
Elliot, A. (1992) *Social Theory and Psychoanalysis in Transition*. Oxford: Blackwell.
Glenny, M. (1999) *The Balkans, 1804–1999*. London: Granta Books.
Jay, M. (1973) *The Dialectical Imagination*. Boston: Little, Brown and Company.
Kovel, J. (1988) *The Radical Spirit: Essays on Psychoanalysis and Society*. London: Free Association.

Concluding words

Linda Hartley

Perhaps it has never been so vital as it is today to reclaim the subjective body, the 'body experienced from within' (Hanna 1975), from the over-objectification of modern culture. Embodied practice in psychotherapy offers a way to support clients to re-inhabit their bodies in a meaningful way, when that connection has been lost or never fully experienced. For the body psychotherapist this is a fundamental premise; the subjective experience of embodiment, the therapist's own and the client's, is a source of immediate, extensive, and subtly nuanced information about the client and the client–therapist relationship.

The work presented throughout these chapters also points to a sophistication of attention to the embodied relationship – a complex, multi-layered experience of intersubjectivity enlivened through a mutual engagement with sensation, emotion and image. It points towards a way to be in authentic relationship to oneself and another simultaneously, engaging with all levels of process as they come into awareness and expression. In the therapeutic encounter, the dialogue between two bodies in the room can be raw, challenging, frightening, exciting, moving and deeply meaningful. Attending to this level of relating demands courage, awareness and a highly tuned somatic perception.

At the Chiron Centre, a way to engage with this multi-layered task of embodied relational work has emerged through the integration of approaches once felt to be polarised, seemingly incompatible orientations. The results of the alchemical process described here will undoubtedly go on developing through the work of Chiron-trained psychotherapists, providing the ground for new integrations and transformations in the future. New developments, some of them described or hinted at in these pages, might occur in group, social and political arenas; through our changing relationship to planetary and environmental issues; and in the unfolding of spiritual awareness through embodied relationship, for example.

I trust these chapters have shown that Chiron body psychotherapists are already engaged with breaking new ground in terms of theory and application, and it is hoped that this will make a valuable contribution to the wider field of counselling, psychotherapy and psychoanalysis, as well as to body psychotherapy theory and practice.

Reference

Hanna, T. (1975) Three elements of somatology. *Main Currents in Modern Thought* 31(3): 82–87.

Appendix: Professional bodies

Chiron Association for Body Psychotherapists (UK) (CABP)
www.body-psychotherapy.org.uk

European Association for Body Psychotherapy (EABP)
EABP Secretariat
Leidsestraat 106–108/2
1017 PG Amsterdam
Netherlands
Tel: +31 20 330 2703
Email: eabpsecretariat@planet.nl
www.eabp.org

United Kingdom Council for Psychotherapy (UKCP)
2nd Floor
Edward House
2 Wakley Street
London EC1V 7LT
Tel: +44 (0)20 7014 9955
Email: info@ukcp.org.uk
www.ukcp.org.uk

US Association for Body Psychotherapy (USABP)
7831 Woodmont Avenue
Suite 294
Bethesda
Maryland 20814
USA
Tel: +1 202 466 1619
Email: usabp@usabp.org
www.usabp.org

The Chiron Centre is a private institute in London, offering a variety of psychotherapy services to the public as well as advanced training and continuing professional development (CPD) events for practitioners:

Chiron Centre for Body Psychotherapy
26 Eaton Rise
London W5 2ER
Tel: +44 (0)20 8997 5219
Email: chiron@chiron.org
www.chiron.org

Index

abandonment 168, 173, 195, 198–9, 202, 205, 222

Ablack, Carmen Joanne 5, 61, 63, 100, 121–32

abuse: borderline personality disorder 195; people with disabilities 167, 170; sexual 40–1, 91, 136–7, 167, 212–25; trauma therapy 180, 185, 186, 188, 189

acting-out 68, 234, 238

Adler, G. 195

Adler, J. 1

Adorno, Theodor 233–4

affect regulation 101, 108, 141, 186; borderline personality disorder 195, 197, 199, 201, 205; empathetic attunement 208; *see also* self-regulation

aggression 56, 108, 189

Alvarez, D. 130

Amini, F. 1–2

analytical psychotherapy 26, 28–9, 67

anger 172, 173, 189

ANS *see* autonomic nervous system

anti-psychiatry 67, 71

anxiety: borderline personality disorder 194, 195, 198–9, 203–4, 205; interpretation 22; pain link with 147; peristalsis 39; psychosomatic distress 151, 156, 159

arguments 101–2

armouring: biodynamic massage 34–5; body armour 16, 34–5, 108; borderline personality disorder 202; character armour 16, 90; muscular armour 19, 20, 34, 37, 197, 202; therapist's 125, 126; touch impact on 108; visceral armour 34

arousal 97, 127, 139; affect regulation 208; breath techniques 158; childhood 36–7; limbic system 155; mother–infant interaction 95, 96; psychosomatic distress 151, 152; *see also* hyperarousal

Asheri, Shoshi 5, 6, 61, 62–3, 96, 99, 106–20, 158

attachment 17, 23, 29, 94–6; avoidant 154; borderline personality disorder 195, 196, 198, 199; disability 168; disorganised 179, 186, 198; insecure 153–4, 179; neuroscience 143; secure 209; self-regulation 138, 139–40, 142, 186; trauma 179, 191

attunement 68, 95, 98, 127, 191; borderline personality disorder 201, 202, 204; empathetic 208, 209

auto-regulation 96

autonomic nervous system (ANS) 15, 19, 34, 139, 182; borderline personality disorder 198; limbic system 155, 156, 178, 184; psychosomatic distress 151; vasomotoric cycle 35

avoidance 101, 178, 179, 180–1

avoidant attachment 154

bare attention 47, 48

BDNF *see* brain-derived neurotrophic factor

Beebe, B. 97, 98

Beisser, A. R. 48

belly 21, 49, 55

Benjamin, J. 107, 109

Bernard, Claude 38, 89

biochemistry 140, 142

biodynamic cycle 51